The Lies They Tell

A Journey through America

Tuvia Tenenbom

gefen publishing house
JERUSALEM ◆ NEW YORK
Est. 1981

Cover Drawing: Shay Charka
Cover Layout: Leah Ben Avraham/Noonim Graphics
Typesetting: Benjie Herskowitz, Studio Etc.
Organization, Advice and Photos by Isi Tenenbom

ISBN: 978-965-229-911-6

1 3 5 7 9 8 6 4 2

Gefen Publishing House Ltd.   Gefen Books
6 Hatzvi Street   11 Edison Place
Jerusalem 94386, Israel   Springfield, NJ 07081
972-2-538-0247   516-593-1234
orders@gefenpublishing.com   orders@gefenpublishing.com

www.gefenpublishing.com

Printed in Israel   *Send for our free catalog*

To Isi, my Woman of Valor

*For gracing every moment along the
journey with your loving voice*

For capturing every image with your shiny lens

For chasing the unknown with fervor

For being who you are

The New Israeli Bestseller
(Print and digital bestseller lists)

• • •

"Savage, disturbing, comical ... Tenenbom has again written a book that is unputdownable. "
– The Jerusalem Post

"*The Lies They Tell* exposes the real America, the one where racism and anti-Semitism lurk just beneath the surface.... Not to worry, Tenenbom knows how to serve his dishes in an easy, palatable manner, which won't allow you to put the book down until it's finished."
– Israel Hayom

"Special and unique. "
– Channel 1 TV

"An excellent book!"
– Channel 2 TV

"An excellent, wonderful book!"
– Channel 20 TV

"Sharp in its observations, pointedly direct, highly humorous and a very readable book...that will make you laugh out loud at the same time that it paints for you America's saddest stories." **– Makor Rishon**

• • •

A Spiegel Bestseller

"A New Yorker travels through Trumpland ... gives a voice to people of all social classes, from the homeless to the oil tycoons; all faiths and minorities ... his description of America's ghettos and homeless colonies is impressive..."
– Spiegel Online

"A great, sharp book with deep insight, never sugarcoated, into the reality of a country torn apart. Skillfully, Tenenbom interweaves the dialogues into the text and the result is an entertaining and authentic book. Detailed and shocking, this is the best of Tenenbom's books."
– Deutschlandradio

"After reading this book, it is no surprise that Donald Trump has won the election." — *Stuttgarter Zeitung*

"Packed with Jewish humor.... Reading this book is a delight.... Tenenbom is honest, free of political correctness and he doesn't shy away from recounting embarrassing experiences." — *Titel-Kulturmagazin*

"Tenenbom is not interested in what is on the surface but in what is underneath it, and he digs ever deeper. In what at first seem like harmless chats, he uncovers an America that you won't find in the news: the shadowy side of the American Dream. He does not judge people who share with him the darker corners of their hearts, but he quotes them mercilessly." — *Mitteldeutsche Zeitung*

"Entertaining and frightening." — *Fantasia 637e*

"Incredibly funny, entertaining, revealing and, at times, nasty." — *Hamburger Abendblatt*

"A terribly funny journey of discovery through a shallow America ... Tenenbom's book is entertaining and shocking at the same time." — *Die Welt*

International Praise for
Tuvia Tenenbom's Previous Work

"Highly engaging and emotional, eminently readable, brutally honest." — *Publishers Weekly*

"Irresistibly fascinating…seductive and engaging." — *New York Times*

"Illuminating and alarming." — *Wall Street Journal*

"Read what Tenenbom has to tell us, without bias. We don't have the privilege not to know." — *Haaretz* (Israel)

"Tenenbom's laughter touches our soul in places where mere intellect could never reach." — *Die Zeit* (Germany)

"One of the most iconoclastic and innovative of contemporary dramatists." — *Corriere Della Sera* (Italy)

"Tuvia Tenenbom is Michael Moore and Borat in one." — *Die Welt* (Germany)

"A force of nature…provocative, satirical, intellectual." — *La Repubblica* (Italy)

"A free artist who fights for truth and tolerance." — *Le Vif/L'Express* (Belgium)

"A mystical provocateur." — *Le Monde* (France)

"Brilliant." — *Deutschlandradio* (Germany)

Contents

Acknowledgments

MY WARMEST THANKS TO EVERY AMERICAN WHO GAVE OF HIS OR HER precious time to satisfy my curiosity into the depths of their souls. My thanks also go to those who revealed the inner reaches of their hearts provided I wouldn't quote them by their full names.

I am grateful to the following professional organizations that were there to help when needed: Philadelphia Convention & Visitors Bureau, Destination Gettysburg, Laurel Highlands Visitors Bureau, Visit Pittsburgh, Destination Cleveland, Circle Michigan, Visit Milwaukee, Circle Wisconsin, Meet Minneapolis, Visit North Idaho, Rust's Flying Service in Alaska, Hawaii Tourism Authority, Visit Denver – Convention & Visitors Bureau, Colorado Tourism Office, Kansas/Oklahoma Travel & Tourism, Dallas Convention & Visitors Bureau, Jekyll Island Club Hotel.

I am indebted to Lori Lowenthal Marcus and David Mills for going over the manuscript and graciously sharing with me their comments, remarks and corrections.

To my spiritual brothers, Dr. Jonathan Landgrebe, head of Suhrkamp, and Winfried Hörning, my editor: I will forever cherish your trust.

To my dearest friend, Rotem Sella, for enlightening my eyes with his most endearing personality and for being there for me whenever I needed it.

Lastly, to my mother-in-law, Isa Lowy, who treats me like her only son: I love you, Mama.

Prologue

I LANDED IN THE USA THIRTY-FIVE YEARS AGO WITH $400 TO MY NAME, AND America has been good to me ever since. From the start I believed in the American Dream, and I've lived to see it come true for me. I owe this country a debt, the debt of gratitude.

I was born in Israel, the land in which I spent the early years of my life and where I was groomed to become a rabbi, just as my father was. I left Israel and moved to the United States of America – to New York City, to be exact – and instead of becoming a rabbi I spent fifteen years in various New York universities, where I collected degrees and half degrees and left the rabbinate to other people. These days I still live in New York, but also in Europe, mainly Germany, and in other parts of the globe. But beginning in just a few weeks, I plan to stay only in the United States for six months, spending my time traveling across the country.

I am the artistic director of the Jewish Theater of New York, which I founded about two decades ago and where close to twenty of my dramas have been produced. I'm also a journalist, writing for the German highbrow paper *Die Zeit* and its online edition *Zeit Online* for over seven years now. In addition, I'm an author for the prestigious German publishing company Suhrkamp, where both my previous books, *I Sleep in Hitler's Room* and *Catch the Jew!* (the American titles), were *Spiegel* bestsellers. I am also a contributing columnist for a liberal New York Jewish paper called the *Forward*.

Following the success of the two books, my devoted editor, Winfried Hörning, asked me to add another book to the series. The first book was about Germany, the second about Israel, and Winfried thought that the time had come to have a book about America as well.

Now you know why I'll soon be traveling across the US of A.

The idea in this series is quite simple: travel around a country for six months, meet as many people as possible and portray the character of the country and its people. Although the idea is indeed simple, executing it is exhausting. It requires a workload of more than sixteen hours a day, every day, relentlessly. Yet the rewards are immense. I love to meet people, and the more I meet the better I feel.

I know that getting around America is going to be different from Germany and Israel. In those countries I used public transportation, which allowed me to get closer to the people, but America is huge and most people drive cars, not buses. If I want to mix with the people and meet them I'd better drive alongside them and to them. There is only one little problem here: I haven't driven a car in decades, and now I'll have to do it day in and day out. Hopefully, I won't get into an accident or three.

What will I find in America? I don't know, but let me make a comment first. Whatever I find, whatever I discover, will no doubt be influenced by the education I received: the years that I spent studying the Talmud, mathematics, literature, religion, theater, journalism and computer science. Other people, of different backgrounds, might come to different conclusions – and I respect that.

Like many New Yorkers, I don't know much about the other forty-nine states that make up America. Of course, as a person residing not only in New York but also in Europe, I did acquire a prejudice or two about Americans. Americans – don't you know? – are shallow and dumb. Is this true? Soon, I hope, I'll find out.

And there are other things that I'd like to find out.

For the past few years, especially during the presidential reigns of both George W. Bush and Barack Obama, America has been experiencing continuous bouts of polarization that defy logic, especially for a country such as the United States that often defines itself as a melting pot. Now Americans seem to want to melt one another (but not themselves, of course) in a boiling pot. Who, exactly, are the warring parties? Who are the American conservatives? Who are the American liberals? What do they stand for? Why do they fight?

Being Jewish, I can't avoid noticing one major political difference between America and Europe. European countries, in general, tend to be more pro-Palestinian than pro-Israel. America, on the other hand, is too often the one lone voice in international forums that still supports the Jewish state, and I'm intrigued to see whether the American people as a whole also support Israel.

Residing partially in Germany, there is something else that I'd like to find out. I've read somewhere, don't ask me where, that fifty million Americans claim Germany as the land of their ancestors, topping the list of all other countries of origin. Is that true? If so, who are the "German Americans" and what influence do they have, if any, on America?

America, outside of New York, is a big puzzle to me. I know that the largest majority in this country are the people of faith, mostly Christian, but who, in God's name, are they really? There are many megachurches in this country, as anyone flipping their TV remote control on Sunday will notice, but I've never seen a single megachurch with my own two eyes. I'd love to see them. To be surrounded by multiple thousands who believe in an ancient Jew will, I think, be quite an experience.

Then there are the Native Americans. In New York I've often heard people talking about the great spirituality of the Native Americans, also known as Indians, but I have never had the chance to actually meet a single Indian, not to mention visit a reservation. I hope that in the next few months I'll get to see these people and be inspired by them as well.

Of course I also want to meet Muslims, Jews, Mormons, Jehovah's Witnesses and whatever other witnesses live outside of New York. Will they be different from the people of this city? Don't laugh at me, but I'd like to meet rednecks as well. I've heard that they are horrible people, and I wish to be in their company. Being a man of the theater, I know that there is no character more exciting than the villain, and I can't wait to meet them.

My wish list doesn't end here, mind you, for there are many others that I'd like to meet: playful KKK members, religious environmentalists, handsome gang members, gun-toting conservatives, bleeding-heart liberals, soulless capitalists, No-Smoking hotheads, cannabis enthusiasts, fanatic atheists – and everyone in between.

Will I meet them all? I don't know.

Will I get to all fifty states? No. There are only twenty-four hours in a day and I won't be able to visit every state, but I'll try to visit more than half of them. In addition, and based on the size of this country and the number of states I would like to visit, I know that I won't be able to share all the experiences that I will go through, all the people that I will meet and all the places that I will visit. That said, I will do my best to share a representative sample.

I love America, but I won't let this prejudice of mine cloud my judgment.

In order to draw the fairest portrait of America, I make no specific plans as to which places to visit and which people to meet. I will let the winds blow me wherever they may.

Gate One

One thousand people come to say "I love you"

THE NUMBER OF PEOPLE RIDING ON NEW YORK'S SUBWAYS TOTALS 5,597,551 on an average weekday, according to the Metropolitan Transportation Authority (MTA).

The "1" at the end of the number is me.

I'm on a subway car, going to Penn Station, and I engage in an activity that no New Yorker would even dream of doing: I look at the people around me. New Yorkers don't do that. No matter where their bodies meet – elevator, train, café, Macy's – their eyes don't. The iron rule is this: unless you know the other people, you don't even think of looking them in the eye. This is Rule #1 in New York City. I don't follow this rule.

Thirty-five years ago I came to New York from Israel and I still behave like an uneducated foreigner. Years ago, truth be told, I tried to partially follow the eye-contact rule. I would look at women, especially if they were attractive, but not at men. Kind of semi-educated. But times have changed. Today, if you look at a woman, attractive or not, law enforcement agents could charge you with sexual harassment and you will end up in jail. And so, to have some kind of an alibi for such an eventuality, I look at men, too.

Slowly the train reaches Penn Station, a major transportation hub, and I get off. Outside I see a man who, for one reason or another, is wearing a bra. He shouts this smartest of lines: "Get yo' fucking bitch ass outta here." Nobody pays any attention to him.

And this is Rule #2 in New York: You don't get involved with other people's business. If a person urinates in front of you, creating a pool of unpleasant fluid in your path, you don't see it. You do not look at him. You keep walking. This is life, New York style.

As night falls in the Penn Station area the homeless arrive, filling up the sidewalks of nearby streets. They lie down in this city that never sleeps, and they fall asleep on the sidewalks. Some bring cardboard boxes with them, creating semblances of houses, while others just bring big plastic bags to protect themselves from rats, streetlights and winds. I know this place. My office is right across the street.

In Israel I saw stray cats on the sidewalks; here I see people.

I like New York. Chiefly, I like it because of the predictability of its people. There are millions here; some are black, some are Spanish, some are white, some are Asian, some are Jewish, some are Arab, some are Russian and then there are a couple of Mormons. No matter who they are, you can rest assured that whatever you say to them they will respond with: "That's awesome!" "Oh my God!" "Really?" "Great!" "Oy!" "Yo, man!" "Cool!" "Absolutely!" "Love it!" and "What a fucking fuck, motherfucker!"

Predictable.

Of course, you can't really say "black," "Spanish," "Jew," "Asian" or "Arab" because these words are not PC (politically correct). You can't even say "homeless" anymore. You have to say African Americans, Hispanics (or "Latinos"), American Jews, Asian Americans, American Muslims and "otherwise resourced," which are the homeless. "Whites" can stand by itself, because they are the ones who have made up this rule, and "Mormons" can also stand by itself because Mormons don't count according to present-day PC. Why? Because.

We also have super-PC people, those who say "Caucasians" when they talk about whites, wish everybody Happy Kwanzaa on Christmas (long story), and will never tell me that I'm fat, which I am. In super-PC lingo you can call me Otherwise Skinny, if it makes you feel better.

Oops. I forgot another major group, sorry: Gays and Friends, which includes lesbians, bisexuals and transgender. This group, known as LGBT (or LGBTQ), is one of the holiest groups on earth, and if you make fun of them you will be ostracized, lose your job and your spouse will divorce you. Why? Because. There are also asexual people in New York, but they don't count. Because.

These rules, part of a long list of more rules, are what makes New York kick, and why an apartment the size of a small toilet costs $5,000 a month.

New Yorkers are also known for their busyness. In fact, every New Yorker I know is extremely busy, even if he or she has nothing to do and has been unemployed for the past five years.

• • •

Should I get busy as well? Perhaps, I say to myself, I should interview a couple of people in New York before I start my long journey. Kind of a warm-up. Well, why not?

There's an Irish pub across the street from my office and I walk in, looking for my first interviewee. I find him in the image of an Air Force officer, a handsome young black man, who seems to be having the greatest time of his life with a beautiful lady, merrily drinking beer while diving into fish and chips. I approach him.

The national anthem, I say to him, describes America as the Home of the Brave. What does it mean?

"We kick everybody's ass."

Why?

"Because we can."

For the record: he is sober. God only knows what he'll say once the alcohol starts kicking in.

I go to my office. It's not nice to start a journey on such a note, I say to myself.

Brandy, a bright lady who dreams of becoming a writer, comes to my office, and I ask her to lend me some of her wisdom and answer a question or two. She gleefully agrees.

Why did America invade Iraq in 2003? I ask her.

"In America nobody asks these questions! You don't understand America. To ask 'Why?' is so un-American!"

But why did America invade Iraq? I mean, what do you think?

"You really want to know? Okay. There was a bad guy there, what's his name, and we went there to fight him, and when we were there, other reasons came up why we were there, and that's it."

Brandy is an American, born and raised, and this is how she sees herself: "I like the bad things about America. Greed, the big cars, the indignation when needs are not instantly met. And for this we go to war."

I gotta do better, I say to myself, and find myself people who will be more positive about this country. At least at the beginning!

• • •

To achieve this honorable goal, I think I'll have to move my fat ass, get out of my office and go beyond my comfort zone of Penn Station. But where?

Why not a press conference?

New York is where things happen: private clubs where the rich mingle with each other and decide which project they will sponsor next, "power lunches" where the super-rich mingle with the politicians they bankroll, and then there are those press conferences designed to entice journalists to write favorably about this cause or that. I've been to power lunches and clubs more times than I care to count or remember, mostly with people speaking off the record, but press conferences are on record. And so I go to a press conference held by a PR company whose sole reason for being is to instill love of gay people in the hearts of journalists.

Come to think of it, it's funny how things work.

At the press conference, a journalist from abroad has this question: Just a few days ago, he says, the chief rabbi of Moscow said that while he would not kill gays, he condones the killing of gays. Will the PR company do something about it?

This is a strange story. If it's true, I want to fly to Moscow and interview this rabbi. It's so bizarre! But is it true? To find out, I head over to the one man in New York who most likely would know. His name is Abe Foxman, leader of the Anti-Defamation League (ADL), whom I happen to know personally.

Abe has no clue what I'm talking about. He has never heard of this story and he doesn't know why anyone would tell it.

Perhaps, I say to myself, that foreign journalist is a little anti-Semitic. It wouldn't surprise me, because I know the European media and often enough they are anti-Semitic. Which makes me think: Is America anti-Semitic?

No, according to Abe. "While in Europe anti-Semitism has gone up," he tells me, "here it has come down." Abe should know. His organization, the ADL, continuously invests huge sums of money on surveys that determine the levels of anti-Semitic attitudes around the world. "Today," Abe tells me, "America is not immune, but the level of anti-Semitism is about 10, 12 percent."

Nice. But this does not mean that American Jews feel secure in this country. In fact, they don't, according to Abe; not even the more famous of them, such as producers and directors. These particular Jews produce untold number of films and theatrical shows about every segment of American society, but rarely about Jews or Israel. "Tell me the movies on Israel! You can't name five!" Abe says to me

The "five" part is a bit of an exaggeration, but in essence he is right. Is he also right about the "10, 12 percent"? I don't know, so I ask him: Will I, in my journey, find the same low percentage of anti-Semitism in this country as in the ADL's surveys? No.

"You are going to find a lot more anti-Semitism than what we find," Abe answers. "What will you find? I predict you will find twice as much. Why? Because you will, in your inimitable style, remove their inhibitions. You will release their innermost feelings, which are prejudice. Americans are prejudiced, but they know better than to express it or act on it."

I am thankful to Abe for his compliments and at the same time am surprised to hear from him how unreliable his organization's surveys are.

I depart from his office, but I'm not done with him. Abe is leaving the ADL soon, retiring after decades at the top, and in about a week the "Tribute to Abe Foxman," a goodbye party in his honor, will take place at the Waldorf-Astoria.

Of course, when the day arrives I arrive as well. Wow! What a party this is! The place is packed with about one thousand people, all here to say "I love you" to him, and Abe is returning the favor – he feeds them. And how! I've been to many events at the Waldorf, but this one tops them all.

First off: the food. I've never tried pierogies with honey, until this tribute. "Delicious" is a word that barely describes them. What's more, everywhere one goes, even just in the reception area, there are mountains of food of all sorts, all kinds, all tastes and all sizes. Abe loves big sizes and he cherishes the best of tastes, and on this evening he shares his taste and portion size with all of us. I have never, ever seen as much sushi as I see here. And it's so tasty! Look at the cakes – oh my God, they are almost as big as the whole of Brooklyn!

Second: the people. Among many others, here you can see the US ambassador to the United Nations, Samantha Power, and National Security Advisor Susan Rice, and both give speeches of praise in Abe's honor. There are others who deliver their praise in pre-recorded messages, including former president George W. Bush and President Barack Obama. I don't know why, but I like this S&S team, Samantha and Susan. I will go everywhere they go, especially if there's food around them.

Food aside, I do have a few questions: Why do such high-level officials, not to mention the two presidents, care about a retiring Jew? Would a Jew in today's Europe command as much respect as this American Abe? Is there something unique in the way America relates to its Jews?

I ponder these questions when the latest news breaks out. Far away from here, in Charleston, South Carolina, a white man walks into a black church, takes out a gun and shoots nine people to death. America, if one can judge by the media here, is shocked and shaken.

• • •

It is time I leave New York and journey into America, the America I don't know. I pack my suitcases and get ready to go. Where to? My first instinct is to go to South Carolina, but on second thought I decide that I'm not ready yet. I have to know more, and learn more, before heading south.

Across from my office, at Penn Station, workers have put up big signs all around: "XOXO. Philadelphia." This might actually be a good idea! Philadelphia, Pennsylvania, is the city where the Declaration of Independence was adopted and where the "We the People" Constitution of this country was written and signed, effectively making Philadelphia the birth city of the USA. I should be there, shouldn't I?

The Declaration of Independence, adopted by the thirteen American colonies in 1776, declares that the colonies are no longer part of Great Britain but an independent United States of America, a new entity created by this very declaration. The Declaration, may I add, is an eloquent document, containing some of the most memorable passages composed by man: "We hold these truths to be self-evident, that all men are created equal, that they are endowed by their Creator with certain unalienable Rights, that among these are Life, Liberty and the pursuit of Happiness."

Years ago, just before I became a citizen of this country, I learned this stuff, and now it all comes back to me. Both the Constitution and the Declaration came to life, if I'm not mistaken, in a place called Independence Hall in Philadelphia.

Philadelphia, here I come!

Gate Two

If you are a straight woman, you must call your
husband "partner" or else gay men will be offended

WISHING TO START MY JOURNEY ON A HIGH NOTE, I POSTPONE MY DATE
with the steering wheel, a date marked with a high statistical prob-
ability for a severe car accident on my first attempt at driving in
decades. In a week or so I'll either get myself into a driver's seat or
buy me a private jet equipped with a personal pilot, but for now
I board the train to Philadelphia. The train ride is nice, and soon
enough I reach my destination, get off the train and start walking
the streets of the USA.

My journey into the unknown has begun!

In front of me I see a street preacher, a black man with a message. If you don't believe in Jesus and ask for forgiveness, he says,
"You'll go to hell.

"If you say, 'I'll survive 'cause the preacher prayed for me,' this
ain't gonna work. You went to school. You studied. You can read
what Jesus said! You say I'm makin' a fool of myself, preachin' on the
corner, but the Bible in your home is collectin' dust!"

The "you" here is me, since I'm the only one listening to him.
I stick around for a while, listening to him a bit more, and when I
depart he says, "Thank you." This touches me. I'm probably his only
audience in a long while.

I continue to walk, and soon enough I bump into the National Museum of American Jewish History. How did the Jews get in here?

I enjoy walking the streets of Philadelphia, which locals call "Philly," and then I notice that almost anywhere my feet take me I end up in a pothole. I start counting the potholes, but when I reach twenty-two I stop. Enough!

I proceed to my hotel, the Hilton at Penn's Landing. The images on all the TV screens at the reception area are of the murder in Charleston's black church. The name of the white man is Dylann Roof; the name of the church is Emanuel AME.

America is scared.

But I have to keep cool. I take my room key, a plastic card, and proceed to my new abode. The first thing that I notice in the room is a little note advising me that if I smoke in my room I will be fined $300.

Murder, hell, fines. What a wonderful start!

I try to settle at my desk. I sit down on an interesting-looking swivel chair, but this chair swivels all the way down and I fall to the floor.

I call the front desk and ask for their advice. The hotel people tell me that they will send an engineer to look at the chair.

Engineer? Yes, engineer.

I love this new PC world of our time. In the days of old this kind of "engineer" was called a room attendant, fixer, cleaner, jack-of-all trades and a bunch of other precise terms. Now it's "engineer"!

It takes time for this engineer to show up, and I go down to smoke.

• • •

You can smoke outside, a hotel employee tells me, but only in the smoking area. I walk outside only to realize that there is an invisible line outside the hotel, probably drawn by this hotel's famed engineers, that divides between the smoking and the non-smoking peoples.

That's racist, I say to the hotel employee, a black man.

A white man, who looks like a natural bully, yells at me. "Why the fuck are you calling this racist? Are you not an American and you fucking don't know English, or what? What a dumb thing to say. You dumb!"

I'm shocked by such behavior. I wish the street preacher were here to save us.

A lady, perhaps the white man's wife, snatches him away. Other people in attendance stare at me as if I were Dylann Roof. I let them stare, smoke three cigarettes, and when I'm done I go to my room and quickly fall asleep.

• • •

When I get up I join a Constitutional Walking Tour. Don't ask me what it means. I don't know, but I am impressed by the name.

The guide, a young man, says that during this walk we'll be "following in the footsteps of the Founding Fathers," meaning those who founded the United States of America.

As we walk, our guide speaks of the bravery of those who signed the Declaration of Independence. At that time, he says, what they did was an "act of treason." What made those people so brave? I ask him.

"They didn't want to pay taxes [to the British]."

Some people would call this capitalism; he calls it bravery. He loves those people, I can tell, and he is highly taken with them. "Thomas Jefferson," another Founding Father and the third president of the USA, "invented the swivel chair," he says with a loving voice.

If only that Thomas were alive today, I think to myself, I could have asked him to fix my chair!

We pass by Independence Hall, which the guide reminds us is "the birthplace of the United States," but we don't go in. We are walkers, and we have to keep walking. And when we pass the house of Benjamin Franklin, the Founding Father whose image adorns the one-hundred-dollar bill, our guide tells us that "Ben invented bifocal glasses."

Those early Americans were amazingly inventive. Swivel chair, bifocal glasses, but no engineers. Engineers came later.

We walk around more and more buildings, museums and historic locations, but most of what the guide says flies over my head. He talks like a machine, a zillion details per second, and I start paying attention to the other people on this tour.

Here is a well-dressed man from Seattle, who seems to be of retirement age. I chat a bit with him and he tells me that this is his first time in Philly. What do you feel walking here? I ask him.

"Pride."

In what?

"My nation."

Is America a "nation"? In over three decades in New York, this thought has never crossed my mind.

Slowly but surely we reach Christ Church Burial Ground, where we stand near Ben Franklin's grave, which has many pennies on top of it.

"If you toss a penny on Ben Franklin's grave," our guide shares with us an old belief, "you will absorb some of his intelligence."

I toss a penny.

And it brings me good luck: the tour ends.

A sign nearby reads: "David Salisbury Franks (c. 1740–1793). Distinguished Jewish officer and aide-de-camp to Gen. Benedict Arnold during the Revolutionary War." Another Jew in Philly.

I chat with a group of three people standing by. I ask them to tell me what's special about America.

The youngest of them, twenty-three-year-old Ann, says: "In this country everybody can go from rags to riches. No matter how low on the social ladder you are, if you apply yourself you can reach the highest rank."

Do you believe that you, personally, will reach the highest rank of the ladder?

"Yes!"

What's the highest rank of the ladder?

"A high school teacher."

Wow! That's high!

I bid them farewell and we depart.

• • •

And now that I'm on my own, I walk over to Independence Hall – the very reason I came to Philly to start with. I enter the building. It is not what I expected.

I expected Independence Hall to be opulent in style and design, even more grand than the Waldorf-Astoria in New York, but this is not the case. The Assembly Room in the Independence Hall looks more like an old restaurant in an Eastern European village,

where lunch costs pennies, rather than a super major American historic building. Perhaps it indicates a humble beginning for this huge country.

The Liberty Bell in the steeple of this structure is not the original one, I'm told. The actual Liberty Bell is a five-minute walk from here, standing on the floor at the Liberty Bell Center.

I gotta see the Liberty Bell, an iconic symbol of American independence. I want to touch American history with my bare hands. I walk over to the center.

There's an inscription on the bell, which reads: "Proclaim LIB-ERTY throughout all the land unto all the inhabitants thereof." Interesting: these words are taken from the Bible (the Book of Leviticus), and they were written about the Holy Land of Israel.

Were the founders of this country, deeply religious, trying to build a new Israel in the New World? Maybe, just maybe, this was the beginning of America's relationship with the Jews. It did not start with Samantha.

• • •

I head back to my hotel. In the smoking area, now that I know where it is, I meet a middle-aged white couple. "There are neighborhoods in this city," the man, James, tells me, "that you wouldn't want to go in, unless you have a gun. Watch Channel 6, Action News, and you'll see."

Do you carry a gun, James?

"I have a gun, but not on me at the moment."

I go to my room to check James's Channel 6. Here is what I find: "Police are looking for the gunman who shot a fifty-year-old man in an alley near his home in the Frankford section of Philadelphia." "Authorities say a male juvenile was shot in the leg in Philadelphia's Juniata Park section." "Police in Southwest Philadelphia are hunting for the man who they say raped a woman while she waited for the bus."

Dr. Engineer comes in. He turns my chair around, this way and that, but nothing happens. He's an engineer like I am Ben Franklin.

Can you fix it?

"Can't."

But he'll try to replace it. That's Philly of today: engineers, rape and murder.

Somebody out there must take all this to heart and pray for the lost souls of Philly, wouldn't you say so? I do, and on Sunday morning I check around for the best church one can find in Philly. I pick the Religious Society of Friends, known worldwide as Quakers.

• • •

I am about to attend a Quaker service or, as they call it, Meeting for Worship – and I'm excited. I don't even know why.

The Quakers played a big part in the establishment of the United States of America. To start with, the founder of Pennsylvania, William Penn, was a Quaker, and he founded this state as a haven for them. In addition, the principles that he set forth, such as equality and religious freedom, would later be adopted as the leading principles of the United States of America.

How do I know?

I read this stuff in this Quaker house. But enough history. It's time for service.

No cross, crescent or any other symbol is evident anywhere in the prayer room – or whatever one would call this room, where about sixty people have gathered for service. There's no prayer book either. There are rows of benches here, three on each of the four sides of the room, and people sit on them, facing one another.

They are quiet. They are silent. Nothing really happens.

Are they waiting for the Second Coming? Perhaps, but no one says anything or shows any sign.

Time passes and nothing happens.

Are they waiting for somebody? Doesn't look it. They are thinking.

More time passes. Slowly.

And then a lady, a white lady in her sixties, stands up and speaks: "I want to confess for feeling numb. When I heard the news, what happened in South Carolina, I felt ache but no pain."

She's talking about Dylann Roof. Nobody says anything.

Quiet again.

These are the American roots, if you hadn't guessed by now. Quakers. Quiet Quakers.

I'd never have guessed in a million years that America is rooted in silence.

I learn.

The clock continues ticking and nothing happens. What patience these people have!

And then a white man, about the same age as the lady, stands up and speaks: "I saw on TV that some of them say that this was the beginning of a religious war. Which is what the son of Osama Bin Laden said." Bin Laden was reportedly the founder of Al Qaeda, the organization that took responsibility for blowing up the Twin Towers in New York on September 11, 2001. "We have to pray that this doesn't succeed."

He sits down. Nobody talks. All are silent.

The clock continues to click and tick, but nothing happens. And then a black lady, a bit younger than the other two speakers, opens her mouth. She sits as she speaks. "I saw on TV," she says, "the talking heads, and some of them were saying that what happened in South Carolina was an act against Christians. Act against Christians? That was not an act against Christians; that was a racial crime, a murder because of race. Murder because of race!"

Nobody reacts. Silence.

More silence. More silence. A white lady gets up and agrees with the black lady. And then a man gets up and says, "We have a lot of cakes, and all are invited."

Food time.

• • •

Sitting next to me is a lady by the name of Audrey. Everybody goes to have cakes, and I talk with Audrey. "Are you German?" she asks me.

How did you know?

"Very easy to know. I see how you are dressed, your bag, your manners."

I never knew I was so German!

Audrey is a Quaker, a devout Quaker. Explain the Quakers to me, I ask her.

"Quakers is an English word, to quake. George Fox, the founder of the Quakers, quoted the Bible saying that you have to tremble before the Lord, from which the word *quake* and later *Quakers* developed. The original name was Religious Society of Friends. As you could see in the service, it's quiet; you speak only when you have the need, when something quakes inside you, something that makes you open your mouth and speak."

Are you a descendent of the original Quakers?

"No, I was not raised a Quaker."

Catholic or something?

"No, no. My parents were reformed."

Reformed? Who are the reformed?

"Reform Jews."

Ah! So you grew up Jewish?

She looks at me as if I've just found out her biggest secret and am about to out her.

Are you Jewish?

"My parents, they were reformed."

Another Jew in Philly. This time in the flesh.

David, a member of the community, joins in. He is very happy, he says, with President Obama because Obama is favorable to the Palestinians.

I go to the cakes table and find myself half a Berliner (a dough-nut). It's really good, it has more jam than dough, and I quietly enjoy every bite and every lick. God bless the Quakers!

I get myself some coffee, which is not really good, and sit down to talk with other Quakers. Almost all of them are white, and they all love blacks and deeply care about them. That's what they tell me, at least. I tell them I'm a tourist and ask them for tips.

"Don't go to Germantown; it's not safe there," one of them says, and all agree.

I write a note to myself, "Go to Germantown!" and continue listening to them. All of them, they share with me, love Obama.

Why? Because he is "showing more support for the Palestin-ians, he is tougher with the Israelis, and he is lifting the embargo on Cuba." Cuba is America's neighbor, but Cuba is the last on their list of Obama's good deeds.

Later, I check out the news to see if anything especially horrible happened in Israel that would make them feel this strongly about that country, but all I can find in today's top news is Channel 6 reporting that "police are searching for two suspects after a shooting at a West Philadelphia block party injured ten people, including two children and a one-year-old baby."

While the Philadelphians around me can't stop worrying about Palestinians who live thousands of miles away from them, not one Quaker here seems to quake about people being fired upon within walking distance of them.

Why are these people so interested in Israel? I don't know. All I know is this: I gotta go to Germantown.

• • •

When I arrive in Germantown I go into a side street, where I notice people sitting in groups on the front steps and porches of small houses. Everybody is black. There are no Germans here, not a single German. The only white color around is on the walls.

I stop by one group of people, perhaps members of the same family, and I start talking with them. How's life in Germantown? I ask them.

I don't have a better question.

"Life's good here," a woman tells me. "Thirty years ago it used to be bad, but now it's good."

I'm happy to hear this, I say to her. I explain that I'm a German reporter and I came here, to Germantown, to see how you live.

"Our mayor is not good, he's corrupt, but otherwise it's okay," she adds.

How are you getting along with the white people?

"Very good."

A man, standing near, listens to this short exchange, and interrupts.

"Where you from?"

Germany.

"How long have you been here?"

Just came.

"Never been here before?"

Never. I'm a journalist and I came here to report to the world about you. I just heard that everything is good in Germantown. Is that correct? Is this what I should tell the world? Whatever you say, I'll tell. Don't matter to me.

"You want to hear the truth?"

Only the truth, my new friend.

"This place is shit."

Why?

"'Cause they may beat you whenever the fuck they want."

I have no idea what he's talking about, but I go on. Give me an example, I say to him.

"'Cause the police, they only want guns, they only want violent stuff. We, they don't give a fuck about we. They only give a fuck if we have a gun on us."

Another man, Horace, says: "There was shootin'. Four gun shots. Two kids, ten-year-old, twelve-year-old; two adults, one lady, one man."

I don't know what he's talking about but, again, I go on. Today? I ask.

"Four thirty. A few hours ago."

What was the reason?

"No reason. Could be gang-related. Lookin' for your enemy. No enemy on your block? You go round there shootin'. Hopefully you get him. If not, whoever else got there gets shot. If you can't catch the person you're lookin' for, you go at his brother, his sister, or his mother. However you get at him."

I get it, I think. Somebody was looking to shoot somebody but he didn't find that somebody, so he shot somebody else, a few somebodies. How often does this happen here? I ask.

"Every other day."

Do you personally know any of those who got killed here?

The first man answers: "My bro, that I grew up with him all my life, got shot two weeks ago, execution style."

What is "execution style"?

"In the head."

Did the police catch the killer?

"No."

Horace: "The killer never get caught. That's why you don't know when he's comin' again."

This is a very hard life –

"You live life to the fullest, 'cause you never know when it gonna end. You be humble and you just try to survive."

The first guy adds: "We live in war every day. A lot of stuff on the street not been reported on the news."

Horace: "If a brother [a black person] walks on the block and he get shot a couple of times, it ain't gonna make it to the news."

Both have been detained by police at one time or another, but they claim it's racially motivated. "They stereotype me 'cause I'm black," Horace says.

Horace explains to me how you stay alive in the 'hood [black neighborhood, black ghetto] despite all the dangers you are surrounded by: "If you feel, whenever, when your heart tell you somethin' ain't good, run fast. Listen to your heart!"

We take a photo together. Horace's friend makes a three-finger sign (denoting gang membership) and Horace pushes his friend's hand down. "No gangs now!" he tells him.

· · ·

Rachel, a young lady, approaches me. "My dream," she says, "is to move away from here." US authorities, she tells me, "treat minorities very, very bad. It all gotta do with skin color."

To the people of Germantown I am something of a UFO. No white man, to their recollection, ever walked on this street. This area, I realize, is de facto segregated. For blacks only. Whites might pass through in their cars, perhaps because their GPS has directed them to drive through Germantown, but they won't get out of their cars to walk here.

It is sad to watch this 'hood.

I have been to poor neighborhoods before. I have spent time, time and again, in Middle Eastern refugee camps, and the difference between them and this 'hood is glaring: here the Angel of Death rules supreme.

As I stand here I understand why the Quakers advised me not to come here. They love the image they have created of themselves, that of a caring people. But do they care? They won't lift a finger to help their poor, dying neighbors. But they deeply care, of course, about "Palestinians."

English has a word for this: it's called hypocrisy.

I leave Germantown and go back to my hotel. Near the hotel is the Independence Seaport Museum, and across the street from it an ATM machine. On it someone has scribbled one word: "Jew." The meaning is clear: if it's a cash machine, there's a Jew attached to it.

As if I needed another ugly reminder after being to Germantown. I've come to Philly to learn how America was born, and I leave it with images of death; I have come to see tolerance and I find prejudice.

I ready myself to leave Philly. But how? I don't think a private jet is really doable, which means that I have to rent a car.

Oh, my God, now I'll have to start driving!

I hope I make it. I schlep myself to a car rental company and get a red Chevrolet Cruze. A small car with, I hope, great promise. I love red. In Europe red is associated with communists, in the States red is associated with capitalists, but I like red for no political reason; I just love it.

• • •

Philadelphia, Pennsylvania, is the place where the Second Continental Congress adopted the United States Declaration of Independence and where the United States Constitution was written and signed. And then there is Gettysburg, Pennsylvania, one of the bloodiest battlefields of the American Civil War and the place where, in November 1863, President Abraham Lincoln delivered what would later become known as the Gettysburg Address, a speech that to this day is viewed as one of the most important ever given in America.

The Civil War of 1861–1865, between the South and the North, between the Confederate States of America and the Union, undoubtedly shaped America into what it is today.

I drive to Gettysburg to follow in the footsteps of this part of American history.

Within the first half hour of my driving, I almost get into an accident with a huge semitrailer. Luckily, the driver of the vehicle is an experienced driver and at the last second he flies to another lane. He blares his horn at me, but I'm not upset; I deserve it.

I keep on going, driving and driving, and with time I feel a bit more comfortable. Tomorrow, I hope, no truck drivers will have to fly on the road because of me.

At a rest stop along the road I check for a specific starting point in Gettysburg, and I find out that there are guides there who will take people like me along the route of the Battle of Gettysburg.

Perfect!

• • •

I hook up with one of those guides, a man by the name of Paul. Paul gets into my red car and directs me. From time to time we stop and get out of the Cruze, and Paul gives me the exact number of dead and the total number of mortar shells that exploded in each particular location of the battlefield. He also informs me that not all the dead were buried. It is likely, he says, that there are remains, bones and such, right under my feet.

Thank you.

Personally, Paul prefers the northern Unionists over the southern Confederates, but when he guides people from the South he's very careful with his tongue. "Emotions still run high," he explains to me, and visitors from the South object to his use of the words *Civil War*.

Do they have another name for it?

"Yes. They call it 'The War of Northern Aggression.'" And there are others, he tells me, who refuse to step on the ground that 150 years ago served as the Union side on this battlefield.

I have no problem with it. I drive and I walk on the ground that served the two sides in the war, stop next to this cannon and that, next to this number of dead and that, until, suddenly, my belly starts screaming: "I need food!"

I have no problem facing up to any Southerner or Northerner, but I can't face up to my belly. She is the king and the queen of me. I go to a fine restaurant.

I'm not the only one at the restaurant, just so you know. Robert, sitting at a table behind me, is one of those Americans who can recite the Gettysburg Address, with only minor errors, by heart. How do I know? He tells me.

What's the most important line in the address? I ask him.

"That this nation shall not perish from the earth," he answers.

Robert is missing a few words in between, namely, "That this nation, under God, shall have a new birth of freedom – and that government of the people, by the people, for the people, shall not perish from the earth," but that's okay with me.

We continue our talk.

Over half a million people lost their lives during that war, if I remember correctly. What was the war about?

"Slavery." The South wanted to keep their black slaves; Northerners wanted to abolish slavery. His wife, Kim, disagrees. She says that the people of the southern states believed that the US government was taking away too much power from the states and they fought for their states' rights.

Robert and Kim disagree on almost everything. Robert thinks that America supports Israel because the Jews in America give money to American politicians. There's a strong Jewish lobby here, he says, and the Jews pay politicians to be on Israel's side. Kim thinks that Palestine already exists, in Jordan, and that the Palestinians don't want to have peace with Israel to start with.

These two also don't agree on what to eat.

When it's time for dessert, Kim orders a big plate of chocolate cake with ice cream, but Robert doesn't order anything. I have long noticed that white intellectuals who side with the Palestinians are into "health" foods and are against chocolate cakes with ice cream as a matter of principle. Israel lovers, on the other hand, have no principles and eat everything.

Kim is immensely enjoying the heavy cake and fat-rich ice cream, and her face is shining with pleasure. Robert takes out his smartphone to read while she eats.

I do as well.

The battle between the Confederates and the Unionists, I read on my smartphone, still resonates in America. Breaking from Fox News: "South Carolina Gov. Nikki Haley called Monday for the removal of the Confederate flag from statehouse grounds but defended the right of private citizens to fly it."

This, of course, is in response to the widely spread, undated photo of Dylann Roof in which he is pictured with the Confederate flag. If not for the Confederate flag, Governor Haley's reasoning must be, Dylann wouldn't have killed anybody.

• • •

Belly full, I cruise with Cruze away from the Gettysburg dead and the chocolate cakes. We reach Grantsville, Maryland. I don't know how we got here. We drove north, or was it west, and we ended up here. The main thing: Cruze seems happy to take me anywhere and is not at all complaining about Maryland.

Is this a nice town? I ask a young woman at a local gas station who is collecting garbage bags from various bins and tossing them into one huge container.

"I love this town," she tells me. "I grew up here. No crime here, everybody knows everybody."

Feet away is a pickup truck on which the following is written in big letters:

Dodge the father

Ram the daughter.

You stay home and stroke it

I'll go to her house and ram it.

What's that? It sounds like a rape scene and I thought there's no crime here?

She laughs. "It's not about a woman, it's about a car. 'Dodge,' you know?"

Truth be told, I don't. This pickup truck, with its most loveable poem, wouldn't survive more than eight seconds in New York City. Somebody, a white free-speech professor at Columbia University or his teenage Mexican maid, would stone this pickup into a little mound of unrecognizable pieces before anybody could say Jack Robinson.

I get intrigued.

Let me find out where I am.

Inside the station's shop I see Tim, an unemployed man, and ask him to tell me where exactly I am. "This is redneck town," he says. "Not much to do here, but if you drive up the road you'll have a nice view."

What's redneck?

"You don't know what a redneck is?"

You tell me.

"I'll give an example. The other day a black man was here and everybody was looking. Some approached him to ask him if he needed anything, telling him that he could get it somewhere else. That's rednecks."

What would happen if a Muslim or a Jew moved in here?

"I would advise them not to come here."

What's the problem with Muslims?

"9/11."

And Jews?

"I don't know. I never met a Jew."

But the Jew better not show up here?

"I'd say so."

A lady walks by. Tim asks her: "How would you describe redneck?"

"Ask the kids over there," she says, pointing to her right, in the back. "They call themselves rednecks and are very proud of it."

One of the "kids" is Brooke, an attractive eighteen-year-old, and she says that she's not a redneck but a "country girl." She explains: "Girls are not called rednecks; they are called 'country girls.'"

It's time for me to play a little.

Let's play a word game, I say to her. I say a word and you tell me what you associate with it. Okay?

"Okay."

Black.

"I don't know." She chuckles.

Muslim.

"I'm not sure."

Let's try again: Black.

"City."

Muslim.

"A different country."

Give me better!

"Better?"

Yes.

"Okay."

Muslim.

"War."

Jew.

"Holocaust."

Black.

"Money."

What?

"A lot of black guys have a lot of money."

How did they get the money?

"They sell a lot of drugs."

Will you marry a black, a Muslim, or a Jew?

"No."

What did your parents tell you about blacks, Muslims, and Jews?

"Not to bring them home. They don't like them."

How about people who grew up as Christians but no longer practice? Any problem with them?

"No."

Is there a way to tell if somebody's a redneck?

"Yes. Rednecks have their baseball hats cooked in."

I have no idea what "cooked" is and ask her to show me a "cooked" hat. She takes off her baseball cap, folds the visor tight, puts the hat on my head and then tilts the hat rightward. "That's a redneck."

I'm a redneck! I'm so damn proud!

• • •

The new redneck is reading today's news right at this moment. Here is this from the *New York Times*: "In a long-sought victory

for the gay rights movement, the Supreme Court ruled on Friday that the Constitution guarantees a nationwide right to same-sex marriage." Great news for gays, provided they don't ask the chief rabbi of Moscow to officiate.

I drive on, on and on. The roads in America never end. I try to avoid highways and use byroads instead. This way I can learn more about the people.

Alongside the road I'm driving on right now I see churches all over, and where I don't see a church I see huge billboards. Here's one: "In the beginning God created," which is taken from the Book of Genesis. Other signs encourage people to believe in Jesus.

I turn on the radio, randomly picking a station, and I listen. A female pastor teaches us listeners how great it is to be silent. Silence, she says, is the best medicine. On and on she goes about the importance of silence, and she won't stop talking for a second.

I need to take this lady to a Quaker church!

Meanwhile, she keeps talking, and I'm driving. When I reach a place called Ligonier I turn off the radio and I get out of the red lady. I am in Pennsylvania again. Go figure. The Cruze took me here.

• • •

Ligonier. What the heck is Ligonier? I never heard of Ligonier, but it exists. I go to a café for a healthy shot of caffeine, which is where I meet Michelle. I know about Michelle as much as I know about Ligonier, but she knows everything about me. For example, that I am a "European intellectual."

How fast I changed! I was just a redneck, and now I'm a European intellectual!

Not to disappoint her, I ask her an intellectual question: Is Ligonier red or blue? (Red means Republican and blue is Democrat.)

She examines me up close, trying to figure out which party and ideology European intellectuals like me might prefer, and then says: "This is a liberal town. Most people here vote Democrat."

She must think that I'm liberal, I say to myself, and I try to play a little game with her. I'm German, I tell her, and Germans are red. Did the people of Ligonier, I ask, vote for Obama?

"To be honest," she now says, "I don't really know. I don't understand politics, you see. How's the coffee? Have a wonderful day."

She leaves.

Lesley, a lady I don't recall ever meeting, comes to sit next to me as if we've known each other from Biblical times. Ligonier ladies like me! I think I'm staying here.

Lesley tells me that Ligonier is a redneck town, which is more than just red. Lesley doesn't wear a baseball cap, cooked or not, and I assume that she's no redneck. But I say nothing; let her talk. And talk she does.

"I am Jewish," she says to me. The only Jew in Ligonier, as even her husband is not Jewish.

American Judaism is disappearing, she informs this German intellectual; there used to be a Jewish temple not far from here, but no more. America is a melting pot and the Jews, a people in love with pots, have given up on their culture.

She probably assumes that as a German I'd be happy to hear that the Jews are melting.

• • •

Devyn, a gorgeous young girl who dreams of becoming a Supreme Court justice when she gets older, walks by. Describe "America" for me, I ask her.

"America is a country where you can live the life you so choose freely."

Do you think that in Germany, for example, you are less free?

"In America you have more freedom than in Germany." How so?

"The gun laws in Germany are much stricter than ours."

Do you have a gun?

"I do!"

What gun?

"A rifle."

A rifle?

"Yes. I hunt deer!"

When was the last time you hunted?

"Not this past fall but the fall before."

How many deer have you shot so far?

"I've never shot a deer. I've tried but never gotten one."

You shoot, shoot, shoot and nothing happens...?

"No. I just sit in the cold and wait for the deer to come. They never come and I just get very cold and I come back the next day and I sit in the cold and I wait..."

Is it exciting?

"When you see a deer it's exciting. I also do target shooting, just with targets."

What's the big deal about having a gun?

"I like the excitement. The excitement of shooting. I enjoy it. For some people cooking is fun. I like shooting. Shooting guns is not the *only* thing that gets me excited, but it's one thing that gets me excited."

What's more exciting, sex or guns?

"I don't know because I'm saving myself."

You're saving yourself?

"Yes. I have a promise ring."

What's a "promise ring"?

"I live a Christian life and I promise to not have sex before marriage."

You don't have a boyfriend?

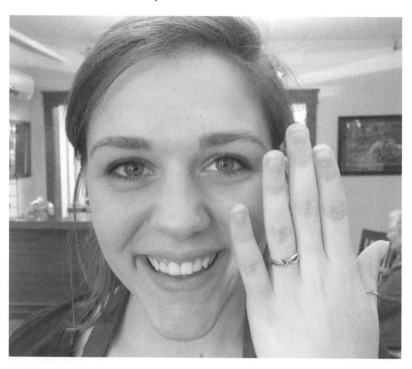

"No."

How old are you?

"Nineteen. And I plan to be celibate until I'm married." Devyn shows me her promise ring, a silver ring that she wears on her left hand. She's damn proud of it.

Lesley, the Jewess, likes to be surrounded by people like Devyn, to be totally melted by them.

• • •

Of course, not every woman in Pennsylvania wears a promise ring. Kelly, a young intellectual white woman, never will. I meet Kelly at the Cathedral of Learning at the University of Pittsburgh.

Yes, I'm in Pittsburgh. Why? No particular reason. "Pittsburgh." Don't you like the way it sounds?

In any case, I am at the Cathedral of Learning, which looks like any good, old, but very, very tall Catholic cathedral, only this cathedral has no religious symbols. This is not a church, but a protective structure for young souls wishing to be inspired. Something like that.

I am sitting down on a chair, trying to suck more intellectuality into my system, when this Kelly shows up, accompanied by an Indian man, severely interrupting my scholarly inspiration. "He's my partner," Kelly introduces her non-white companion to me.

Partner?

"Gay people use the term *partner* for their mates and I think that if I use the word *boyfriend* it might be offensive to gays, since they use the term *partner*, and I don't want to offend anybody. *Partner* is good. This way we all use the same term."

In non-intellectual, non-super-PC terms, this is what she's saying: He's my husband.

Is this your first time here? I ask her.

"No. I'm a graduate of Pitt. I know this place well. There's a reverent feeling here, a quiet and safe space to study, resembling a holy place. Ornate architecture. It always made me feel good."

Is it like a church? I mean, I don't know if you ever went to a church –

"I was raised Catholic. Yes, it feels like in a church."

I'd assume that you are a liberal –

"I am!"

And that you voted for Obama?

"Certainly!"

Are you happy with him?

"Generally yes, but not so much in his approach to foreign affairs issues."

Could you elaborate?

"Obama should be more vocal on the Palestinian issue, not stick with Israel as he does. He should be more supportive of the Palestinians."

What's wrong with his approach?

"I don't know very much about the Palestinian-Israeli conflict, but I think people don't know enough about Palestine."

What's wrong with Obama's approach to the issue?

"He supports Israel and I think it's wrong."

This is the last place on earth I'd expect to hear about Israel and Palestine.

• • •

Come Sunday, I go to a real church, the Covenant Church of Pittsburgh. Somebody's got to pray for the Palestinians, to make Pennsylvanians less worried, so why not me? On to the church!

The guest speaker for today, someone named Dr. Mark Chironna, tells us that "Jesus is the new temple. Jesus is the new covenant."

Intellectually speaking, I have no clue what he's trying to say, but the people in the audience flow with him. And when he says, "If the Lord takes something, it's because He's going to give you better!" they shout, "Hallelujah!"

The preacher is dressed in a floral, Hawaiian-style shirt that he wears over his pants, which makes me think that in real life he's a plumber.

"My mamma didn't raise no fool," he yells, by way of introducing himself.

"I've got the power," he shouts, and the people shout back: "Yes!"

This reminds me of Obama's election campaign: "Yes We Can!"

The Hawaiian plumbing preacher walks right and left on the stage, then goes down to the audience and screams, "You just need to say, 'God, talk to me! Jesus, talk to me!'"

And then he instructs the flock: "Put your hands on your belly and say, 'God, make me bigger'!"

They do as instructed and they feel great. Hallelujah.

What I'm witnessing here is an instant-gratification Christianity, similar to a Big Mac.

"Give Him another shout!" he yells. And, oh boy, they shout!

"If you believe me," he goes on, "get on your feet and give God a shout."

On their feet they are, and they shout.

"He who is depressed come here," he says, and most of them come forward.

In fifty-two days, he promises the depressed, they will conquer their depression. He asks them to shout "Yes!" if they really believe that they will conquer their depression in fifty-two days. They shout "Yes!" and he suggests that each of them donate an "offering" of one dollar per day, fifty-two dollars in total.

This is the best healthcare in America, and the cheapest. Fifty-two bucks and you will have no depression.

I, watching this, get depressed. Are we humans so naïve? I need to entertain myself now.

I go to a baseball game.

I can't believe that I forgot to pray for the Palestinians. What a German shmuck I am.

• • •

Playing now, at the PNC Park stadium: the Pittsburgh Pirates against the Atlanta Braves. Pirates and Braves. Who came up with such lofty names?

Maybe some bored pastors.

PNC Park has thirty-eight thousand seats; one of them should be mine. I pay whatever it costs, go in and sit down to watch.

Baseball is an American game, a game that outsiders have a hard time following. It lasts hours, goes pretty slowly, and only future Einsteins know what is really happening in the field.

Still, baseball is fun. There is music, there are constant cheerful announcements coming from the loudspeakers, and there is food all over: hot dogs and cinnamon buns, ice cream and colored popcorn, cookies and hot pizza, beer and ice pops. Each food item here costs on average five times more than anywhere else, but that's okay. If the food cost less, nobody would have as much fun. Yeah, Hallelujah.

From time to time the fans roar in approval or in boos. I'm not sure why, and, possibly, they don't know either.

Before the seventh-inning stretch the audience stands on its feet, and we are treated to a live performance of "God Bless America."

A few minutes later the line "Make some noise" is projected on screens, and the fans shout. For a moment there I think I'm still in the church.

A young man in a seat next to me says, "I love baseball!"

What's so great about baseball?

"During the game you can go to the toilet, you can relax. It's great!"

I bend the visor of my hat and walk out. This redneck has had enough.

The journey must go on; time to cruise with the Cruze.

Gate Three

Fine dining and white people look well together

THERE ARE CERTAIN FEATURES ONE NOTICES WHILE DRIVING. ONE IS THE greenery. Everywhere I drive I see green. This is a blessed land. The other noticeable element is the frequency of American flags; there are so many of them! Are Americans so patriotic?

I press on the accelerator, hoping that no cop will stop me, and soon enough I reach Cleveland, Ohio.

I know I'm in Cleveland because everywhere I look I see the name of the Cleveland Cavaliers, a basketball team. The baseball teams I saw in Pittsburgh call themselves Pirates and Braves; these guys call themselves Cavaliers. Who came up with such titles? Oakland, for example, has the Golden State Warriors. Warriors? Since when? If I owned a sports team I'd name it New York Thieves. Sounds better than Pirates and is more accurate than Warriors.

Cleveland has more than just Cavaliers. The Rock and Roll Hall of Fame and Museum is also in Cleveland, and I go to see it. I have no idea why the Rock and Roll Hall of Fame is in Cleveland, since Cleveland is not known to be a music city, but here it is.

The list of people who have been inducted into the Hall of Fame is long, and some are my favorites: Aretha Franklin, Ray Charles, Billie Holiday and Madonna.

Yes, I like the Material Girl.

Walking up and down the floors of this building reminds me of America's huge contribution to music in years past, be it soul, R&B, jazz, country, or just plain rock 'n roll – music that influenced millions upon millions in scores of countries. American singers and musicians from, roughly, the twenties through the eighties of last century, shaped many of us into what we are today. They made us feel positive about ourselves, they made us believe that love was just around the corner and they made us think that we'd forever be young.

Here you watch them and you realize, more than ever before, that some of the best of American music was made and performed by black America. Their contribution to the field is immense.

Walking in downtown Cleveland after I leave the museum, I hardly see blacks. I spot some, but for the most part they are the poor who'll ask you for a cigarette, for food and for cash.

On East Fourth Street, where a section of the street is for pedestrians only, there are a number of fancy restaurants. The diners, at least on this day, are all white.

I take my seat at a fine restaurant called Lola Bistro, and I have a blast. The food is great; best I have had so far in America. Yes, most of the food in America, at least this far, stinks. Even the bread in this country, and I know this from New York as well, is most suitable for dead dogs.

But Lola is good.

• • •

Belly full, I go to meet the poor. I learned this trick long ago from some very successful politicians. On the next street I meet a black guy and ask him how's life in Cleveland.

"I love Cleveland."

What's special about this city?

"I was born here."

Let me ask you something else: I walked on the street with the fine dining and I noticed that those who were enjoying the good food were all white. Did I get it wrong?

"No, that's correct."

Blacks live the hard life?

"Yes."

Why?

"It's always been like this here."

Will it always be?

"Yes."

Why?

"That's the way it is."

Did life not change for black America once Obama was elected?

"Yes. One black family moved to a better house. That's it. He lives in the White House; we live here. No change for us."

I ate. I walked. Time to rest. Tomorrow I drive. Where to? Detroit.

Why? Because there's nothing more American than Detroit. How do I know? I just made it up.

Gate Four

Blacks kill blacks because they're "niggas" – If you don't know who you are, you are a German American – If an Indian mosquito bites you, you will become a Native American

ON THE WAY TO DETROIT I SEE FEWER AMERICAN FLAGS ON THE ROAD THAN I saw before. I don't know why. Are Michiganders less patriotic?

Soon enough I spot a mosque. I have arrived, I believe, in Dearborn. Dearborn, if I remember correctly, is one of the most concentrated Arab towns in the USA.

There must be some good Mediterranean restaurants around. And just thinking of this, believe it or not, makes me hungry.

Yep. My belly is calling again. It had good food at Lola, but that's long gone.

Let me make one point very clear. There are two obligations that I must meet on this journey: supply Cruze with enough liquids to drink and supply my belly with enough food to eat.

And I will.

Cruze is doing okay at the moment; I poured enough gas into her belly this morning, and now it's my belly's turn. Where shall I find the food?

I drive on residential streets, and when I see a guy walking on the sidewalk I stop the Cruze to ask him for good Arab food. He sends me to some hotel. No, I say to him; I want to eat with the people!

"You are on the end side of Dearborn," he says to me. "If you want to go to where the Arabs live, all I can tell you is that you better not."

Why?

"That's a dangerous place."

I love dangerous. Can you give me directions?

He directs me to the highway. Why does he think he can fool me like this?

I drive a bit more and when I see a man getting out of his SUV I stop next to him. Where can I find good Arab food around here? I ask him.

"There are some around," he says, and suggests a tourist restaurant.

No, I say to him. I want to eat with the people.

"What people?"

Arabs!

"What do you mean?"

Where the Arabs go to eat!

"The restaurant I suggested to you is –"

I cut him off. I want to eat with the real people of Dearborn. You know what I mean? The Arabs!

"I'm afraid you don't understand what I'm trying to tell you."

Explain!

"You want to be in the heart of Dearborn, where the original mosque is?"

I have no idea what he's referring to, but I say: Yes, that's exactly where I want to go!

"That's a scary, dangerous place. I'm sure you don't want to go there."

I love "scary" and I admire "dangerous," my man!

"You sure you know what you're doing?"

Yes!

Now convinced that I'm totally deranged, he gives me the right directions.

• • •

I drive there. While driving I pass deserted buildings that look like old factories, and I drive over the biggest and deepest potholes imaginable in any developing country. Am I really in America? What's the story with these potholes?

While driving in and out of potholes I repeatedly see this sign on the road: "Injure/kill a worker $7,500 + 15 years."

Whatever this is, I'm sure it has nothing to do with Islamic law. I don't remember reading this in the Quran.

Yes, I studied the Quran. Actually a nice book.

I keep on driving until I see signs in Arabic. I've arrived in food paradise! There is only one little problem: the restaurants are closed.

How didn't I think of it before? It's Ramadan! The Muslims are fasting during the daylight hours. What an idiot I am.

I get out of the car and look for some humans who can tell me when the Islamic day ends and the Islamic night starts in Dearborn. A young man, wearing his baseball cap backwards, tells me that the breaking of the fast today is at 9:14 p.m., about two hours from now. What shall I do till then?

Well, I could talk with the guy. Tell me something, I ask him, do you know what people around here say about you?

"What?"

That this place is dangerous. Is it?

"Where you from?"

Jordan.

"I'll tell you why they say it: because they are liars. Here, dangerous? You know that we Muslims are the best. Don't you? Detroit is the murder capital of the USA. Not Dearborn! We are the best!"

My brother, I don't know if you read the news lately, but we are not doing very well. Look what's happening in the Middle East, Daesh (ISIS/ISIL, the Islamic State of Iraq and the Levant) is beheading people right and left and everybody is seeing the pictures.

"Don't believe anything you see on the news! They are all liars!"

Where are you originally from?

"I was born here, but my family is from Yemen. Everybody here is from Yemen. If you want the Jordanians or the Palestinians or the Lebanese, they are a fifteen-minute drive from here."

Where will you break the fast today?

"Not with my parents; they went for a vacation in Yemen."

They vacation in Yemen? There's a huge war there!

"Who told you? Don't believe the news!"

Since it's so good in Yemen, why aren't you moving back?

"Why? What's wrong with here? I'm an American! I have the freedom to stay here!"

• • •

I bid him farewell and drive to the Jordanian, Palestinian and Lebanese section. And I meet an Iraqi man named Muhammad. I ask him who lives around here.

"Arabs."

Muslims?

"Yes."

Only?

"Yes. It's good."

No other people here?

"What people?"

Let's say, Jews.

"Where are you from?"

Germany.

"Okay. I have a sister there."

Can a Jew live here?

"No."

Why?

"He can pass by here, but not live here."

Why?

"That's the way it is."

Why?

"There are Jews about ten miles away from here, but not here."

Why not here?

"That's the way it is, I told you."

He reminds me of the black guy from Cleveland. Both say, "That's the way it is." The blacks won't have fine food, and the Jews can't live here.

Yeah. That's the way it is.

• • •

I move on to an Arab sweets store, where I find three young women. All are Lebanese. Do you like America? I ask the one who seems the youngest of them.

"No."

Why are you here?

"I study in a university here. I study interior design."

Why here and not in Beirut?

"It's too expensive there."

What will do when you finish college?

"Go back home, to Lebanon."

I heard that there are some problems there.

"No! Hezballah is strong and they protect us." All present agree.

Hezballah (the Party of God) has been on the United States State Department list of Foreign Terrorist Organizations since 1997, but I don't raise this issue. Instead, I say: You are probably right. I like Hassan Nasrallah (the leader of Hezballah) very much!

"We love him!"

The others agree again.

• • •

I buy some sweets and drive around the neighborhood. I can't spot one American flag flying from anyone's home. Yet it's America here. A visit to a local hookah store, where they sell tobacco for nargilas, makes this clear. These tobaccos come in different flavors, such as apple and orange, but in Dearborn they also come in the flavor of "Starbucks Coffee."

The Fourth of July is coming in a couple of days, and here you can't tell. What you can tell here is that today is Ramadan.

I'm starving.

I go to a restaurant called Al Ameer, which is open for Arab Christians who don't observe Ramadan. I order hummus, baba ghanoush, falafel, kibbeh, Turkish coffee, and for a moment there I imagine that I'm in Bagdad. The food is great, just like Mama made in Iraq before America invaded the country.

Is Arab Dearborn scary? No. Is it dangerous? No. Are its Arab residents racist? You bet, but no more than their racist neighbors who call them scary and dangerous.

• • •

I drive in this land and I meet blacks, Jews, Arabs and Quakers. No Germans.

I am looking for Germans, those fifty million Americans who claim Germany as the land of their ancestors. Where the heck are the fifty million Germans?

I keep on driving.

By the way, I'm starting to get used to driving and I am loving it. From time to time I go over the speed limit, run a red light or two, but all in all Cruze and I are getting to know each other well. It feels like dating.

At this moment I am driving on the roads of America's famed "Motor City," Detroit, and I – new driver that I am – feel a certain connection between the city and myself, as if it were my homeland. Your lost son is home again, Motor City!

I reach Michigan Avenue, which I think is in the direction of downtown. Driving along Michigan Avenue, though, I notice something sad. Block after block is deserted, desolated and ugly. Condemned buildings are the rule rather than the exception.

What happened to my hometown? I don't know. I just drive.

When I reach a sign saying "Heidelberg," I stop. Heidelberg is one of my most favorite German towns. Have I reached its duplicate city? Have I just found the fifty million? I drive there.

I see two German tourists, standing close to their car, but that's it. The rest are blacks.

I leave Heidelberg and I go on driving. Where to? Let my Cruze decide.

I make a few turns on side streets, and then I reach a place that – I can't tell what it is. It reminds me of a place I was in years ago: Fukushima, Japan, right after the tsunami and the nuclear reactor meltdown. As in Fukushima, there's an air of total mayhem here.

Once upon a time this place must have been a lovely neighborhood, with nicely laid out private homes. Now those homes look more like rotten monuments, some of them just skeletons, but I can tell that there are creatures moving inside them, maybe ghosts or rats.

This area must have been abandoned decades ago. Wild shrubs and advanced decay are almost everywhere, and then I see debris here and there, there and here. I drive closer.

And I notice people.

Yes. People. People who, in this setting, look like ghosts. Frightening.

As if from under the earth, a black guy with a bicycle appears near me. His name is Jay and he's a twenty-six-year-old father of four. What's going on around here? I ask him.

"Black people killing each other."

Why?

"'Cause they're niggas [niggers, meaning blacks]. They do it 'cause they do it."

Why?

"If they think you didn't look at them right, they shoot you. No other reason."

That's it?

"You know where you are?"

What do you mean?

"You know what this place is?"

I want to say Fukushima but I say "not really" instead.

"This place called Red Zone."

Red Zone?

"Yeah."

Red Zone of what?

"Last zone."

After here, death?

"Yes. Here you don't know who will shoot you."

Is it always like this?

"Always like this with black people. They shootin' each other."

The situation is getting worse, he says, because it's summer. "It's hot, and people shoot."

Across the street is a burned-out house. How did that house get burned? I ask.

"A black drunk man lived there. He was drinkin' and he lied down by the fireplace. The house was burned and he was burned."

Did he burn himself on purpose?

"No! He was a black drunk, that's why."

The Fourth of July is coming. Are you proud to be an American?

"Yeah. *Black* American!"

The houses here look like they've seen better times. What happened?

"We didn't build them. They are ours 'cause they were abandoned and if you fix an abandoned house and live in it, it's yours. Squatters' rights. We didn't buy them. We moved in. But people are stealin' all the time. A door, a window. Anythin'. And we kill each other, black against black. Is the red car yours?"

Yes.

"You want me to keep it for you, while you're walkin' around?"

No, thanks. Tell me: Do you need a gun to live here?

"Yeah!"

Do you have a gun?

"Not on me."

We shake hands, and I depart.

How long will Jay stay alive? I don't know.

• • •

A few houses down the road there's this sign on an empty house: "Reduced Price. 5,000 or best offer." Yes, there are places in the country that boasts some of the world's most exclusive real estate where you can buy a home for $5,000 or less.

Everything's possible in America.

This place, what can I say, makes Germantown look like a nice, cozy neighborhood.

I enter one of the abandoned properties and am shocked to see the level of destruction. Everything and anything that could have been stolen from here, down to wires and switches, has been stolen.

I walk around the neighborhood and I see death lurking on every corner. The Last Zone is here, and the train of death is moving fast. How and why is this place allowed to exist in our day and age?

I can't answer this question.

There are countless Western humanitarian organizations, funded to the tune of billions, that send activists all over the world to improve the lot of the downtrodden. Why aren't they here? Come here, Human Rights Watch. Visit this place, Amnesty International. Issue a resolution, United Nations. Bring your shiny vans, Red Cross. Do something, Save the Children and Save Africa. Fly over here as fast as you can, NGO activists, if you dare.

Where are those activists and organizations when people die like flies? Are they all Quakers?

• • •

My hotel in Dearborn, DoubleTree by Hilton, is offering shuttle buses to downtown Detroit. I jump on the opportunity. There's no point in driving to downtown and then looking for parking.

The driver, Matt, tells me that Dearborn is a historic place and that it's here that Henry Ford created the American auto industry and built the headquarters of the Ford company. Why here? "Henry Ford liked this place."

So be it.

Detroit, he also tells me, used to have eight million residents, but most left and now only about two million live in the city. I like learning history from van drivers. It's special.

What happened? I ask him.

"Race riots."

Six million people running away during "race riots" must have been quite a deadly scene.

"Not like in the Civil War, but bad enough."

It's hard for me to imagine six million people running away from their homes, probably because I'm a bit sensitive to the "six million" number.

But, hold on! Maybe it did happen, maybe that's what the Red Zone used to be, long before Jay started calling it home.

What were the race riots about? Maybe Matt will tell me next time. Now he drops me off at the General Motors Renaissance Center, a skyscraper by the Detroit River and across the river from Windsor, Ontario.

Yes. Canada is just across the river.

I don't cross into Canada. I stay in the United States and enter the Renaissance. I have no idea what I'm doing here. All I know is that this place looks much better than the Red Zone, and that's enough for me.

I see some people on a guided tour, and I join them. A woman who seems to be twenty years past retirement age leads us along escalators and elevators, amid GM cars on display. She tells us about the time when America's auto industry almost collapsed: "The decline started in the seventies, when people started to buy foreign-made cars. But that era is over. Today the Big Three [General Motors, Ford, Chrysler] are back to their old glory."

We follow her into a see-through elevator and we go up to the seventy-second floor, where there's a 360-degree view of Detroit.

Lovely. Yes. From here, let me tell you, Detroit looks plain gorgeous. What a rich, beautiful and fascinating city!

Our guide points to different parts of the city and advises us where we could go to eat, shop, shop a bit more, dine, drink, shop again, see shows, take rides, shop more, walk and shop more. Detroit is there for us, and anything we desire could be ours today. No Red Zone and no Last Zone, only pleasures and beauty.

These tourists will never know of the Red Zone. I leave the tourists and the guide and walk on my own. Somewhere in the midst of this building, between the escalators, I meet Frank. "The biggest ethnic group in Detroit," he tells me, "used to be German." That was around one hundred years ago, but today it's a different story. "With the exception of downtown, Detroit is 98 percent black."

Would be very lovely to see the reactions of the Canadian tourists if I told them this.

I ask Frank about the Red Zone, but he doesn't know what I'm talking about. He knows Detroit, extremely well, but he has never heard of the Red Zone. I describe the place to him: It's like a ghost town, a place for walking dead.

Oh yeah. Now he knows of the place, except *place* is the wrong word; *places* is more exact. In other words: there are many red zones in Detroit. Jay's Red Zone is not an official name; it's a name based in reality.

"What you saw is just a small section of many similar places that exist in Detroit, spread around an area of 139 square miles."

That's huge; that's too many ghosts.

In the sixties, Frank tells me, blacks were rioting on the streets of Detroit, burning and looting the city, which caused a "white flight" from it. Race riots. White flight.

Historians disagree on what happened here in those days, Frank tells me, and some reject the term *white flight*. But he is from here and this is what he knows.

What started those riots?

"Martin Luther King gave his famous speech first here, before he did it in DC. He tried it out first in Detroit."

You are referring to the "I Have a Dream" speech, I assume.

"Yes. After he gave that speech, and 200,000 people followed him, one thing led to another, the streets of Detroit were burning, and the Caucasians abandoned their properties, fleeing Detroit."

This Frank is super-PC; he wouldn't say "whites." Are you telling me that those "red zone" homes belonged to whites who were running away from the rioting blacks?

"Yes."

In other words, there's another story here: not that of the suffering blacks that we usually hear, but also of rioting blacks and suffering whites.

Where was Martin Luther King in all this? American people are always told, by officials and the media, by intellectuals and by various leaders, that King's movement was non-violent and that a racist murdered him. But somehow the part of the white flight is rarely, if at all, mentioned.

Personally, I never heard of it.

• • •

The Fourth of July starts in just a few hours and I go back to Dearborn, to my DoubleTree by Hilton.

If you're curious: the swivel chair in this hotel works perfectly. Almost everything does here, with just a few minor exceptions. For example: the toilet doesn't always flush. Sometimes it does, other times it doesn't.

It's the Fourth of July in the morning and I need a cigarette. Down near the parking lot there are two benches and a table, a metal structure that is welded together, and two ashtrays are next to it. It's the smoking section. And that's where I go.

I light up my Indonesian cigarette, which I bought a couple of days ago, and soon enough three men join me. They are visitors from Jordan and they want to smoke.

They are real Jordanians, by the way; unlike me. Welcome to the lepers' section, I say to them, and they smile in appreciation.

"America," one of them tells me, "is a fake place."

What do you mean?

"It's all fake here. People don't relate to people, not even to their neighbors. All fake and wars. Who do you think blew up the Twin Towers? America and the Jews. You think that Arabs did that? Who are Daesh? American agents!"

Of course, when one calls the other a "fake" he'd better be without fault. This is not exactly the case here. These guys are Muslims and today is Ramadan, when smoking is forbidden during the daylight hours. But they smoke, something they wouldn't dare do in Jordan.

What's your name?

"Ghazi."

Nice to meet you.

"The food here in America," he goes on, "has no taste. The Americans export terror but they don't know how to cook."

I found myself just the right place to begin the Fourth of July. Now I need to do better. But what?

The hotel staff gives me a few suggestions and I pick "America's greatest history attraction," as the Henry Ford Museum defines itself. Seems like a good idea, and I go there.

• • •

The museum features a gorgeous display of the history of the auto industry. In a section called "Driving America," I read this: "Americans didn't invent the automobile, but we embraced it and quickly made it our own."

So true! I personally feel it. Yes, I embrace driving and, yes, I make it my own. I can vouch for every single word here!

"The car," it continues, "led us to reshape our culture and landscape like no other invention."

I think that my constant driving these days, after a life of almost no driving, is indeed shaping me. I'm not sure into what, but that's beside the point.

Henry Ford is credited here as the inventor of the assembly line. For him this was the best way to make the car affordable, not only for the rich but for the rest of the people as well.

Henry's car-to-all idea was an inspiration to Adolf Hitler, who embraced this idea wholeheartedly. Sadly, this is not the only thing these two men shared in common.

To put it mildly: Henry was a flaming anti-Semite.

Among his many activities and possessions, he owned the *Dearborn Independent* newspaper, which ran articles, and also a series called "The International Jew: The World's Problem," accusing Jews of every bad thing under the sun. For years he made public his accusations that Jewish bankers were responsible for World War I and that they killed Christians for their personal enrichment. Following a lawsuit, he in effect apologized for his anti-Semitism, but later on in life he repeated such claims over and over.

I'm not in the habit of thinking about this Henry, but shortly after entering the museum his history pops up in my brain, and when a guide approaches me to ask if I need any help I ask her to show me the section in the museum that deals with this particular part of Henry's history. The guide, a nice lady, looks at me in total disbelief, as if I had just asked her to commit a major crime.

"What did you ask, again?" she asks. I repeat the question.

"I am not aware of what you are saying," she replies. "I don't know anything about that. But, if you want, you can use our help screens. If there is anything to what you say I'm sure you'll find all the necessary info in our computers."

She gives me a card to be used with the research computers on the floor.

Great!

First, I have to register with the system, which I do, and activate the card, which I also do. That done, I can now start using the most authoritative database about Henry Ford in the world.

Fantastic!

I start my research. I put "Henry Ford and Jews" in the search area and I get this: "This search returned no results." I try "Jews" and I get the same response.

I give up and walk around until I reach a big sign, "With Liberty & Justice for All." This must be interesting. I go over there, and another guide approaches me. Would I like help? Yes, with pleasure. Could you direct me to the section that deals with Henry Ford's anti-Semitism? I ask her.

She gives me a sweet, innocent smile.

Were you never asked this question before? I ask her.

"No. Nobody has ever asked me this question."

It's a historical fact, as far as I know –

"My husband worked all his life for the Ford company and he never mentioned anything about it."

I give her a friendly smile, one of my more stupid ones, and I ask her: Is this the first time you're hearing about it?

"Since you put it in those words: Yes, I heard about it. But not here."

Do you know why they don't deal with it here?

"Here it's all 'hush hush.' Why are you interested?"

I'm a journalist.

"I didn't say anything. Don't quote me. It's between you and me."

I won't use your name.

"Then it's okay."

Why don't they –

"Here we talk only about positive stuff, not about problems."

But this is not exactly true. This museum does deal with this country's problematic black history. It features, for example, Martin Luther King and Rosa Parks.

In Rosa Parks's case they even have the actual bus on display here. Rosa Parks became famous in this country for refusing, in 1955, an order by the bus driver to give up her seat in the front of the bus for a white man, which was the law of the land in those days. I go on the bus and ask for the exact seat Rosa Parks was sitting on, and then sit in it.

Within minutes another lady from the museum comes by to help me with my historical Henry question. I'm inside the bus, she's outside – and we chat. The guide, of a higher rank than the guides I've encountered before, tells me that there's a reason the issue of Henry's anti-Semitism is not dealt with in this museum. No, it has nothing to do with trying to hide anything. The reason is much simpler: the Henry Ford Museum is about cars, not about history.

I'm sitting on Rosa's seat, correct? I ask her.

"Yes."

Hello. I'm Rosa, not a car.

She feels like a total fool. "I don't know what to tell you," she says in a low voice.

And this is how it works in the Information Age, as our era is often described: Henry was a nice, pleasant man and Detroit is a city of stores and restaurants.

Good.

I get off Rosa's bus and move on to look at some exhibits. As I walk around I see a chart titled: "Population of Detroit, 1900–2010." Here I read that at its height, in 1960, Detroit had a population of about 1,800,000 and that in 2010 the population of Detroit was less than 700,000. These are different figures than the ones I was given by Matt the driver. Somehow I think that on this issue, the museum got the history right.

At Greenfield Village, which is part of the Henry Ford Museum complex, the concert "Salute to America," in celebration of the Fourth of July, is about to take place. Thousands of people have shown up here, and we are treated to musical compositions such as "None So Beautiful as the Brave."

This event is a "salute to our troops," a speaker at the podium says.

If you dropped from Mars into this place you'd think that America is in the middle of a huge war, and that its survival is at risk. "Our troops." Salute to our troops. Beautiful Braves. I never think of "our troops" in New York, but this is not New York. This is Michigan.

The people here are in a celebratory mood. Some carry the American flag and some wear it – a hat in the image of the flag, or a shirt or pair of pants. Almost all the people here are white.

But not everybody is happy. A young employee, with not a trace of a flag nor a hint of happiness, arouses my curiosity. I approach her.

What's cooking, girl?

"Welcome to the Land of the Free!" she says, sarcastically. "This is the Henry Ford Museum. Do you know who Henry Ford was?"

Yes. A Nazi sympathizer. But the other girls wouldn't admit it.

"True. During training they teach us that if a visitor asks about Henry Ford's racist history we should say that we never heard of it. We have to pretend to help the visitors and we give them research cards to research on their own, knowing full well that they won't find anything."

Where can I smoke here?

"Nowhere. We are outside, but you can't smoke anywhere. Land of the Free. Where you from?"

Europe.

"I wish so much to move to Europe! We have new healthcare, you know, in this country. In theory it sounds so good, but in reality it's a whole different story. My husband used to have a good health-care plan. Everything was included and no additional expenses. Not anymore. Since the new healthcare took effect, the insurance companies make us pay more because now they need to subsidize the Obamacare [the Affordable Care Act, which President Obama pushed through Congress and which is considered his "signature" legislation]. My husband and I are $20,000 in debt, which we incurred in the last two years in medical expenses. Healthcare? I want to leave. I'm sorry I dropped this all on you, but it just came out."

What I'm learning here today is immense. The Henry Ford Museum, a mainstream giant, is shamelessly engaged in spreading lies. In the enlightened age of the twenty-first century, nobody says nothing.

Where is Abe Foxman when we need him?

• • •

Michigan is not a small state, and so I keep roaming within its borders to get over its Ford. I reach Frankenmuth. Sounds and looks Germanic.

Am I finally going to meet the Germans? I shall see. Frankenmuth celebrates Christmas all year round, and as you enter it – we are in July, to remind you – you are greeted by a big sign: "Merry Christmas." And as you drive through, you feel as if you were in a Bavarian village on Christmas – only the signs are mostly in English, and Santa Claus, America's favorite grandpa, is presented in very large scale. Frankenmuth's specialty is Christmas goods, as becomes ever clearer while walking through here.

In Frankenmuth they serve German food and the waiters are dressed very cutely. The girls at the restaurant that I go to, the Bavarian Inn Lodge, look like an exact replica of the Nazi-era photos that featured beautiful German girls greeting Hitler. I can't believe this image comes to my mind.

The food here is good, if you care to know. At this very moment they serve brunch, buffet style, and I get myself a bread pudding that reminds me of home, wherever that home is, and a mouth-watering cherry strudel, a little bitter and a little sweet, just as I like it.

But enough about food. Let's get spiritual.

Today there is a "Patriotic Prayer Service," which is to take place at the largest building in Frankenmuth, the Festhall. About four thousand people attend, which is almost everyone that lives in Frankenmuth.

In a brochure printed for this occasion, I read:

We are glad you're here today!
We welcome you to this special time of praise as we worship God and the gift of His Son and for the blessings we enjoy as citizens of the United States of America. This is also a wonderful opportunity for us to honor all who have served our nation and those who continue to protect the freedom we so deeply cherish.

Are these people "German Americans"?

I walk in. As I enter the Festhall, which is decorated with a huge American flag and a shiny cross, a group of people carrying flags and machine guns enter as well. To my right I see two soldiers, both black. I talk with Walters, a soldier wearing a US Army uniform.

What's America for you?

"Opportunity."

Can you be more specific?

"Yes. I grew up very poor. In my family we shared pants, but now I'm doing very well."

Are you a rich man today?

"Compared to where I started, I am."

Did you serve in battle?

"Yes, I did."

Where?

"Afghanistan."

How was it?

"Scary."

Why did you serve there?

"'Cause I'm Christian."

From the stage comes the sound of music: "Glory, glory, Hallelujah."

• • •

I need a cigarette. I walk out. Not far from me is a square, called Military Space, where a huge American flag is flying proudly above a plane and a tank.

I am in Germany.

The thousands of people here must be German, I say to myself. They are so Germanic! Germans, in case you've never met one, are very extreme people. That's their culture. If they decide to be nice, they will be the nicest humans possible. When they decide, for example, to be liberal, no liberal the world over will match them, not even close. If, on the other hand, their mood sweeps them in the exact opposite direction, no one will match their cruelty. One day they can be the Weimar Republic and the next day they can become the Nazi empire. They are, in a word, extreme.

Look at the people here. Extreme. They want it all: flags, planes, tanks, machine guns and a prayer. But that's not enough, of course. They got themselves two black soldiers; looks really cool. Is it enough now? Nope. They also have here a monument made of a steel beam from the wreckage of New York's Twin Towers, which was given to them by New York City's Bravest.

Give me a break, patriotic Frankenmuth! I smoke my cigarette.

There's a lady here, and she tells me that Mackinac Island is a great place to be. There are no cars on the road, she says, and it's really a very quiet place. To get my mind off the Military Space and the Red Zone, I proceed to my next stop: Mackinac Island, Michigan.

• • •

The name of the island was coined by Native Americans, I'm told, due to its shape (*mackinac* means "the great brooding turtle"). The only way to get to Mackinac Island is by either private jet or by boat. Since I don't yet own a private jet, I take a boat across Lake Huron, where I'm picked up by a horse-drawn carriage to my new abode, the Grand Hotel.

The first thing I notice when I get there toward evening time is the hotel's employees who are taking down the American flags for the night. Why? I ask a lady whose name I don't know.

"Because the American flag must not fly in the dark. At night it must be taken down unless a source of light is shining on it. But since they don't want to have lights on every flag – they have many flags here – they take them down and fold them. I wouldn't say it's a federal law, but this is the custom."

Each flag, I notice, is folded by two people. Can't one do this alone? I ask.

"No. The American flag must not touch the floor, that's why you need two people. These flags are big, and if only one person folded them they might touch the floor."

Oy vey, as they say in Yiddish.

Another person, a middle-aged man, wants to share with me his thoughts about the American flag. "For me," he says, "the flag represents freedom. I revere the flag. We fought for it, for our freedom," and now his voice is cracking with immense emotion: "I'm a patriot, and I'm not ashamed of it. I'm proud of it, I'm proud of my country!"

I look at the man and I wonder: Is this the face of the Brave?

The Grand Hotel has 390 rooms, and it's almost full. Average price per person per day is $285, two meals included. Dinner is a four-course meal, and all the diners are white. We are served by the darker-skinned, who are mostly from Jamaica.

Diet Coke is not included, and no alcohol. No smoking anywhere on the property.

I go out to smoke. As I puff with pleasure, Bryan joins me. Bryan is from Texas, he tells me, and he is interested in foreign affairs. To demonstrate his wide knowledge on foreign issues he shares his opinion with me that Israel should stop building settlements in Gaza. Should I tell him that no living Jew exists in Gaza? No, I'm not going there.

I think he should join the Henry Ford people; he would be a great asset for them.

I go to my room and check the news, perhaps I'll find something about the new Gaza. Here's something from the *Huffington Post*: "Greeks on Sunday decisively rejected a bailout deal proposed by the country's international creditors, which demanded new austerity measures in return for emergency funds. The vote amounted to a stinging rebuke of the austerity measures imposed on Greece since 2010."

And this is the news from CNN, reporting from South Carolina: "A bill that would remove the Confederate flag from statehouse grounds was approved by state lawmakers in a 37-3 Senate vote." CNN does not indicate how many people will be required to take down this flag.

New York's *Daily News*, in a report about a white man who was beaten unconscious by a group of blacks, writes:

> Cold-hearted bystanders jeered and laughed at an unconscious tourist lying at their feet after a vicious beating in Cincinnati, a video showed.
>
> "Damn, n---a, you just got knocked the f--k out!" shouted one of the callous witnesses.
>
> The man's face was covered in blood as he lay motionless late Saturday in the city's Fountain Square neighborhood.

The accompanying video is hard to watch.

N---a stands for nigger, or nigga (in black dialect). *F--k* stands for fuck. American media won't spell out nigger, because that's racist. They also don't like to spell out fuck because it's not a nice word.

Not only media. The other day I asked Siri, the iPhone "secretary," What the fuck is wrong with you? The response: "I'll pretend I didn't hear that." When Siri is in a preaching mood, which happens, and I use the "f" word, Siri responds: "Tuvia! Your language!"

Rooted in Quaking Puritanism as this country is, the mainstream media spells out no explicit sexual terms. If you are in the United States and you want to tell somebody in writing that he's an asshole, this is the way to write it: a-----e. In a generation or two, cigarette will be spelled c-------e.

I'm going out to smoke one more c-------e.

· · ·

It's a new day in Michigan state and I am in Sault Ste. Marie in Michigan's Upper Peninsula, also known as "Soo."

There is an Indian reservation here. What's a reservation? A reservation is defined in official dialect thusly: "An area of land reserved for a tribe or tribes under treaty or other agreement." In simpler lingo, it goes like this: Once upon a time, and for God knows how many thousands of years, this land was populated with people of many tribes and languages, none of which was white and none of which spoke English.

These people, who would later be known as "Native Americans" or "Indians," lived in this land on their own until one day a white man dropped by and desired the land for himself. The white man, who brought some friends along with him, killed the natives, raped them, starved them, stole from them, and once he was done he declared the land as a land of We the People, a shrine of democracy and freedom, and renamed the land as the Land of the Free and the Home of the Brave.

Of course this didn't look so nice, and so the white man, a man of supreme intelligence, kept some of the natives alive and proclaimed chunks of land here and there, there and here as the natives' inheritance until the end of days. Those chunks of lands are called reservations, sovereign lands, and God knows what else.

In a reservation, I am told, no white man roams. Why? A reservation is a sacred ground, reserved for the great Native American Indians.

I love sacred. And so I drive through the Soo reservation, looking for holy Indian inspiration, but I can't spot anything "Indian." It's just a bunch of houses and roads, but no holy rays anywhere in sight. Have I gone blind? To be on the safe side of knowledge, I go to meet the leader of the people here; maybe he will be able to show me the way and teach me about the sacred.

His name is Aaron Payment and his business card describes him as the tribal chairperson of the Chippewa Indians in Sault Ste. Marie. He is, in short, the tribal chief, and I'm delighted at the opportunity to meet such a man.

His hair is salt and pepper and he has a ponytail as well. He is dressed like a normal American – no Indian feathers.

What does it mean to be Indian today? I ask him, just to get acquainted.

"Recognizing your origin and spirituality," he says in beautiful English.

What does that mean?

"I was raised both in our traditional beliefs and in Christianity."

You are Christian, then.

"Yes, I am."

What does it mean to be Native American if you're Christian?

"To completely live with respect to other people and to the environment."

I really don't know what this means, and so I say: That's what every Christian on the liberal side in New York would say; what's unique to the Native American?

"Our struggle with surviving the American attempt to annihilate us. But we don't give up, we persevere," he answers with a serious face.

That's what Jews say as well, and blacks too. What's unique to the Indians?

"I don't know that there is a difference."

Do you speak any Native American language?

"No."

What makes an "Indian"? How do you decide if somebody is Indian?

"Some states have a blood quantum, and only those who have one-quarter Indian blood are considered Indian. This was challenged up to the Supreme Court, since this is racist. The court agreed and decided that the tribes themselves will have the right to determine who is Indian."

How do you determine who's Indian?

"If you can prove that you have one-thirty-second of Indian blood in you, then we will recognize you as Indian."

That's racist as well, isn't it?

"No. One-thirty-second of Indian blood is our way to determine who's Indian, since we need some way to measure – "

Why is one-quarter blood racism, and one-thirty-second is not?

This he cannot answer. And in any case he is in a hurry. Mr. Payment is traveling today to Washington, DC, on Indian business; he is looking for more government grants to help keep the Indian culture and people strong and good.

Is what I see and hear here a fair presentation of "Native America"? I should visit more reservations, because what I witness here is not culture but business.

Aaron, by the way, tells me that he's one-quarter Austrian. I wonder what I am? Maybe a n---a.

You can never tell.

• • •

I leave the Soo and ramble around for miles. I mix in with some Yoopers (people of the Upper Peninsula) until I reach Munising, where I take a three-hour Lake Superior cruise offered by Pictured Rock Cruises. One of the first things I hear once seated in the boat is this: "Lake Superior is as large as Austria." They love Austria here.

We cruise near caves situated at the bottom of the rocks at the water's edge. The rock formations, multicolored, are brilliantly reflected on the surface of the water. It is bewitchingly glorious! Simply divine.

This divine place, our captain maliciously interjects into my thoughts, used to serve as an excruciating hell. When Indian tribes fought one another they would take the captured of the other tribe, bring them into the caves by canoe and leave them here to die.

Finally, I see, I get in touch with something that's uniquely of the Indian culture. What they did here, whether I like it or not, was brutal.

There's no escape from these caves. The captured would have few choices: jump into the water and die fast or stay in the caves until the waters swept their bodies into the lake. If, by any chance, the water didn't carry them away, starvation would take their lives. A slow, painful death.

This, too, is part of Indian culture and history.

As the boat cruises along, the mixture of ever-changing rock formations and ever-mesmerizing water colors does not end. Here nature reveals itself in its full might and glory.

My whole being is captivated by the beauty around me. There's no painting – realistic, impressionistic, surreal or modern – in any multimillion-dollar New York museum that matches the images unfolding in front of my eyes. Here's where the master artist of all, call it God or nature, practices his art and performs his magic. The water is clear like a pure diamond, the rocks are mighty as eternity, and no race – Indian or whatever – is strong enough or capable enough to lord over either of them.

• • •

Government grants and funding, no matter how large, are never enough for those on the receiving end. Native Americans are no different from anyone else, and they have found a way to make more money – not from the US government but from US citizens.

Since they are a government within a government and a land within a land, they make their own laws and rules, and they build whatever they want on their lands – like cash machines, popularly called "casinos." To the Indians (interchangeable with "Native Americans") it doesn't matter whether the particular state in which they live allows casinos within its borders, since they make their own laws.

There are Indian casinos all over this country, and today I'm going to one of them, the Soaring Eagle Casino and Resort in Chippewa, Michigan.

Frank, of the casino's PR department, greets me as I arrive. FYI: Frank is one-quarter Indian, one part French, and God knows what else. Naturally, when we meet Frank first goes into PR mode and tells me that in just a few days the twenty-seventh Elijah Elk Competitive Powwow ("Gathering and Competition") will take place at the Soaring Eagle Casino and Resort.

What the heck is that?

"A cultural exchange of competitive dance and drum of the Indian people."

Sadly, I'm leaving today and won't be able to attend such a cultural event. But no worry: If I want, Frank says, he'll take me to the local museum, where I can learn about the culture of the Indians.

That's how PR people think: always have a Plan B. He drives me to the museum.

A very nice place, I must say. Images of Indians, with clothes and hairstyles that one would see in movies, are presented here. Highly recommended if you're into feathers.

This museum is also for those among you who are into "touch" technology: you touch a word or image on one of the screens provided and you hear it pronounced in a Native American language. For example: sugar is *ziibaakwad*, chair is *pabiwin* and paper is *mzinigan*.

I ask Frank if he speaks any Native American/Indian language. "A few words only."

I too, by the way. I know *ziibaakwad*, *pabiwin* and *mzinigan*.

Frank tells me that Indians are "First Nations people." What's that?

"The Jewish people believe that they are the children of God, and we believe this about ourselves. We were the first people on earth, from which all other people came." Christians and Jews think that the first people on earth were Adam and Eve, but the Indians believe that the first people on earth were Jibbawaba or Chippewa.

Not bad.

Frank is Christian, by the way. The one real difference between him and any other American Christian is that the Christian would say he that he or she believe in the "creator" while Frank says that he believes in Jimanadu, which means creator.

Jimanadu sounds much nicer than creator, I agree.

Plus: If you believe in Jimanadu, you don't have to pay state income tax. Indians in reservations don't pay that.

Frank is a very capable PR person, but even he cannot put his finger on what makes an Indian an Indian.

Is this all just a little racist scheme to erect big casinos? One way to find out is by visiting a reservation and speaking to its residents.

• • •

Not a very easy task. There's this proper white etiquette, alluded to above, which dictates that no white shall go to an Indian reservation and talk to its people. But I try this anyway and I ask Frank if he wouldn't mind showing me around the reservation, because I want to schmooze with some Indians who are not working as PR executives. He complies.

Being a PR man, he first gives me the following info.

Name of reservation: Isabella Indian Reservation. Tribe: Saginaw Chippewa. Center of Michigan.

Members total: 3,490 people. Living on these grounds: 1,100.

Finances: Every adult member gets $64,000 yearly, and those under eighteen years of age get $32,000 each.

Where do all these bundles of dollars come from? From the businesses that the tribe does. The Soaring Eagle Casino is an example.

How do you decide who's Indian? Could I become one? "Sadly, no."

It goes by quantum blood, I learn. "Here the quantum blood to determine membership is one-quarter."

A tribal chief I met recently told me it's one-thirty-second.

"You were in the Soo? There, if you get bit by a mosquito you become a member of the tribe," Frank says, laughing.

Frank drives me around the reservation, and all I see are houses. When I finally see a person, a woman standing outside her home, I ask Frank to stop. Her name is Dawn. Dawn is forty-nine years old; she strikes me as a warm person, and I'm curious what she thinks of Indian culture.

What are the basic elements of Indian culture? I ask her.

"It's family, community, hmm, I'd say mostly it's community."

Most people of other cultures would say the same about themselves. What's the difference between you and them? What's unique to your culture?

"We're not different; we're not any different from the Japanese. We're all the same. We all got God, our creator, and we all got our family values and we all got our cultural values."

Is there anything unique about the Indian culture that you could sum up for me in a sentence or two?

"Well, I don't know. Being the original people, I guess. And we got special protection from the world."

Simple. Concise. Straight. No PR here. The uniqueness of the Indian people is that they have a "special protection" by the white man.

If there ever was a great Indian culture here, it no longer is and not a trace of it remains.

Time to visit the casino. Frank drives me there.

There are 4,300 slot machines here, and most of the players are old white ladies. These slot machines project phrases in multiple cheerful colors and shapes:

"Win! Win!" "Golden Money." "Reward!" "$81,624."

"Wild Multipliers." "Free Games." "Players' Party." "Sizzling."

"Queen of the Wild." "Double Gold." "Double Diamond." "$21,344.36."

I like the "Queen of the Wild" the most.

The old white ladies empty their life savings into these machines. What a sweet Indian revenge!

Nature calls and I go to the toilet. At the entrance I see a box, "Gratuities," where we, the naïve visitors, are supposed to drop green bills.

Genius!

The Indians, let me tell you, are the most brilliant people in this country.

• • •

What's new in the world? NBC reports that "after weeks of long, emotional debates, South Carolina governor Nikki Haley signed into law a measure to take down the Confederate flag from the state capitol on Thursday – but, across the country, politicians and regular citizens alike are clamoring to remove similar iconography."

This flag flew high for God knows how long and nobody took it down. Until now. Why now? Because Dylann Roof was pictured with a Confederate flag. Doesn't make much sense unless you happen to think that blacks might start the race riots once again and you want to appease them.

In Greece there is also news. From the *Washington Post*: "Greece offered to make painful spending cuts and hike taxes Thursday in a final gambit to win one more bailout from Europe before the country descends into bankruptcy."

As for me, I am to leave Michigan tomorrow. Destination: Washington, DC.

Gate Five

A few thousand Christians love Jews and
thousands of Jews fly to sit next to them

WHY DC? WHAT HAVE I LOST THERE?

Well, after hearing often about "Jews" on this journey I want to explore the American thinking about Jews a bit deeper.

A few months ago I was invited by a member of a group calling itself "CUFI" to join their next yearly conference, or "summit," as they call it, which is to start later today in DC. CUFI, which stands for Christians United For Israel, is headed by a famous American pastor, John Hagee, and a couple of Jews. Yeah. There are two Jews at the top of this organization, and they are the ones who actually run it, but nobody likes to talk about this, so I won't either.

I don't know much more about this group, but I do remember reading somewhere that they are a major lobbying group, which is another thing that I would love to explore.

Some people tell me that CUFI members are a bunch of lunatics who blow shofars on the streets of DC, and that I would do better to avoid spending my time on them.

Whatever they are, I want to see them.

I get a cheap plane ticket with Frontier Airlines, which then charges me an arm and a leg for having a suitcase, and fly. In due time I arrive safely and in one piece at Dulles International Airport. Moments after my arrival there is a PA announcement notifying interested passengers that a Catholic mass will take place at 6:30 a.m. at the interfaith chapel. Thank you.

On my way to pick up my extra-costly suitcase, I see this sign: "Welcome to Washington, D.C., our HEROES of AMERICA! Thank you for your services & sacrifices." It is signed by Washington Dulles International Airport, and in the background there is an image of three people with machine guns. They are evidently shooting, God knows at whom, amidst smoke clouds, but no specific explanation or location is supplied.

Would be nice to be a hero and be welcomed like this, don't you think? Hero or not, DC welcomes me with warmth, and too much of it. It's hot here, and it's humid.

I go to my new hotel to rest a bit, and when it's time to go to the CUFI conference I take a taxi. I'm not going to rent a car in DC and spend precious time finding parking. The cabbie, a black man by the name of Tom, strikes me as just the right person to teach me about this city.

Why is this place called DC? I ask Tom. "DC" stands for "District of Columbia," even though this area is not a State of Columbia, and there's no "Columbia" in the United States to start with.

"Because they don't want to give us power."

What are you talking about?

"We are – were – 80 percent of the people here and they wanted to control us, that's why they didn't want it to be a state."

Who's "we"?

"Blacks."

He drives and he talks. And he says: "They always cover it up and don't talk about it."

Who's "they"?

"The whites. It's time we tell it the way it is. Maybe if we are honest the reality will change. There's a gentrification going on in DC; we are now fifty-fifty. When they are the majority, after they get more of us out, I bet you that DC will become SC, State of Columbia. I've lived in DC for thirty-six years, I know something."

I give him a nice tip, just so, and I get out.

• • •

The first CUFI day, it's just a hello kind of a gathering. Nothing's really happening. I should come back tomorrow morning. At least I learned something from a cabbie.

The next day I go again. I walk into the conference, or summit, whatever it's called.

Diana Hagee, the wife of Pastor John, welcomes us and says that together we are an impressive four thousand people in total. We all look at each other and are impressed that so many of us have shown up here.

The conference this year, I learn, is special. CUFI leaders want to achieve a specific goal this year. Namely, to prevent a deal between Iran and world powers, mainly the United States and Europe, that would see the end of sanctions against Iran. The deal is supposedly intended to lower Iran's capacity to manufacture atomic weapons. Almost nobody knows what it really is. The American secretary of state John Kerry, a super-rich man by virtue of his marriage to the heiress of Heinz, the world's major ketchup maker, desperately wants to make a deal.

And understandably so. John Kerry cannot point to a single major achievement in all his years as secretary of state, and this could be his best chance. Europe wants a deal, the Russians want a deal, China wants a deal and of course Iran itself wants a deal. The question is, what will the terms of the deal be? Conservatives, and some liberals as well, believe that the deal now on the table is bad and that Iran will end up manufacturing atomic weapons sooner than anybody publicly admits. Liberals, most of them, support the deal.

CUFI, which claims to have over two million members, is here to use the strength inherent in such a large membership to make sure that this deal never takes off. Will they succeed? I don't think so, but I've been wrong before.

Looking at the people gathered here, my assumption is that at least one-third of them are Jewish. It's quite easy, I think, to figure this out. When the words "Holy Spirit" are uttered on the stage, fewer than half of the people clap. When something like "Support Israel" is mentioned, almost all clap.

Surprisingly, nothing special is taking place at this conference. Some low-ranking lawmakers show up, but they have nothing special to say. There are speeches, all kinds of them, and the people network – but that's it.

Between sessions many people go out to eat at their favorite restaurants and everybody seems happy. The happiest here are the Jews, who have come to this conference for one purpose: to see non-Jews love them.

How do I know? They tell me.

It's sad to watch their need to be loved.

As for the lunatics: I don't see them here and I don't hear them here. How did the CUFI people get such a bad name? I don't know.

Toward the evening, at about five, some demonstrators appear in front of the convention center. They are about twenty altogether, white people with big Palestinian flags and signs such as "End the Occupation." They are part of the group Jewish Voice for Peace (JVP), a far-left Jewish organization associated with Professor Noam Chomsky and playwrights Eve Ensler and Tony Kushner.

Nobody is paying them any attention, which is something that these American Jews don't like, and so they start screaming at the people who are entering or leaving the building.

It's a Jew versus Christian show in the funniest way imaginable.

One of them, trying to poke fun at Christians, is a bit overdoing it. "God loves the Palestinians," he shouts, but not even an echo answers him. As the media piles out, these demonstrators get out their loudspeakers and make even louder noise.

I watch all this while writing on my iPad. Jonathan, one of the demonstrators, sees me writing and assumes that I'm part of the media. He tries talking to me, but I don't reply. He tries again, but I still don't react. He tries one more time, and fails again. He's getting upset, and he tells me that I'm an "ugly man with fat fingers." In case I didn't get the message, he goes on: "You are pissing from your shoulders. You make me lose my appetite, you fucking filthy Jew. Your fat fingers will break your iPad, don't you worry about that? Fucking Jew!"

Now he got me. Definitely.

Would you like to say this on record? I ask him.

"Yes!"

I turn the video on and he changes his tune and tone. He loves all people, he now says calmly, and he wants a "free Palestine."

I protest. I want you to repeat what you just said to me, I say to him. You know, that I'm an ugly Jew and the rest –

He denies he said it, so I repeat his words while the video goes on. He realizes that this might not sound good, and he says: "You're weird."

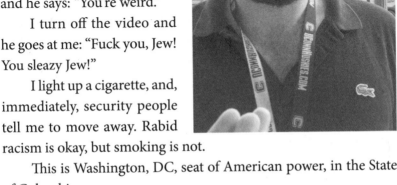

I turn off the video and he goes at me: "Fuck you, Jew! You sleazy Jew!"

I light up a cigarette, and, immediately, security people tell me to move away. Rabid racism is okay, but smoking is not.

This is Washington, DC, seat of American power, in the State of Columbia.

• • •

It's time I go out to eat as well. Where's the good food? People tell me I should go to Georgetown, where I can find great restaurants facing the river. Georgetown, home to prominent Democrats such as President John F. Kennedy in the days of old and Secretary of State John F. Kerry of today. Sounds like an excellent idea. I take a taxi to Georgetown, to no specific address, and the cabbie drops me off near the waterfront.

I look around. It's beautiful!

Two young men pass by me. One of them, Will, tells me that Georgetown is one of the richest places in DC.

What kind of people live here?

"People who have money and want to keep it for themselves."

Who are they?

"Here we call them Republicans."

Not bad, man! Any recommendation for a good restaurant around here?

"Do you like Thai?"

If it's good.

"Go up to Avenue M. They have a great Thai restaurant there, I Thai."

I walk in that direction but I don't find I Thai. I approach a man walking his dog on the street and ask him for I Thai.

"Where you from?" he asks me. I'm tired of saying Germany. No excitement there. And so, I say Israel.

"Hmm," the man says, as if the name Israel had some kind of special meaning to him.

What do you think of Israel? I ask him.

"I'm surprised at the ability of people to colonize after two thousand years."

Interesting thought. Would you mind if I record your response? I'm a traveling journalist and I collect peoples' thoughts. What's your name, by the way?

"My name is Andrew and I'm a lawyer."

Great. Let's talk. I turn on the recording app on my iPhone and ask him again: What do you think of Israel?

"I think it's a miracle that after two thousand years people can rebuild a homeland."

Before I recorded you, I asked you what you think about Israel and you said that you're amazed that after two thousand years they've colonized –

"Is there an incorrect use of the word?"

No. I just want you to repeat that sentence because I found it very interesting.

"*Colonization* is not quite the right word."

But you used it, right?

"I don't know if the word was *colonize*, I think [I said] *coalesce*, to come back and organize a homeland – "

I turn off the iPhone. He pulls his dog closer, looks me straight in the eye and says: "What the Nazis did to you, you are doing to the Palestinians!"

He is angry. He is full of hate. And he wants me to know how much he hates me.

I think I should have said to him that I am German. So good to be German, so hard to be a Jew. I've lost my appetite.

I go back to my hotel and read about what's going on in the world at large. "Europe Takes Hard Line with Greece," goes the cover story of the *Wall Street Journal*, adding: "Germany Flexes Its Muscles in Talks."

Day follows night and here's the news, per the *New York Times*:

> Iran and a group of six nations led by the United States said
> they had reached a historic accord on Tuesday to significantly
> limit Tehran's nuclear ability for more than a decade in return
> for lifting international oil and financial sanctions.

Oops. The Obama administration is not impressed with the Israel-loving Christians. The negotiations with Iran, which had lasted for years, finally end. The game's result: Heinz 1, Jesus 0.

President Obama, meantime, vows to veto any lawmakers' attempts to derail this agreement. To override his veto, two-thirds of the lawmakers in both the House and the Senate must vote against the "Iran Deal."

· · ·

Iranians are happy with the deal and, as reported by the media here, they are dancing in the streets. CUFI members, on the other hand, are totally not in the mood to dance. They are in the mood for walking, walking to Capitol Hill to register their dissatisfaction with members of the House of Representatives and the Senate.

I've read much about this "powerful Christian Zionist lobby" before, and today, to witness it for myself, I join CUFI members as they get ready to mount buses and cars for a lobby invasion of Congress. This phenomenon of "lobbying" in America is not new to me, but I never personally experienced it before.

Before we mount the invasion vehicles we are divided into groups, as each group is assigned to visit a lawmaker of their home district. I join the Tenth District group, which I think is the Manhattan group.

Our group is to visit three representatives and two senators. CUFI officials tell us that we have appointments with the senators but not with the representatives. But no worry: we should leave printed materials at the lawmakers' offices, and that's very important, they say.

We are driven to the Hill. First we go to visit Congressman Jerrold ("Jerry") Nadler.

Jerry is Jewish. A few years ago I had a meeting with him, and, based on what I know of him, he will endorse the Iran deal. Jerry is a flaming Democrat and there's no way under the sun that he will join the Republicans, creatures that he hates with a passion. I say nothing of it to my group. I'm here to observe, not to influence results.

Personally, I can't say much about this deal. The deal is 159 pages long, none of which I have read. In addition, and as far as I know about political deals, there must be about a thousand riders to it – which so far no one is talking about. And even if I had all the material I would need to know law, international law, physics, military history, Iranian political history and loads of other fields in order to form a learned opinion. I did study various topics in various universities for quite a number of years, but none of them are relevant to this case.

I am here to watch.

We enter the House office building and take the elevator to Jerry's office, but we don't get to see Jerry. Instead, a foreign affairs aide to the congressman comes out of a back room to talk with us. We just got the Iran deal, he tells us, and we didn't have a chance to look at it. We will examine it, we will speak with various specialists and then the congressman will decide if he approves it or not.

I believe in full disclosures and I tell him that I'm not a CUFI member but a journalist. Hearing this, his composure immediately changes. He thanks me for telling this to him and asks that nothing of what he just said be quoted. God in heaven, the man said nothing!

Still, to honor his request I don't quote him straight and don't give out his name, but I'm quite surprised at this behavior, at how afraid people are of the media.

These are the Brave, and this is the House of the Free.

We stop by more congressmen and congresswomen, but no one talks to us. CUFI activists drop printed material for the elected officials, and then we cross to the Senate office building.

We go to New York Senator Kirsten Gillibrand, only to be told that she ain't here. Appointment, shmapointment, she's not going to meet us. Instead we get to meet an aide, a heavy-set lady who clearly enjoys having so many people listening to her.

The Christian Zionists tell her how much they are against the Iran deal, and that it's against the Bible. She doesn't seem impressed, but the CUFI people take pictures with her. All smile, even before anyone tells a joke.

Time to see the next senator, Chuck Schumer, also of New York. We have an appointment with him, but he ain't showing up either.

After twenty minutes or so, while we are waiting outside his office, an aide comes out and speaks to us. He says, almost word for word, what Jerry's aide said. Did these two go the same PR school? Probably.

And now we are ready to call it a day. The lobbying is over. We ride back to the convention center.

A nice party is taking place here, a CUFI donor's party. Diana says that six thousand people came to the summit this year. Where did she get the extra two thousand? Jesus might know, but I don't.

All in all, this CUFI organization – which many Jews think is a powerful lobby that will help them in time of need – barks, but it can't bite.

I'm ready to leave DC. Where should I go next? Chicago, known to some as Crook County, "is still No. 1 for public corruption," according to *Crain's Chicago Business*. I think I should go there. Let me see how politics really works.

Gate Six

*The mayor's office prints fake business
cards to confuse the dumb press*

ON THE PLANE TO CHICAGO, ILLINOIS, AMERICA'S THIRD-LARGEST CITY (THIS
time I missed the Catholic call to prayer), I read the news. Here's the
BBC: "Greek MPs have approved tough economic measures required
to enable an €86 billion Eurozone bailout deal to go ahead."

The Europeans, following the long tradition of inter-European
hatred, trust the Iranians much more than they trust the Greeks and
happily do their best to make the Iranians richer and the Greeks
poorer.

Brilliant.

On the way from the airport to downtown Chicago I see signs
all over in Polish. What are the Poles doing here? I don't know. All
I do know is that I like Polish food. And so I ask Siri to take me to a
Polish restaurant near me.

Siri directs me to Staropolska, the nearest along my route. Once
I get there I order a brandy called Christian Brothers, in honor of
the CUFI people. It's not bad. Try it. You don't have to convert in
order to drink it.

A young waitress, Silvia, asks me what I'd like to order. In lieu
of a reply, I ask her what she thinks of the Iran deal.

"What is that?"

You don't know?

"No."

How long are you in the United States?

"Five years."

Do you like the United States better than Poland?

"I love Poland! Much more!"

Then why are you here?

"To make money."

As a waitress…?

She gives me a shy Polish smile and a shake of the head in reply. Lucky me, my family is Polish and I understand. What it means is this: "I thought I'd make a lot of money here but I didn't. I got stuck and the years just passed by. Maybe one day I'll gather the strength to admit to myself that nothing will change and have the courage to take the first plane to my beloved Poland."

Yes, Polish is a complex language.

After the meal I get myself to downtown Chicago and go to City Hall to request an interview with Mayor Rahm Emanuel for my column in the *Zeit*.

• • •

I take the elevator to the fifth floor and walk into the office of Mayor Rahm Emanuel. Rahm is a famous man, in case you didn't know. Prior to serving as mayor, he was White House chief of staff, senior advisor to President Obama, and a member of Congress. He is also Jewish.

I introduce myself to the mayor's press aide, a man by the name of Andy, and we have a little talk. The conversation goes well and he promises that he'll try to arrange the interview for tomorrow morning. The *Zeit* is a major paper and it will be great for His Honor to have this opportunity to speak to Germans. Andy gives me his official business card, which has his email address on it, and asks that I shoot him an email in order to make this official. Makes total sense, and later on I send him an email.

I try, is a better word.

The email address that Andy gave me does not function. My email to him immediately bounces back by the City of Chicago email server with the message: "The recipient's email address was not found." I try again and again, but to no avail.

ANDY ORELLANA
PRESS AIDE
MAYOR'S PRESS OFFICE

121 North LaSalle Street   312 744-4351
City Hall   312 221-3047 Cell
Chicago, Illinois 60602   andres.orellana@ex.cityofchicago.org

All attempts to reach Andy by phone, per his phone number on the card, fail as well.

Life.

And life goes on.

• • •

Down the road from City Hall is my hotel, and next to it is a theater. I tried to suck some culture into my bones while I was with the Indians, but that didn't work. Now that I'm with normal Americans, and they hopefully have culture to offer, I think I should grab this opportunity.

I walk to the theater. The name of the theater is Cadillac Palace Theatre. Interesting name for a cultural organization, though I'll probably feel more cozy in a Chevy Cruze Theater.

Anyhow, currently playing at the Cadillac is the Broadway show *Kinky Boots*, with music and lyrics by Cyndi Lauper. Sounds promising and I go to see it. What's *Kinky Boots* about? For the most part it's about drag queens of all kinds and sorts.

Kinky Boots is very "American," laden with "positive thinking," as is evident in the closing number:

> Just be.
>
> Who you wanna be.
>
> Never let 'em tell you who you ought to be
>
> Just be. With dignity.
>
> Celebrate yourself triumphantly.

Culturally speaking, *Kinky Boots* fails at almost every turn. It has as much art in it as the average Indian slot machine. But as entertainment it succeeds at almost every turn. How does it manage these two opposites? Simple: it's a flatly written show, but Cyndi Lauper's club music is exact, hearty, elevating, merry, smart, strong and powerful. No wonder this musical is beloved by this audience.

The Cadillac Palace Theatre has over 2,300 seats, and practically all of them are taken at this performance. When the show ends, I go outside to watch the audience as they pile out of the Cadillac. These theatergoers are for the most part older rather than younger, more females than males, and include three blacks.

Three.

I walk to my hotel, the Allegro Hotel, formerly the Bismarck Hotel. Yeah, that Bismarck, Chancellor Otto von Bismarck. Always good to be in a place that has German history speaking to you from the walls before you go to sleep, especially in a city with a Jewish mayor.

• • •

Morning comes and I'm back at the mayor's office, trying to figure out why the email address I was given does not work. At the receptionist's desk I see a man wearing the Chicago Police Department's uniform, obviously a cop, and he has a gun. I have to be nice.

Could I please speak with Andy? I ask him.

"Andy is not here."

Could I speak with His Highness, the mayor?

"Do you have an appointment?"

That's the issue, my dear friend: I don't know.

"Why don't you write Andy an email?"

I tried, but the email address on his card is not working.

"Could I see the card?" asks the man with the gun. I show him the card, and he looks at it. "This email address is incorrect," he says. Good to hear this from a man with firepower.

I go downstairs.

At the lobby I meet another employee from the mayor's office and I tell him the story, same story. He asks to see the business card. He looks at it and he says: "This is a fake address."

What should I do? I ask him.

He points to an elevator across the hall and says: "You see that elevator? Andy just pressed the button. He's trying to run away from you. Go fast and catch him. What he did is inappropriate."

I run and catch up with Andy just as the elevator doors open. Why did you give me a business card with a nonexistent, fake email address? I ask him.

His face turns red. No journalist has ever dared to question him before. With a voice full of anger and spite he utters these words, emphasizing every syllable: "There will be no interview! I tell you right now!"

He steps into the elevator and disappears.

Crain's Chicago Business was right. Chicago is No. 1 for public corruption.

• • •

I leave City Hall and go for a walk on Michigan Avenue, also known as the Magnificent Mile or Mag Mile. Here you can shop till you drop. Store after store offers everything you never knew you needed until you came in. As a sign of our time, here are two shops that define our era: the Apple Store, which is partly a store and partly a shrine to our digital self-esteem, and the Under Armour store, which will sell you the underwear that will make you look trim, masculine and ever proud of the armor between your legs.

Walk a few more steps and you'll hit the Harley-Davidson store. "Great riders aren't born, they're made," reads a digital ad at the entrance.

How are they made? For that you need to buy a Harley. Brilliant marketing.

Marketing, I think, is one of America's biggest contributions to humanity, if not the biggest of them. You'll buy anything, even a Big Mac, because you've been convinced that this is the best, tastiest, greatest product ever made by man.

Chicago, at least in this area, is gorgeously beautiful. It's cut into two parts by the Chicago River, but it is united by multiple bridges. Venice, if you wish to call it that.

But what really makes my day here is a man by the name of Oscar, who calls himself SoulO, for he sings like a million birds. Oscar, a young black man, understands soul music and he knows how to bring out its real soul. When he schleps out the word *long*, rendered by him into *l-o-o-o-o-o-o-o-o-n-n-n-g-g-g*, you can see the skyscrapers of Chicago dance to his tune, something no Apple product could ever duplicate. You see him and you fall in love with humanity.

Tell me, Oscar, I ask him: Where in America can I find good people?

"Go south, my man. Go south. Go to Georgia, go to Mississippi, go to Texas. The good people live there. Go south. South is the place."

That's what I do in a city whose leader won't talk to me. I talk instead to the finer of that city's people, to a soul man with a voice.

• • •

There's a sticker at the entrance to many businesses that says "No Gun." What is this about? Over a year ago, residents tell me, the state of Illinois passed the Firearm Concealed Carry Act, which allows residents to carry a gun with them, provided it's concealed.

In simple language: carry your gun, but drop it on the sidewalk before you walk in through the door.

I don't have a gun, only a cigarette. And a cigarette is even less welcome than a gun. There are many more No Smoking signs in this city than No Gun signs.

And so I stand on a street corner and smoke. About five puffs later a high-level Washington official, on political business in Chicago, approaches me. He is trying to quit smoking, has no cigarette on him and asks if I mind selling him a single cigarette for one dollar. I tell him to keep his money in his pocket and I give him a cigarette, and another one and then another one, and we chat in between puffs.

I tell him what happened with Andy at the mayor's office and he explains to me the whole nine yards of politicians and journalists. This conversation is off the record and I cannot share the name or the position of this man, only his observations.

"The way Rahm's press aide behaved is utterly stupid and it will come back to haunt him and the mayor because, I believe, you will write about it. That's your obligation as a journalist. The aide should have never given you an email address that would come back to you and you'd know that it's an invalid address. The proper way would be to give you an email address that would not bounce back and then send you a form letter or email apologizing that the mayor is not available due to a big volume of tasks and previous obligations."

Or arrange the interview –

"No. You have to understand something: we don't want to give interviews unless it's for local media, where we know the people and we know what they will write. Otherwise, almost all of us prefer not to grant interviews to national or international media. In today's American politics, especially after the Supreme Court decision in 2010 making it legal for donors to donate unlimited amounts to political groups, interviews carry huge risks."

What does an interview have to do with donors? "Everything. If you said something that you shouldn't have said in an interview, somebody will drag it out from the newspaper and feature it in a multimillion-dollar ad campaign against you."

I don't get you.

"Because of campaign contributions you want to make sure that you don't say anything that your donors don't agree on, but you don't always know what they think. The rule of thumb is: don't give interviews when you don't have to."

Is this democracy?

"I'll admit that it's not. Is there freedom of expression in the country? No. Is this the honest way to deal with issues? No. This is capitalism in politics. This is the system, and this is the way things are. This is America, at least now. I don't like the fact that today this is the way of doing politics, but I can't change reality. Sorry. I am honest with you and I tell this to you off the record. If we had an on-the-record conversation, where you would mention my name, I would say totally different things, but they wouldn't be true. It is what it is and it will stay this way for a long time to come. Are you surprised? Don't be."

We depart. I have no doubt that this official spoke truth to me. In practical terms, for me, this means that I won't be able to interview many politicians in the Land of the Free, Home of the Brave.

Too bad.

For some time now I've been harboring the hope of interviewing President Barack Obama, but after what happened with Chicago's mayor, who is President Obama's friend, and what I just heard from the official, I realize that I shouldn't waste my time even trying to arrange such an interview.

But I do want to know about him, and as much as possible. Can I find his inner self by other means? The late leader of Hamas, Sheikh Ahmad Yassin, reportedly used to say: When all doors are shut, Allah opens a gate.

And sometimes a gate means a different understanding.

• • •

What I would like to know is very basic: Does a man who ends up being president really care for the people who put him in office, those who gave him the power that he has?

This would take an interview, at the end of which I would either get the answer or not.

But, it occurs to me now, there's another way – maybe even a better way – to get the answer to this question: meet the people who first put him in power and see how they are doing today. How are the people of his Chicago district, those who first voted for him, doing now, some fifteen years later?

Obama started his political career as a state senator, representing Illinois's Thirteenth District. When he was first elected, in 1996, the Thirteenth District was drawn along Chicago's South Side neighborhoods, from Hyde Park-Kenwood south to South Shore and west to Chicago Lawn, according to the information I have.

Let me, I say to myself, go to that area and see how it's doing – talk to the people and see how they fare.

As a first step toward this goal, I go to my hotel's front desk and ask the staff for directions. A smiling-faced lady tells me that she doesn't know of the area I'm looking for. She needs an address, she says. I give her the boundaries of my search area again, but the smiling lady says, "I don't understand you, but I suggest that you go to Hyde Park. If you want to experience Chicago neighborhoods, Hyde Park is a good place to visit."

I want south of Hyde Park, I insist.

"How do you plan to get there? Do you have a car? Do you need a taxi?"

I don't want to get there by car, and I don't want a taxi. I want to get there by public transportation. I want to meet people.

"Take the Green Line."

Green line? "Yes, the Green Line. That's the train that will take you where you'd want to go. Green. Not red."

Why not red?

"The Red Line is not good."

Why?

"I don't take the Red Line, and I live in Chicago!"

Why not the red?

"It's not recommended."

Why not?

"It's not safe."

Well, Dearborn was also not safe and I damn well enjoyed it. I take the Red Line.

The train, much nicer than New York trains, moves smoothly ahead. I love this modern train: cool, new, effective. Can't get better. I look at the people around me. And I notice a pattern: every stop more whites get off the train and more blacks get on. This goes on until all the whites are gone.

By now the train has only black people on it. And me.

Where is the best place to get off? I ask a man sitting next to me. He asks me what I'm looking for. The heart and soul of the people south of Hyde Park, I say to him.

"You know where you are?"

No.

"South Side of Chicago."

Good to know. At what stop should I get off to experience the heart and soul of South Side?

"That's me!"

Makes me very happy. Where do I see more people like you?

"This is a dangerous neighborhood, man!"

I love dangerous.

"Get off at Sixty-Third. I'll show you where it is."

He does, and then he suggests I take a bus that will take me deeper into "the 'hood." I take the bus until its last stop. As I'm about to get off, the driver, a black guy, asks me what I'm doing here. Shouldn't I be here? I ask him.

"You better stay on this bus until I go back. This is not a good neighborhood. Not good. Here they have guns. They shoot here. Why are you here? Stay on this bus or take another bus out of here. There," he says, pointing to a bus that's about to depart, "he's leaving. Catch him!"

I won't hear of it. The people here are the people in whose name Obama entered politics and they are the ones who made him. I want to see them and learn what he's done for them.

I get off the bus. A few people walk by. Most are black, some are Spanish. I start walking around.

One word comes to my mind: hell.

As I walk, all I can see is poverty staring in my face. Store after store is locked, forever shut and clearly abandoned; even churches. I walk for some time on this hottest day of the summer, stare at the poverty and despair that this place projects in a deadly gaze that never ceases, and I am shocked that this exists in the same city as the Mag Mile. I have not even encountered such images in the Third World.

I want to scream: Is this America? Am I in America? I am in Obamaland.

Often, too often actually, I get "personal" emails from President Obama. Here's one of them:

> Tuvia –
>
> When I was just getting my start as an organizer on the south side of Chicago, things weren't easy. Sometimes I called a meeting, and nobody showed up.
>
> But with patience and persistence, folks who lived in the community started to come around. Soon we were spending hours together, talking about the problems they saw and going over the best ways to tackle them.
>
> The more active and engaged they became, the easier it was to affect the change that we sought. I believe that same concept applies today. Organizing is the building block of everything great we've accomplished.

Who is he bullshitting?

In a corner street I see a Spanish man sitting on a stoop while holding on to a cane. What's the name of this neighborhood? I ask him.

"I live here many years and I never asked this question," he responds.

But what's the name of it?

"I don't know."

A gray van stops by. The windows roll down to reveal two men wearing bulletproof vests, both armed with guns and all sorts of communications gear. "What are you doing here? Where are you from? Where do you live?"

I live at the Allegro Hotel downtown.

"How did you get from there to here?"

Train and bus.

"You know where you are?"

Not exactly, but I'm trying to find President Obama's district.

"Not here. Go to Hyde Park."

I was told it's here.

"This is a dangerous place, a shooting range."

Who are you, by the way?

"Police."

Driving a civilian car?

"Unmarked car. We know this area. Please leave."

I'm a journalist. You have your job to do, and I have mine. Where should I go from here to –

The cop cuts me off. "Home!"

What?

"You should go home."

Why?

"Believe me, you don't want to be here."

Is this not Obama's district?

"No, this is not Obama's district. It's way deeper the other way."

Is this not the Thirteenth District?

"No."

I take out my iPad to show him the information that I have. "Why are you taking your iPad out? You want to be robbed?"

The other cop, in the passenger's seat, says, "He doesn't know where he is."

The cop at the steering wheel: "Listen, you don't belong here."

I stop paying attention to his warnings and just go on with my business, showing him the info on my iPad.

In 1996, if I'm not mistaken, the Thirteenth District was drawn differently, I say to him.

The cop changes his attitude. "Correct," he says. "You are now in the district that Obama represented at that time. That's correct."

Were you a cop here at that time as well?

"Yes."

Has anything changed here since then?

"Here, changed? Nothing changes here. If anything, it's gotten worse."

Well, let me talk to some more people and see if you're right.

"It's a free country. Be well and be safe. But, please, get out of here as fast as you can."

The cops drive off, and I'm left to my own devices. Abandoned businesses, some with iron gates all around them as if to protect the decaying emptiness inside from spilling out, continue to be the common sight. I walk, walk, walk and walk and store after store, business after business is abandoned.

Only a few stores still function: a Salvation Army station, a gas station, a check-cashing business, liquor and lottery stores, and then a couple of restaurants.

I enter the restaurants and in each of them I am welcomed by poor lighting, broken toilets, dirty floors, broken chairs and dirty walls. And they are empty of diners, save for one of them that has two people.

The houses in the area, surprisingly, actually look nice. Many are private homes, which gives the impression that this is a nice area.

But it's not.

How do the people, who are dirt poor, get to live in these houses?

Part of the neighborhood, which some tell me is called Englewood, is black and another part has Spanish people as well. Alex, a sixteen-year-old Spanish boy, tells me that he likes his neighborhood but that life is not easy. "All gangs are here," he says.

How many gangs are there?

"A lot. A lot of different gangs are here."

And they kill each other?

"Yes, they do."

How often is there violence here?

"Every summer everybody gets killed around here."

How many and how often?

"Once a week somebody gets killed here." Pointing ahead of him, he adds: "They just killed somebody right there, in the gas station."

For what?

"Gang member. Shot in the head."

Is he dead?

"Yes."

When was the last time you heard gun shots?

"Two days ago."

As far as you remember, did anything change here in the last ten years?

Two older men, both Spanish, are listening to Alex. He looks at them, not knowing what to say, but then says: "It did."

For better or for worse?

He looks at the elders and says: "For the better."

What's better?

He does not reply, as if afraid to say anything.

Be honest, Alex.

"To be honest? No."

What "no"?

"No. Nothing changed."

Are you scared?

"I'm not scared."

Do you go out at night, like you're doing now?

"At night? No."

What's the difference between the gangs?

"On this street there are two gangs. One gang, they walk with baggy pants and blue shirts. The other gang, they walk with baggy pants and red shirts. That's how they know who is who and they kill each other."

How is it between the Spanish and the blacks, do they kill each other?

"Yes, sometimes."

Two Spanish youths pass by; one is a teenager and one a ten-year-old. Did anything change, I ask the older, since Obama became president?

The teenager says that there's no difference, and the ten-year-old tells me that there is. How a ten-year-old can answer this question, given that Obama became president about seven years ago, is a mystery to me. Still, I ask him: What's the difference?

"More food stamps!"

"Food stamps" is a government program that helps the poor buy food. The government used to give out stamps. Now it gives out debit cards.

Walking about here and there, I see a lady across the street. She's old enough to remember Barack Obama who, in his first campaign to an elected office in 1996, said he was running because he wanted to "empower the disenfranchised citizens." I should talk with her.

Her name, she tells me, is Cynthia. She's a Spanish lady, seems older than I initially thought, and she leans on a dirty wall.

Her right hand is encased in an orthopedic cast; she is quietly smoking a cigarette, fear emanating from her eyes.

No point in talking to her about twenty years ago. What happened to your hand? I ask her.

"I was coming out of a grocery store. I had my groceries and someone came up and pushed me, I fell on the ground and they robbed me."

Did your robbers get caught?

"No. They escaped in a car. They also stole $300 from me."

Who were the robbers? Spanish, black?

"Black."

I wish you well, my lady.

"Thank you."

She pauses for a minute or two and then says: "At least I have my life."

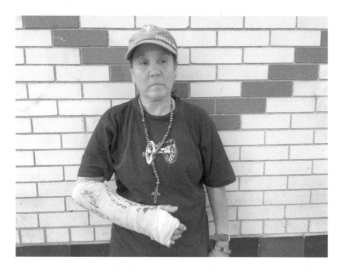

I talk to more people, and the stories repeat themselves. I'm ready to leave the neighborhood, despondent and despairing.

None of the people I talked to, excluding the ten-year-old kid with his food stamps, could point to even a single improvement in their lives since Barack Obama first started representing them years ago, and no one cares about Obama one way or the other. For them he's just one black man, a "nigga brother," who made it to the top. It has nothing to do with them.

As for President Obama, if one is to judge by deeds rather than words, he cynically used these people's hardships to get ahead of the other contenders, but he doesn't care a bit about the people who put him in power. Lucky him; he doesn't live here.

I go to a nearby bus stop and wait for the next bus out. At the station I read that a "march to end rape culture" will take place tomorrow. In moments, long moments, the bus arrives. I mount the bus that will take me, I hope, to a better place.

A number of stops later a lovely, friendly and gorgeous teenage black girl asks me if I need any help. She's not used to seeing white men on this bus and wonders from what planet I have dropped. I tell her that I'm here because I wanted to check out a few things about President Obama.

"You went to the president's house?" she asks.

President's house? What's that?

"You don't know?"

No.

"What are you doing here?"

I just spent a few hours in Englewood.

"You??"

Yes. What's the problem?

"You were in Englewood??"

I wanted to see people.

"In Englewood??"

Yes.

"I'm from Englewood! I *hate* Englewood! It's a dangerous 'hood. You didn't go to the president's house?"

What's the president's house? Where is it?

"You want to go? Take bus number 15."

Well, it takes me some time but slowly I get it: President Obama has a house in Chicago, where he lived before he moved to DC. The house is in the historic Hyde Park-Kenwood neighborhood of Chicago, which is somewhere around somewhere, and bus number 15 goes there.

I take that bus.

I get off where the driver tells me to get off, and I walk toward President Obama's Chicago abode. He is not there, but some Secret Service agents are. Their mission is to protect the house, and they have blocked off the street where the house is. The only way to see the house, actually just a fraction of it due to the many trees surrounding it, is by looking at it from the other side of East Hyde Park Boulevard, which is perpendicular to the blocked-off street.

This is a rich neighborhood with stately townhouses. This is not Englewood, and nobody will rob you here.

Whatever the difference, I want to see more of the house and I contemplate ways to outsmart the Secret Service. I try schmoozing with one of the agents, but this leads me nowhere. What I do find, however, is that there's a tremendous structure right across from the president's home, and I ponder ways to enter that place. As I approach it I see Hebrew words at the entrance. What is this place? Well, it's a synagogue by the name of KAM Isaiah Israel.

Hallelujah! All I need to do is to take part in some services and I'll get to see the president's home from inside the temple.

The temple's entrance is locked. I check for their schedule of services and find that their last event for today took place at 10:00 in the morning, quite a few hours earlier.

The title of today's last event, if you care to know, is Yoga. What's yoga got to do with a temple?

I leave the area of Obama and yoga and think of what to do next. Perhaps, a thought drops into my brain, I should find myself a temple that teaches Pilates and pole dancing. Would be nice to watch a kosher Jewish woman pole dancing in front of congregants pigging out on gefilte fish. I do a little research and fall upon an interesting discovery: Rahm Emanuel's temple.

Yeah.

Barack's got a temple and Rahm has one too. Only Rahm actually attends services. I mean, I suppose.

I must check the place out. Yoga.

Do the Jews in Chicago have nothing better to do in their temples than practice yoga next to the holy arks?

• • •

The name of Rahm's temple, or synagogue, is Anshe Sholom B'nai Israel, and it is located in the Lake View neighborhood. I get there around evening time. Outside the synagogue a man in black civilian clothes, whose name is Neil, minds the entrance door. Are you the guard? I ask him.

"Kind of. I'm a police detective, specialized in drugs and gangs."

Jewish?

"Me? No. I'm of German descent."

Neil explains his presence: "Years ago a Jewish doctor saved my life. I came into his office and he gave me my life back. What I do here is my personal thanks to him."

Are you armed?

"Always."

Tell me, gang specialist, how many were shot dead in Chicago lately?

"This month, just in the Fourth of July weekend, eleven people were murdered and sixty-three were shot. Maybe there were more shootings, but we know of sixty-three."

I guess you are familiar with the Englewood neighborhood.

"Oh, yes! Englewood is a very, very dangerous place."

They have nice houses there, at least some of them, but at the same time everything there smells of poverty. How can the people afford such houses?

"The government is paying for them. The residents don't pay for them. The original owners were whites, but they left the area. 'White flight.'"

Here too, I see. I wonder how many more neighborhoods of "white flights" exist in this country.

I walk into the synagogue. It's a big place, but very few people have bothered to show up; most of them are about God's age. The event, I read on a piece of paper everybody here gets, is a speech about the Iran deal.

The speaker, who happens to be quite boring, strongly opposes the Iran deal. Couldn't this synagogue bring a more exciting speaker, maybe Rahm Emanuel?

Once the event is over I talk to a Jewish lady, a member of the congregation, and she tells me that, yes, "This synagogue is Rahm Emanuel's shul [synagogue]. He comes here every year for the High Holidays service. He doesn't pay his dues. Everybody else who attends the High Holidays pays, except for Rahm."

Why doesn't he pay?

"He feels that he's above the rest of us. He used to stand during services because he didn't pay for a seat, but now one of our members is paying for him, from his own pocket. He pays for Rahm and for Rahm's family."

A man standing near us intervenes: "You know why he doesn't pay? Because he's stingy, he's a miser. Rahm doesn't spend money, not his own money. That's Rahm."

Time for yoga, I think.

• • •

The American media is very busy these days with Donald Trump. Known as the Donald, he tears to pieces every American pundit's predictions that he will soon disappear from the map. Instead, he just shot to the top of the list of Republican candidates. The Donald has diarrhea of the mouth; he doesn't stop talking dirty, and the people love it. American journalists can't figure this out and so they write long articles about him, hoping that by the time they are finished writing their articles they will have figured something out.

The Obama administration, on the other hand, is not busy with the Donald. It is busy, very much so, with the Iran deal.

Tomorrow morning, for example, its people will try to convince Jewish leaders in Chicago that the Iran deal is not really bad.

I think I should attend.

...

The Jewish Community Relations Council of the Jewish United Fund/ Jewish Federation of Metropolitan Chicago is holding a special meeting today to discuss the Chicago Jewish community's response to the Iran deal. The Jewish Federation is the most important Jewish organization in Chicago, and the meeting today will be attended by members of many Jewish organizations, including the famous AIPAC (American Israel Public Affairs Committee).

Security is tight, with guards, x-ray screenings, and even electronically secured double doors for those going to or coming from the toilet.

Bottom line: only active members of Chicago Jewish organizations, preregistered, are to attend this meeting. I'm not a member of any Jewish organization and, naturally, no guard can find my name on the registered list.

Problem. To solve this problem, I present to the gatekeepers of this ultra-secured building my driver's license.

They let me in. I love it.

I feel so secure!

This is a Jewish meeting, by the way, which means that there's some food around. And actually it's not bad.

Note: when I don't write about food it means that there is nothing to write about it – which, sadly, is what I experience almost every day in the Home of the Brave.

But here, the Jews have performed a miracle: Excellent salmon, warm and fresh, is available to be consumed by the participants. Tuna salad as well, pineapple, avocado, chopped onion, watermelon, coffee (which I don't try) and Diet Coke (which I'm addicted to). No bagels – which reminds me that I'm not at a New York Jewish event, where the lack of bagels is a major crime. No cheesecake either, or any cake.

What's going on with these Jews? For all I know, it's a crime against Judaism not to have sweets at an event like this. But I don't complain. I don't say a word. I don't need any Jew here to ask me which organization I represent. If push comes to shove, I'll say that I represent the State of New York, the issuer of my driver's license. That's an official entity, and as far as I know, Jews love officials.

One official, actually, is speaking to them now as they swallow the salmon. His name is Jon Wolfsthal, senior director for nonproliferation, National Security Council, and he speaks via video from the White House.

"Can you hear me?" he asks. "I wish you could feed me, too." Must be a Jew.

"This deal is an extremely good deal," he says, moving on to talk business. The Iran nuclear deal is an excellent deal, he argues, and it has no flaws. In addition, the United States and its allies will be able to immediately see any Iranian violation of the deal and will act on it at once. Period.

I've never tried it before, but I must admit that salmon goes very well with talks about nuclear bombs. I can't explain it, but it's a reality. In any case, our Jon goes on with a lot of blah, blah, blah, telling us again and again how great this deal is.

What is the deal exactly? Nobody eating salmon will bother to read 159 pages of the deal. Reading, as every child knows, doesn't go well with eating. Especially fish.

What's interesting to note here is that he speaks of this deal more positively than either President Obama or Secretary Kerry have done to date. To them, the deal does have flaws but it was the best that could possibly have been achieved. To Jon, the deal is excellent. No flaws, no issues. Period.

That said, this Jon was of course assigned to speak to these Jews by the White House. And I wonder: Is the White House playing some games here? Who knows! In all likelihood, the White House hasn't even entertained the idea that journalists might be present at this meeting. If they thought that journalists would be here, they would probably be more careful. As far as I care: I hope they are not going to confiscate my driver's license.

The salmon is almost gone, and Jon reveals to us that he has more arguments in his arsenal. He tells us, in confidence, that members of the House and Senate will have access to classified documents and other materials that will show and prove how effective, how good and how great the deal is. In other words: there's more than meets the eye here, and the 159-page document does not stand on its own.

But only lawmakers will get to see the whole package.

As a licensed driver, I have a problem with this. What Jon is basically asking of these Jews here is to blindly follow American leaders to steer them the right way. Would I be willing to drive blindfolded and rely on Mayor Rahm Emanuel giving me instructions from the passenger's seat? No way. Besides: Is this blind trust part of the democratic principles that this country is so proud of?

I ask a person sitting next to me to explain to me what I see and hear. His answer comes in one word: "Jew."

Excuse me?

"Jon is Jewish, and this is how Jews work. They supported Hitler in his early days; they financed him. Why do you think that we have gotten rid of our habit?"

Is he right?

I check out our man Jon. Here's what I read, a little message that Jon tweeted some time ago, speaking of the Jewish lobby, AIPAC: "As a Jew and Survivor son, I'm tired of AIPAC trying 2 play me and push 4 conflict with Iran."

This is interesting, and it raises some questions. Why would this Jon be selected by the White House to speak to Chicago Jews? Couldn't the administration designate someone else to speak to Jews? Why a Jew, and why this Jew? Is the administration trying to send the Jews a message: "Stand with us or else?"

• • •

There is more than one element to the Iran deal. For example, the money element.

A few days ago the *Daily Beast* ran this article about the deal:

> Iran has billions in assets frozen by an international sanctions regime led by the United States and other world powers. Should a nuclear agreement be reached, as is expected later this week, these assets would be eventually released to the Iranian government.
>
> "We are of course aware and concerned that, despite the massive domestic spending needs facing Iran, some of the resulting sanctions relief could be used by Iran to fund destabilizing actions," a State Department official told *The Daily Beast*.

The amount in question, according to a number of published reports in the American media: $150 billion.

Greece would love to get its hands on this bundle. Greece, knuckling under to the strong European countries who are in the midst of teaching the Greeks proper manners, so to speak, is facing severe austerity measures for some time to come. But Iran will soon be richer than it already is, thanks to the Greece-teaching Europeans who are fully supporting the Iran deal.

I get myself another salmon. The meeting goes on.

Next to speak, via audio conference from Washington, DC, is Ambassador Dennis Ross, currently with the Washington Institute for Near East Policy and formerly a special assistant to President Obama, as well as a special advisor to former secretary of state Hillary Clinton.

Dennis, being a diplomat, says that the deal is good but that it needs a few modifications – which is of course impractical because the Iranians won't renegotiate. This Dennis is a diplomat and as such prefers not to take sides. You never know who the next president will be, and so why should you commit to one side against the other?

The next, and last, speaker is Roey Gilad, consul general of Israel to the Midwest. Here's a Jew talking to Jews, an Israeli diplomat talking to American Jews. Roey is straight as an arrow with them, which is quite surprising to witness – since he, too, is a diplomat, except this diplomat is willing to take a stand. And he does. A very strong one.

Roey does not speak via electronic communications but is here in the flesh. He is here with the Jews, he looks them straight in the eye, and he asks them to take a stand against their government. It's actually shocking to witness. And then he adds: "What we are asking you is to stand with us."

This is a very touching moment: a Jewish diplomat imploring his brethren not to desert him and his fellow countrymen.

Israeli politicians and diplomats have spoken publicly against the Iran deal, and from this perspective there's nothing new in what's going on here – but this is not a public event; this is an intimate event, for Jews only. Here we have a Jew, a diplomat who represents the Jewish state, the only Jewish state there is, and he is practically begging these salmon-eating Chicago Jews to stand by him and by their Jewish brethren.

How do they react? They look at him. They stare at him. And they don't react. These Jews have good manners and they do not show emotions.

Roey doesn't go for emotions only; he tries to reason with them as well: "It's the first time that I hear somebody depicting it as an extremely good deal," he says, referring to Jon's assessment that they have just heard. "This deal is like a Swiss cheese; it has many holes in it."

His speech is followed by an announcement that another meeting will be called in a few weeks and that the decision will be taken after that meeting. The Jews of Israel will have to wait before they get to know if Chicago Jews are supporting them or not.

• • •

Life's tough.

Time to move on. I leave Chicago with many questions. This country makes a huge deal out of nine black people murdered by one white man, yet it is peculiarly silent about the thousands upon thousands of black people murdered by other black people.

Yes, I know. The killing in the church is a "hate" crime, unlike the ongoing black-on-black murders. But the truth is, murder is murder is murder, and a loss of life is a loss of life. In addition, the bigger problem here is that talking about black-on-black murders is not politically correct, as it could be interpreted as "racist," but this bizarre political correctness allows for thousands upon thousands to be murdered year after year after year.

Just in Chicago alone, a police officer tells me, it is estimated that six hundred people will be murdered by the end of the year and that thousands will be shot. Where is the outcry about this sense-less slaughter? Where is Andrew, the gatekeeper of justice from Georgetown, to walk the streets of America and shout for justice, peace and humanity?

Before coming to Chicago I had been told that many German descendants live in this city. Maybe they do, but they must be hiding very deep somewhere, or else they have been melted so beautifully that you can't find them without a magnifying glass. Whatever the case, sorry for missing you.

I'll miss Chicago. There's something to this city that's hard to define. The beautiful architecture interlaced and intertwined with ubiquitous rusty elevated train tracks and the people who say, "Welcome to Chicago, brother," when they tell you that their politicians are extremely dishonest.

Yes, they do that.

My only question is: Where should I go next?

Gate Seven

Every family should have at least one hundred guns

"GOV. SCOTT WALKER OF WISCONSIN SAID ON MONDAY THAT HE WANTED to eliminate the state's Government Accountability Board, a nonpartisan agency that oversees elections, ethics, campaign finance and lobbying," writes the *New York Times* about the Wisconsin governor.

Does this mean that Wisconsin is even more corrupt than Illinois, or that Milwaukee is rougher than Chicago? I don't know, but perhaps I should pay Wisconsin a visit. Besides, Wisconsin is Chicago's neighbor to the north. Easy to get there, and easy does it.

I rent a new car, a white Malibu, and drive. Malibu. I love the way car companies think of their cars. Malibu. Who wouldn't like to have a "Malibu"? Malibu. What a name!

The Cruze was nice, I must admit, but sometimes I'm into polygamy, and I want more than one. This Malibu is also bigger, a better fit for rounded people like me.

On the way to Milwaukee I stop at Racine. Racine. Nice name, isn't it? In any case, Racine authorities claim that "Racine County has a proud and long-standing history of grassroots efforts to fight inequity and injustice, as community members work together for the common good," and I want to see this.

I go to a local eatery and order a burger and a brandy, a "B&B" for short.

Next to my table are two men, both white, and they're having beer. How do you get along with the blacks around here? I ask them.

I don't know how much beer they've had, but they immediately become sober when they hear this question. They look at me suspiciously, as if I were a police detective about to arrest them, and both tell me that they get along great with all the blacks there are.

I tell them that I don't buy it. Couldn't be. I don't know what made me say this, but I just did.

They hear me, feel more relaxed, and their tune changes. "There are people who prescribe to a culture of getting instead of giving and working. They are not good," one of them says.

Are you talking about blacks?

"Yes," both say.

Leah, a lovely second-year college student, sits at my table. "Thanks for coming to Racine," she says. "I hope you enjoy it."

I heard, I tell her, that you have a lot of crime here and many gangs. Did I hear this? No, but I'm trying to have an exciting conversation.

"That's true, sadly. We have a lot of gangs here," she says. "GD, which is Gangster Disciples. IG, Imperial Gangsters. Latin Kings. There are more, but I don't know all the names."

Do you personally know gangsters?

"No. I don't mess with that."

Do you know Jews?

"Personally I don't. I never met a Jew, but I certainly know of them."

What do you think of them?

"Most Americans don't like the Jews, but I do."

Why do you like them?

"I'm Christian, and because I'm Christian I like them. They are the people that the Lord likes and I do too."

Not many Europeans would say this.

• • •

I eat my burger, drink my brandy, get up and drive. Don't tell the cops! Once I arrive in Milwaukee I sit down for coffee with a middle-aged blond-haired woman and chat with her. I ask her to tell me a little bit about Wisconsin.

Wisconsin, she tells me, "is 52 percent German American in its Caucasian community." Caucasian; super-PC lingo. This woman, if I'm judging her right, is more PC than the moon. (I don't know why I think the moon is PC, but nobody can prove otherwise.)

Anyway, I think I should deal with this Ms. PC more kindly. Is Wisconsin racist? I ask her.

"I feel very uncomfortable to talk about these things," she answers in a pained voice.

Why do you feel uncomfortable?

"Because I don't differentiate between colors."

I didn't ask you about yourself, I asked about Wisconsin.

"If you push me to answer, I will."

Please!

"We, and I don't include myself in this, are racist. Yes. Quite racist."

Everybody in Wisconsin is bad except for her. Of course.

I finish my coffee and walk around. In a nearby store I read this sign: "Only 2 students at a time in store." Why only two? I ask.

"They come in groups and they steal," the owner of the store says.

"They" means blacks. The owner of the store is Sikh.

I keep on walking and I see Shanta, a black man in his mid-forties who is standing next to his pickup truck. He has written a book, he tells me, and if I want a copy he will be very happy to sell me one.

What's your story? I ask him.

"I moved to Milwaukee in 1984, when I came to meet my mother. Originally, my mother played in bands, and music, so I thought she's Diana Ross and I idolized her. I moved to Milwaukee and I learned that my mother was a long-time criminal. She did prostitution, she did drugs, she stole; a lots of kind of crime she did. She went out for a long period of time with her prostitute friends. For a long period of time I was hungry, I was starving, and I was too young to work and I thought it was a brilliant idea to rob a pizza man. I said: I'm gonna get pizza, I'm not gonna be hungry, and I'm gonna get *cash* because pizza men have cash. I got caught, a juvenile case."

Did you have a gun on you?

"No. A hammer. I was too young to get a gun. I had a hammer."

How did you get caught?

"It was in the snow and the police followed my footprints in the snow. They went into the house and I got caught. I went to juvenile jail and when I got out I had a mental illness. I was trying to self-medicate – "

What kind of mental illness?

"I had posttraumatic distress and bipolar disorder. I didn't know that – "

Who told you that you had a mental illness?

"The one who eventually became my wife. I married my psychologist."

Is she white or black?

"White. She helped me understand myself and I got on medication. Then I started doing drugs again."

Why?

"Because I was depressed."

Why were you depressed? The wife was not good enough?

"She was. I didn't go to jail to leave her!"

Is she beautiful?

"Yes."

But they are getting divorced. "She's twenty-four years older than I am. I'm young, I want a lot of sex."

She doesn't want sex?

"Not as much."

How many times do you want to have sex per week and how many times does she want? Let's talk numbers!

"I want it every day, two, three times."

And she?

"Three to four times a week."

This isn't good enough for you?

"Not good enough."

Shanta had gotten out of prison in August. He'd robbed someone, this time with a gun.

In your old age you got smarter…?

"I got worse!"

Ok, so you had a gun. Who did you try to rob now, a banker?

"No."

A pizza man?

"No, not a pizza man!"

Who?

"A businessman."

What kind of business?

"Well, one of them had a restaurant – "

Again you were into food?

"That was one."

How many people have you robbed?

"Several."

How many?

"Seven."

And on the seventh time, with the seventh man, you got caught. What mistake did you make to get caught that time?

"The mistake was that I used my car and they [police] got my license plate and I showed my face [during the robbery]."

That's stupid.

"Very, very stupid!"

In all the robberies you made, all of them combined, how much money did you make in total?

"Honestly? Probably about $16,000."

Cash?

"Cash."

People carry so much money on them?

"Businessmen."

How did you figure out which people were businessmen?

"I robbed businessmen but also drug dealers. I robbed two drug dealers, and they had lots of money."

The other people you robbed, the businessmen, how much money did they have on them?

"Not even $1,000!"

Did you shoot any of them? Would you shoot?

"If you give me your money I'm not gonna shoot you."

And if I don't?

"I'm gonna hit you. I'm gonna beat you up. And if you hurt me, I'll shoot."

Did you ever shoot anybody?

"Not in my robberies. No."

A van, driven by a white man, pulls up. The driver pulls down his window and asks if I need help. I tell him that everything is all right and there's no need to worry.

Is he a cop? I ask my new friend.

"No, he ain't a cop."

How do you know?

"Believe me: I know cops!"

I can't believe that I'm standing here, spending my time with an armed robber. I take a little peek inside his truck, just to see what's inside, and there I see a woman. I ask the lady to come out.

She does, and we talk a bit. Shanta, it turns out, is not exactly the sex machine he pretends to be. This lady wants more sex, but he won't do it. He's too old...

• • •

America.

This is not the America I expected to find; it is a different America.

For many years I thought that I knew something about America, but do I? The truth is that I have no clue. I am discovering it, bit by bit, soul by soul, state by state.

Who knows where this, my journey, will lead me.

• • •

Today is National Hot Dog Day, and I am going to a Bike Night to spend quality time with Harley-Davidson owners in Milwaukee, Harley-Davidson's headquarters.

That's the real America, some people tell me. Almost everybody here is a Harley owner, but not all.

I meet an old couple who don't ride a Harley but are parents of Harley owners. "My family is from Germany," the lady tells me, by way of introducing herself. "I've never been to Germany but my daughter has. She loved it very much! Until she learned about the Nazis and what they did during the war and she cried out. She couldn't take it."

I tell her I'm German, and she doesn't feel very comfortable standing next to me anymore. This is the one time in my life that somebody hasn't liked me because I'm "German."

I go to ride on a Harley to compensate for the sting of rejection. Well, it's not exactly a ride but almost. The Harley I mount is a 2015 model, only its engine is not connected to the wheels. In other words: it makes the noise that will make me feel "masculine"; I can even change gears, but this bike doesn't move.

And what noise it makes! I can hardly hear the instructor who's trying to guide me. "Be careful not to make contact with the pipes; they are extremely hot."

Takes me less than a second to find out that the instructor is right.

What's the main idea of having a Harley? I ask the instructor, a young lady. Why not other motorbikes, like Honda?

"Harley is the ultimate freedom," she says, meaning every syllable.

Land of the Free.

For the last few weeks I've been asking countless people what it means to be an American, and almost everybody answered with two words: *freedom* and *liberty*. Now I know the ultimate meaning of at least the first word: riding a Harley.

"National Hot Dog Day" is self-explanatory; what's a Bike Night?

Here's how Harley-Davidson officially describes it: "All bikes unite at the Harley-Davidson Museum. Grab your bike. Join other riders for music, fun and plenty of eye candy. Enjoy food and drink specials inside and outside MOTOR Bar & Restaurant including MOTOR Bike Night Koozie Special $2 Miller High Life all season long (Koozies available at The Shop on the Museum campus)."

I don't know what Koozies are but I know what food is, and that's enough.

The sight in front of me is real eye candy: a sea of Harleys and an ocean of people.

We are not inside the museum, but outside. We won't spend this National Hot Dog day in a museum, my dear.

Most people here are males, most are middle aged, many are way overweight like me, many wear sunglasses and many wear black leather jackets. It's hot out here, but they wear wintery jackets. They have all kinds of *shmontses* on their jackets and all kinds of titles, such as "Outlaws," "Riders" and many others.

Quite a number of them are smokers and many have tattoos on their skin.

I approach one man with many tattoos; he has tattoos on almost every visible inch of skin. What do you have there? I ask him.

He stretches his arms and he explains to me his various tattoos: "A Harley-Davidson logo, two guns. And here I have red and white colors, the colors of America."

Should I tell him that these are also the colors of Poland? No; it might destroy his future. Why do you need all of them? I ask him.

"These are my expressions. What's important for me in life."

His wife stands next to him and listens in.

Do you like his tattoos? I ask her.

"They are okay."

Do they make him sexier?

"When I first met him he didn't have them."

From time to time another Harley owner goes to his bike and starts it up; he cranks the gas and makes tremendous sounds. They like noise, these Harleys.

It is here that I meet Greg, a proud Harley owner, and I ask him to explain to me why Harley owners are so passionate about their machines.

"It's hard to explain if you don't know on your own."

Try me.

"It's the wind blowing in your face. You get it? Today I was driving 240 miles, just for the love and joy of it."

You can have winds blowing right into your face while driving motorbikes made by the Japanese or the Germans. Wouldn't it be the same?

"Not the same!"

Why not?

"I told you, it's hard to explain. I tried, but it didn't work."

Try again.

He points to the hundreds of people surrounding us, almost all wearing one or another kind of Harley merchandise, and says: "Look at them! That's Harley. No other motorcycle gets people like Harley. It's a club."

How come Harley succeeded in creating this club and other motor companies do not?

"Look: My father just passed away, and tomorrow it's his funeral. I bet you that between forty to fifty people will come for the procession with their Harleys. I told only one person about the funeral, and tomorrow is a workday, but people will take off work to join the procession. That's Harley people. When I see them tomorrow at my father's funeral, it will be something so special that I will never forget."

Are you sure that they will come?

"I'm sure! That's the HOG."

What's HOG?

"Harley Owners Group."

Harley marketing fellows are genius.

"Perhaps they are. Listen: I have five hundred friends. Good friends. All Harley owners. And I can trust them that they will be there when I need them."

Describe to me what you felt the first time you owned a Harley, if you don't mind.

"I became part of a group. I became part of a family. I gained a family, friends. I was not alone."

How well do you know these five hundred Harley owners?

"Very well. We are one family. There's something you have to understand: every Harley looks different. You can modify your Harley; the company encourages it. Harley is an expression of who you are, beyond just having a Harley. This also helps in creating a unique club, a family. We all have a Harley at the same time that each of us has a different Harley. No two Harleys are alike."

A Harley man and woman sit next to us, neither of whom Greg knows. Not yet. "I don't know them," he says to me, "but I can touch them and they won't feel strange."

Let me see!

Greg lays his hand on the man's shoulders. "I hope you don't mind," he says to him.

"Not at all," the guy responds.

Family.

Harley-Davidson, don't laugh here, is also a religion. There's Christianity, Islam, Judaism, and then there's Harley-Davidsonism. Its house of prayer is the road, the open road. The main difference between Christianity and Harley-Davidsonism is price. Greg's bike costs $24,000; curing your depression at the Covenant Church is only fifty-two dollars. The main difference between Islam and Harley-Davidsonism is that Harleys would never fast for thirty days. The main difference between Jews and the Harleys is their loyalty levels. Harleys are loyal.

There are cheaper bikes than Greg's and there are much pricier ones as well. It all depends on how devout you are.

Blessed be thou, Harley-Davidson, who made man happy, loud, showy and passionate.

• • •

Friday is German Fest in Milwaukee. Good place to spend the day with the fifty million.

When I arrive at the Fest the gates are shut. There's a line of people waiting, and I wait with them.

Milwaukee is an all-American city, but it started as a German city because most of its early residents were German. That's what I'm told here. Some people still speak German, but only very few. One man in my line, with a little beard, tries to speak German but what comes out of his lips is Yiddish, not German.

Is it good to be Jewish in Wisconsin? I ask him.

"How did you know I'm Jewish?"

A wild guess. Is it good to be Jewish in Wisconsin?

"Very good!"

Be'emes ("really")? I ask him in Yiddish.

He's taken aback by the Yiddish. "I don't want to talk about it," he says.

Why not? You just said that it's good to be Jewish here, didn't you?

"You are not from Wisconsin, right? Enjoy Wisconsin!"

By your behavior I can tell that it's not that great to be a Jew here, am I wrong?

"I don't want to talk politics!"

That's not politics –

"Maybe another time I'll tell you. Not now. Leave it."

I think he should get himself a Harley.

Here comes a lady, Eileen, and she's excited to enter the German world waiting for her behind the gates. She is of German descent and she loves everything German, she says.

Do you consider yourself German?

"Part of me is. I speak some German."

Talk to me in German.

"*Ich liebe dich* [I love you]."

Give me more!

"*Auf Wiedersehen.*"

More!

"That's all I know."

And this makes you German?

"It's not just the language. I feel German."

What does that mean?

"How should I put it? I like the German character."

What's the German character?

She thinks but can't come up with anything. She thinks more, and more, and more, and finally she says: "This one is hard. I have to think about it."

The gates open and all enter. First, I go to the stage. Yes, there's a stage here. German Fest is not just about food, it's also about spirituality.

Flanked by many German flags, a nicely dressed man delivers the opening speech in both German and English. He ends his speech: "In the name of the Holy Son, Jesus Christ, Amen." The audience erupts in applause.

Done with Jesus, they sing "I'm proud to be an American" (*"God Bless the USA"*) as a large group of US Navy soldiers, who are on active duty and are here as official guests, sit as one just below the stage and seemingly enjoy every moment of being here.

There's more and more talk on the stage and then the choir ends the ceremony by singing "Ich liebe die Heimat" (I love the homeland) and "America the Beautiful."

In the Germany of today you are not likely to see Germans singing, "I'm proud to be a German." But we are in America, and Americans are proud to be American and its Germans are proud to be Americans.

The navy sailors get up to leave, and audience members approach them to shake their hands in a warm display of love and admiration. The sailors suck up every drop of love for all it's worth.

Should I try to interview the mayor, and see if this city is as corrupt as Chicago? Nope. I don't really care.

• • •

I get into my Malibu, and I drive. On potholes that never end. After some driving I stop in Dodgeville, Wisconsin, where I meet Dan, who works for a nonprofit art organization in the area. When I tell him that I'm from Germany he takes a liking to me, and he opens his heart to this German.

A man's got to unload the pains in his heart to a visiting German. Israel, he tells me, is "shooting rockets on the Palestinians," but America won't stop it, and this upsets him. "American foreign policy is hypocritical. Should I say more?" he asks.

The Arab-Israeli conflict is on his mind, but he doesn't care a flying s--t (shit) about Englewood.

"Where should I start?" he goes on. "With what Israel is doing? We have a double standard here. If you criticize Israel, you'll be labeled anti-Semitic. But, come on! How much more racist can a country be?! What Israel is doing is criminal, Israel is committing injustice, and we are supporting them; we give them millions of dollars every year. Eight hundred million dollars every year. Why? I wish we stopped this. How many settlements are there? Is anybody counting? The Israelis keep building settlements, and we finance them. This makes me mad."

You are very passionate about the Middle East conflict, aren't you?

"Yes, I am."

Are you Muslim, Jewish?

"I'm an atheist. Not exactly. I wouldn't call myself atheist. I am a God hater. What do you call that?"

Why would anybody in Dodgeville have such strong feelings about that faraway country? I don't know. What I do know is that I'm happy I didn't say that I'm Jewish.

• • •

Malibu is also very happy today and drives really fast into places whose names only God knows – mostly private properties. This is how I get to meet Andrea, a hunt club manager in Spring Green, Wisconsin.

I should have this job: "hunt club manager."

Andrea, a thirty-year-old lady, also takes care of the huge private property Malibu and I have driven into, where, among other things, she rides her two horses, sometimes for eight hours a day but usually only two. She is a "spiritual" Christian, as she defines herself; she believes in Jesus but does not attend church services. She loves the countryside, loves nature and she carries a pistol, a Smith & Wesson Bodyguard 380, which has a laser.

How much does this toy cost? I ask her.

"Four hundred and fifty dollars. If you point the laser at a person, that should be enough to scare him."

Have you ever done it?

"Fortunately not."

The reason some people are against guns, she tells me, is that "they are not educated about guns."

I want to be educated. I love education. May I use your gun? I ask her.

"Ever shot a handgun?"

Not yet.

"Let me show you how this works."

She shoots in the air. And then hands me the gun. Loaded. I point at an imaginary bear and I shoot it. And then one more time, at another bear, just to make sure I have enough meat for the week.

To be honest, I have shot before, mostly tank shells while I served in the Israeli army, but I never shot a pistol.

It's a thrill, I tell her. It makes me feel like a powerful entity. I'm like a God. I can take away or grant life.

"This is what I meant when I talked about education. Guns are not about killing people, guns are for protection and for hunting. The other thing about guns: owning a gun is a right, a constitutional right, and that's why I own a gun. Guns are not about shooting people, unless you are in extreme circumstances when your life is in danger.

People have to educate themselves about guns. Here in the country I need a gun, not just for hunting."

Not only Americans hunt, and not only Americans can own guns. But in the United States, the issue of owning guns is more than just about the right to hunt. Here, in America, it seems to me that there is an emotional attachment to guns – either by those who are anti or those who are pro.

Are you emotionally attached to guns?

"The only emotional part of the gun for me is if I have a right to own them or not. My husband and I own at least one hundred guns. Pistols, shotguns and rifles. There is a sentimental attachment to guns because they have been passed down from generation to generation. No different than a grandmother's ring. It's a very sentimental thing. Does that explain it better for you?"

No.

"Why not?"

You're a thirty-year-old lady and you need one hundred guns?

"How many shoes you have?"

You didn't get me there. I have only three pairs.

"Part of the reason we have that many guns is because of the way the government is going for the past few years."

Are you talking about Obama?

"Yes."

You don't like the guy?

"No. When he got voted in a lot of the anti-gun stuff started going on. The price of guns went up, the price of bullets went up, and with it the talk of outlawing certain accessories. When all that happened, we started hoarding."

But why do you need one hundred?

"It's a personal thing."

One hundred??

"Guns are not cookie cutters. Guns are different. Some are with laser, some not. And many other differences. It's a right! We have a right to own one, a lot, or one hundred. You ask me why; I ask you, why not?"

I have a right to buy and own one hundred cars, but I don't. Why do you have so many guns?

"It's somehow hard to talk about, but I truly believe that it all comes down to culture. That's how it all started. A lot of the guns we have now happened in the last five, six years. And what I'm getting to is, politically the country is getting split and I think it's going to be a conflict in this country, and we are stockpiling guns and ammunitions. We had a civil war before, and we can have it again. I'm not saying I walk around and think about it every day. But am I prepared for the next war? Yes."

Is your gun hoarding some kind of a political statement?

"I tried not to take it there, but yes."

What do you think of the black-white issue in America?

"I think it's not an issue other than what the blacks are making of it. If you look at statistics, more cops shot white people than black people, but if you watch the media you only see white cops shooting black people."

And why is the media doing this?

"That's a good question."

What do you think?

"Hard to say. I don't know if it's just a trend the media is rolling on, or a bias. I truly believe that the news is biased and that they tell you what they want you to hear. There is a freedom of speech, that's our right, but you have to be very careful what you say. We, the white people, feel almost like we are becoming the minority and we truly feel that we have to be very careful what we say. But at some point enough will be enough and a war will happen. It will explode at some point. Liberals are doing what they want: abortions, gay rights, anti-gun legislation, and we have to bite our tongues. It will not last forever. We don't talk but we are preparing, we are analyzing, and when something happens we will be prepared. But at this point we are very careful what we say, choosing our words wisely."

Andrea has other issues with the government and its laws. "I don't wear seat belts," she says. "Why is the government getting involved in people's lives and telling them that they have to live until they are one hundred years old?"

Were Andrea not a woman, and had she lived a couple of centuries ago, she would be one of the Founding Fathers. She is exactly what I pictured a Founding Father to be while I was in Pennsylvania. She and they are cut of the same cloth, a piece of the same stone, a drop of the same blood and they share the same soul. But no hair grows on her chin, and she is two centuries late.

Perhaps she's a little bit racist, but the Founding Fathers were as well.

I want to see her home. I want to see one hundred guns with my own eyes. I want to see a home, not an army base, with one hundred guns and thousands of bullets in it. I'm intrigued. It takes her time to think it over, about four minutes, and then she says: "Follow me." She goes to her truck. I go to my Malibu. And we drive. Fast. Yes, she's fast!

It's a nice house and a lovely home, simply but warmly decorated. Her husband is home today and he's glad to show me around. In the living room, a cozy living room, there are two really big safes. He opens one, then the other, and he shows me the different guns: handguns, shotguns and rifles. With immense pleasure he teaches me what to use when, the differences between the various bullets and firepower. He loves his guns. He holds each of them with a display of kindness mixed with kinship. He knows each of his guns personally.

These two safes are just part of this couple's gun collection, he tells me. They have more in the other rooms. Guns are all over. They don't have children, but they have guns. The guns are their children.

I have one little request: Could I shoot?

Of course.

We go to their porch, and I am given a Benelli Super Black Eagle II, valued at $2,000, and I shoot. I love it. Don't ask me why.

They see the smile on my fat face after shooting, and the man walks out fast and lays a shooting target in the backyard. I shoot with the same shotgun. I score five out of five.

Next, I take an Ithaca side-by-side .410 to play with. I score four out of four.

And now I get upgraded: he hands me a Ruger Mini-14 rifle. I score five out of five.

Lastly he gives me a handgun, a Ruger SR40. I score four out of five. I am devastated. But they comfort me. With only one miss, they tell me, my score is fantastic.

When we're done and I'm about to leave, I feel a certain bond between us. We share a close mutual friend: the gun.

• • •

I go to a hotel and relax a bit. What's new today? Here's Reuters reporting: "The Boy Scouts of America lifted its outright ban on openly gay adult leaders and employees."

It's interesting to see how public opinion is shaped and how the crimes of yesterday are the virtues of today. In fifty years or so, I think, every gay person will own at least ninety guns and no Republican will even dream of owning one.

I fall asleep dreaming of one hundred black lesbians doing yoga at the Chicago Jewish temple.

• • •

I am paying tons of money for the right to use Malibu, which includes all kinds of insurances and other fine print, and I better not leave white Malibu parked in some lot, alone and cold.

We unite and drive west. While driving, I see a little memorial monument on the road, and I stop to check it out. Under the name Battle Island, I read this: "Of the 1000 Sacs [Sac Indians] who crossed the river from Iowa in April 1832, not more than 150 survived to tell the story of the Blackhawk War."

The people who came to this continent, whether for a better life or because they were fleeing persecution at home, paid dearly for the right to be here. Yes, this land was won with blood and much suffering – and there is a history to this land predating the Constitution and the Declaration of Independence, a history written by flying souls, a history where European and Indian sought each other's destruction, a history covered with rivers of blood flowing between corpses.

Back in the white American car I drive until I reach La Crosse, Wisconsin. I stop at a store on the main road to get me a Diet Coke and I meet Dan, and he tells me that the city of La Crosse is a great city. I think I should hang around here.

Dan's specialty, I learn, is political science and education. La Crosse, he tells me, is 97 percent white Christian and 3 percent "other." Who are the others? Blacks, Jews and Muslims. He knows much about Jews and Muslims. Not only the ones in La Crosse but also those who live thousands of miles away from here. In 1947 or 1948, he is not sure what year, the United States and the United Kingdom decided to put Jews in the State of Palestine and then they created a new state, the State of Israel. When I ask him what year the State of Palestine was founded, he gets a slight headache and can't remember anything anymore.

He feels much better, and has no headaches, when he speaks of blacks and whites in La Crosse.

Blacks and whites, he tells me, live here in perfect harmony. Are there some poor neighborhoods around with crime problems? Oh yes, he says. I ask him if the crime areas are in poor white neighborhoods, and he shakes his head. Are they where the blacks live? He nods yes.

It's politically incorrect to say anything negative about blacks, but perfectly okay when you use your head, not your tongue, to express what you really feel about them.

After parking Malibu in a local hotel – got to park again, that's life – I walk the streets of La Crosse. Nice city. When I pass by the Weber Center for the Performing Arts, which houses La Crosse's community theater, I enter the complex.

There I meet David, the executive director of the theater company. David is a nice white man and he takes the time to show me around. He's proud of his theater. First, he shows me the view one can see from the theater's lobby: the Mississippi River. Good for theatergoers who come to consume culture and can enjoy nature at the same time.

Then David shows me the main auditorium: the rows are a comfortable distance from one another, offering a wide leg space, and there are even cup holders in front of every seat so that theatergoers can sip some liquids while their brains are working full speed watching high culture. Do you perform political theater? I ask David.

"No."

Why not?

"We are dependent on ticket sales, and people don't want political theater. People want comedies. Theatergoers come to the theater for 'escapism,' not to think, but to be entertained. That's the only reason people go to theater."

People in Europe love political theater. Even Shakespeare was political!

Well, could be, he admits, but not in America. "Americans don't like political theater."

How do you know? Did you ever try?

Not exactly. Actually never.

Why not?

"Our sponsors will pull out. No corporation will sponsor political theater."

Politicians are beholden to their donors, I learned in Chicago. Artists, David says, are beholden to their sponsors. No wonder the Donald, independently wealthy, says whatever will pass through his lips.

Are you a Republican or a Democrat? I ask David.

His face hardens, nervous ticks kick in, and then he shoots back, extremely upset: "I won't answer this question!"

It is a sight to behold.

As the center's name implies, the theater has one main donor: Donald J. Weber. I should get to know him.

After leaving David I inquire about Donald. He is, I find out, the founder and CEO of Logistics Health Incorporated (LHI). What kind of business is this? I read: "LHI's experts provide customized health care solutions supported by a national network of more than 25,000 medical and dental providers." And the list goes on.

That's money.

• • •

Come next day I go to visit Donald, the local celebrity of La Crosse who, I slowly learn, has quite a number of other businesses in addition to LHI. Donald looks like a nice guy, someone you'd like to be your father or grandfather. I read somewhere, I tell him, that Governor Scott Walker describes you as an American patriot. Do you view yourself as a patriot?

"You know, I grew up on a small family farm and then I went to the Marine Corps, so, you know, I'll say that that probably shaped my life more than anything. I have been blessed in many ways."

Do you view yourself as a patriot?

"Well, I don't know, you know."

The answer to this is very short: yes or no.

"I am – I – I'm very patriotic. Yes. Very much so. And I totally, totally support the men and women who serve. Because, you know, they volunteer. Every day we get up we have so many freedoms. You know, we can choose to live where we want to live, we can send our kids to school wherever we want. I have started nine businesses, just from ideas that I had. I lost everything. I lost my home, you know, I didn't have a place to live. I found a place to live, an old house, a shelter, you know; I milked the cows – and I found a way to come back. I took a lot of risk and I've been blessed."

If the election were held today, who would you vote for? I ask. Donald won't say.

What makes Donald proud is this: thousands of people in La Crosse wake up in the morning and have a job to go to, and he's the one who made it happen. Donald is Catholic, a man of faith, and he thinks that he walks in the way of Jesus: he cares for and helps his fellow men and women.

I ask Donald about the theater in the building named after him.

"You know, I don't go to the theater. I'm not a theater person. I mean, I support them because I think it's good for the community. I grew up in a farm."

David won't do political theater for fear that Donald would withdraw his support, but Donald couldn't care less.

Oh, David!

If you had a university degree, would you be as successful? I ask Donald.

"No."

The secret to his success, he tells me, is this: "I always hired people a lot smarter than I am. I don't feel threatened. I can't think in these terms, I only have a high school education."

And he is proud of his children. They don't ask him for money; they work for it. His son just came back from Israel, where he stayed for one week.

What did he tell you about Israel?

"Listen: America must help Israel. What they are facing out there is not easy, you know."

How Israel, a tiny country far away, manages to sneak into the minds of so many Americans is ever surprising.

I ask Donald what I should do while in La Crosse.

"You like steak? We have an excellent restaurant downstairs. Go and have dinner there in the evening. It's on me! They have tenderloin; they have crabs. Excellent fish that they fly right in here."

I certainly will go there. Germans like me love free food. Donald has another suggestion as well: "Go and see the Shrine of Our Lady of Guadalupe. It's just gorgeous. You would never believe it's here."

I bid Donald goodbye and go to see the shrine. Spirit before food, baby.

• • •

The Shrine of Our Lady of Guadalupe, completed in 2008 at the cost of $30 million, was built with donations from private individuals and is not part of any diocese.

Despite attempts by the local bishop at the time, Raymond L. Burke, who initiated the building of the shrine, the Vatican doesn't want to have anything to do with it "because it's too costly," one of the monks here tells me. Instead, and to pacify big Catholic donors, a letter "from the Vatican" which was signed by "+G.B. Re Substitute," was sent to the bishop. It states that "as a pledge of abundant divine graces, the Holy Father cordially imparts his Apostolic Blessing to you."

No apparitions of the Holy Virgin have been reported at this location as of yet, but parishioners have reported miracles happening to them at the site. "Barren mothers bore children after coming to the shrine," Raymond Burke, now a cardinal in Rome, tells me.

For the record: no political theater is performed here at any time, but this place is much better than any show. The shrine is amazing in its beauty, and the windows are lovely. The Shrine of Our Lady of Guadalupe is a 350-seat church built in the old style of Catholic cathedrals, but it's all new.

What I find quite interesting here is the American angle of it: rich people, be they top bankers or big-shot lawyers, sit at their posh saloons and decide to build a church from which miracles will happen. And, guess what? The miracles happen. Even the Virgin Mother, mind you, is beholden to the super-rich.

America!

• • •

As for me, my AT&T cellular service doesn't work here no matter how many times I point my smartphone in Our Lady's direction. Our Lady will create babies for you, but can't provide connection. I am paying good money to get coverage across the United States, as the AT&T

saleswoman promised me, but the No Service signal comes up quite frequently when I'm out of urban areas.

I enjoy the beauty surrounding me, smoke a cigarette or two, and slowly walk back to have a nice meal at the restaurant that Donald recommended, the one that he will pay for.

I order crab cake, Canadian Walleye and cheesecake. All are good, but nothing outstanding. There's money in America, much of it, but not much good food. Not even in expensive restaurants. Virgin Mother, can you do something about it?

Perhaps, just perhaps, what's happening to food in America is what happened to culture here. If all you've got is a melting pot, don't expect the food to be anything but bland.

Should I keep going northwest, or should I go south to Iowa?

Before I go to sleep for the night, a birdie whispers in my ear that Minnesota has got lots of culture. I am a sucker for culture. To the state of Minnesota I shall drive come the morrow!

Gate Eight

Somalis are human beings like anybody else and they,
too, should be allowed to shoot you in the head

IN GOOD TIME, AND WITH EXCELLENT WEATHER, I REACH SAINT PAUL,
Minnesota. Nice name for a city, don't you think?

Of course, when I hear "saints" I immediately think of Jews, the
folks who gave Saint Paul to the world.

I find myself a sizable Jewish temple. Today, it turns out, they
have a lecture/training session about race and racism, which I assume
is about anti-Semitism, given that they are Jews.

The event is organized, I learn, by the Jewish Community Action
in Saint Paul. Good to know that the Jews here are active. About
seventy people attend, two of whom wear skullcaps. The attendees
sit around tables that are spread around the room, and I join one
of them.

The Jews seem deeply worried. I didn't even see sad faces like
these in any of the 'hoods. What happened?

I don't know. What I do know is this: on each table there are
numerous envelopes, for use by those seated around the table who
would like to stuff money into them. Starting amount suggested:
fifty-four dollars.

The Christians asked for fifty-two dollars; the Jews want fifty-
four dollars. No problem.

The first speaker, a young lady, goes to the podium. She speaks about "our system," referring to the American justice system, and says that it is stacked against blacks. This event, I quickly realize, is not about anti-Semitism but white racism.

The Jews here, I slowly find out, feel guilty about the white guy who killed nine blacks at the black church in South Carolina. No, Dylann Roof isn't Jewish, but he is white, and these Jews feel responsible.

Why? Ask them.

Time passes slowly, and then a black lady comes to the podium. American Jews, I have found long ago, love to have at least one black person at their events.

They've got one here. A good one. She's not just black but also a "Jew by choice" black, as she introduces herself, which means that she is a convert. She is, in other words, a black lady who fell in love with Jews.

Well, not exactly.

She has a big problem with Jews, she tells the audience. American Jews, she has discovered since becoming Jewish, are racist, and she wants all Jews present to know that she has blown their cover. As if this is not enough, she adds that racism also exists within the Israeli Jewish community. Ethiopians in Israel, she says, are 2 percent of the population but 30 percent of them have a police record. Who's to blame? Everybody in Israel, including the Israeli government. Israel publicly invited French Jews to come to Israel, she says, but will not do the same for black Jews.

She of course neglects to mention that Israel sent planes to Africa to bring black Jews to Israel, and that that's how the Ethiopians are in Israel to start with. But this is a minor detail, too minor to mention.

When she is done with accusing the Jews, the Jews present here applaud her. Don't ask me to explain.

Next on the agenda is the training part, where people learn how to talk to each other about race. Two people from the audience go to the podium and practice talking about race.

It goes something like this.

One person says: Wow – This is – Wow – This is –

And the other person replies: Yeah. Right. Yeah. So true.

Who is the dumb head who said that Jews are smart?

• • •

Once the event is over I sit down with the executive director of the Jewish Community Action, a guy by the name of Vic Rosenthal, and ask him: Do you think that somewhere out there blacks sit together and discuss how to help Jews against anti-Semitism, just as you are doing about them?

"No."

Does that bother you?

"No."

If I'm not mistaken, Jews have done more than any other group in America to help blacks – in the '50s, in the '60s and ever since. Yet blacks do not reciprocate – and you're okay with it. How come?

"We have not done enough. Maybe we did more than other communities in America, but I expect Jews to do more!"

Why should Jews do more than any other group?

The answer that I get, a long one, could be summed up with one word: because.

To me, the very idea that Jews should do more than others is by itself racist, but I don't think I should say such a thing in a temple.

I also meet Peggy, who is actually Lutheran. Why is she here? "I wanted to see how the Jews deal with racial issues in our country and perhaps do the same in our church."

What did you learn?

"I was very surprised to learn that the Jews are also racist, against the black Jews; I didn't know that."

A good lesson to share with her fellow Lutheran churchgoers.

Next to Peggy is a Jewish lady by the name of Judy. Judy tells me that she works for peace between people and that she fights prejudice against any group whatsoever. Judy also thinks that Jews are racist. But this is not a prejudice. Why not? "I was in Israel and I saw there that all the street sweepers in Israel are Ethiopian and that Jews treat Arabs very, very badly." The church lady is learning a lot today about Jews!

Outside the temple I meet a nice gay guy – he tells me he is gay, not that I asked him – and he tells me that the Jews got it all wrong. "I don't know what kind of metrics they are using, but their conclusions are not correct." Blacks in Minnesota are doing fine.

Not just fine; they are doing great. "The biggest Somali settlement in the world after Somalia is Minneapolis."

This is a piece of interesting news. After all the racism that I've seen so far, I now discover that it all stops at the borders of the state of Minnesota.

Minneapolis is Saint Paul's "twin city," and I think that I should spend some time with the Somalis, to witness firsthand the diversity abundant there.

I register at the Sheraton Midtown – that's midtown Minneapolis – where I get a nice room, and then go for a walk in the neighborhood. Everywhere I look I see black ladies with hijabs, the Muslim headgear, and assume that they are the famous Somalis. Diversity at its best!

• • •

I walk the streets, enjoying the sight of diversity, when suddenly my eyes catch an interesting shop: Koscielski's Guns & Ammo. To enter I ring a bell and wait for those inside to let me in, hoping that they will.

They do.

There are some interesting signs in this shop. For example: "Are you going to listen to me in English?" "I have to speak to you in 12-gauge?" "Keep your hands out of your pockets at all times."

Austria is well represented here by an impressive selection of Glock handguns. I look at them on display and the man behind the counter, a Somali, asks if I would like a Glock.

I ask the salesperson if I can buy a weapon or two right here and now. I want to walk out of this store with some guns, I tell him.

It depends, he tells me. If I want a handgun or an "assault" rifle, I'd need a license, but if I want a shotgun or a rifle that is not "military assault" I could get it on the spot.

Are you telling me, I ask him, that I can walk out of this shop right now with a shotgun without anybody doing a police check on me? You know, just to make sure that I'm not a robber, a rapist or a serial killer?

The salesperson is not really sure now and he asks a man sitting on the other side of the shop if this is indeed the case. The man, O'Neal, who's the owner of Koscielski's Guns & Ammo, says that if I can prove that I'm a resident of the state for at least ninety days, then yes, I could get a shotgun or a rifle of the non-assault kind right away. What's non-assault? Guns that use no magazines.

And then O'Neal, with his loaded handgun, walks in my direction. He asks me what I really want. This O'Neal ain't no stupid. He smells a rotten fish and he wants to stand closer to that fish, me.

Having no other choice, I tell him that I'm writing about America and that I am interested in people of all professions, and that's why I'm here.

"What are you doing in this neighborhood?" he asks. "Where you are now, this street, is a neutral territory. Right and left of this street are gang areas, and they are killing each other whenever they like."

Somalis are also gang members?

"They are human, just like the rest of the people," the Somali intervenes.

They kill each other for what? I ask O'Neal.

"It's dickheads killing dickheads," he says, speaking of blacks.

O'Neal, for the record, is black.

"You take care of yourself around here," he tells me.

What's the problem? Somalis don't like fat white men?

"They see you, they know you are not part of either gang, and that you are not from here. You are like a sore thumb: immediately recognizable."

Blacks are killing blacks and "diversity" is a word not found in the local dictionary.

O'Neal takes out his loaded gun and, just like the "Founding Father" Andrea did, he hands it to me. What for? In case I would like to have a picture of myself with his gun.

O'Neal was wounded in Vietnam when a bullet entered his back and came out of his torso. He shows me the spot where the bullet came out. The scar is still there.

As I'm about to leave his shop he gives me a gift, a stainless-steel folding knife. It's of the heavy kind, a knife not meant to cut bread or apples. I am in midtown Minneapolis and O'Neal wants me to get out of here alive.

His gesture touches me.

• • •

Armed with my heavy knife, perfect for stabbing humans, I go to my hotel. Sitting at my desk, I gather my thoughts. Why are blacks killing blacks? I ask myself. Why are they so cruel to one another?

I think of Greg and of his Harley-Davidson. I shoot him an email, asking how many Harley people had come to his father's funeral.

He answers: "There were forty-six bikes for the funeral procession. I was deeply moved by the generosity."

If only the black community cared for one another like the Harleys. But they don't. It's a "dickheads killing dickheads" mentality and, as Jay from Detroit's Red Zone put it: "Always like this with black people. They shootin' each other."

I came to this state looking for culture, and so far I got a knife.

• • •

I want to see culture, right here in Minneapolis, come hell or high water. In the evening I go to the local theater powerhouse, the Guthrie Theater. Unlike the big theaters in New York, most of which are commercial undertakings, the Guthrie is a leading "regional" theater, a class of theaters that are supposed to be about culture and not commerce.

The Guthrie is an impressive theater even before you enter its doors. It's big. It's awesome. It's a shrine. It's awe-inspiring. In short: it's everything you would expect a highly cultural institution to look. Eye candy, as the Harleys would say. I feel inspired. You can even get a good cup of hot coffee here, to make sure your energy level is high for the theater you're about to see. The show this evening is called *Stage Kiss*. I don't know what it's about, but I'll soon see.

I enter the theater and go to my seat, hoping for greatness. *Stage Kiss*, lasting for over two hours with an intermission, is masterfully acted, especially by its lead, Stacia Rice.

What is it about? The short answer is, nothing. The long answer: you wouldn't care. This play is more about acting than a real story line. It has a gay character, like almost any other modern American show; it doesn't offend anybody and does not even mention the word *politics*. It employs many stage tricks that make you laugh quite often and offers a great dose of escapism.

Message? Forget it. Culture? Don't even mention such a word here. Ideas? That's another dirty word. Art? Not here. Entertainment? Two hours of it.

The Guthrie is not the sole American theater that chooses to be brain-dead. No. New York is full of them. But regional theaters, unlike Broadway, are not-for-profit organizations, ever soliciting tax-deductible donations from every man and woman whose contact information is known to them, in the name of culture and art. If the Guthrie has any ideological agenda, it is this: deactivate all thinking cells in the brains of every American who passes through its gates.

I leave the theater and smoke a little cigarette outside, looking at the people coming out.

Not a single black.

The Guthrie, according to its PR machinery, is for all people, whatever their ethnic background. From what I see, the Guthrie is about laughs, melting pots and boiling coffees.

I stick around for another day in Minneapolis, and I even go to the Mall of America, which has more yearly visitors than Disney World, but I buy nothing.

While in Germany I was told that the second language spoken in North Dakota is German. I want to see this for myself.

Tomorrow I'll drive to North Dakota.

Gate Nine

"Climate change" means Palestinian rights

THE NEXT DAY I REACH FARGO, NORTH DAKOTA'S CULTURAL CAPITAL. UPON arrival I read in *Valley News Live*:

> In North Dakota, a new electronic cigarette law prohibits minors from using, possessing, or purchasing electronic smoking devices, alternative nicotine products, or any of their component parts, and requires child-resistant packaging for liquid nicotine containers.
>
> Gun rights have also expanded. Concealed carry permit holders can bring a gun to liquor stores, public rest areas, and public parks.

In short: fewer cigarettes, more guns.

Doesn't make much sense to me, but not much in Germany makes sense to me either. Big deal.

Jason, one of the first people I meet in Fargo, is an environmental activist who cares a lot about climate change. He defines himself to me thusly: "I am pro-choice, pro-gay marriage, pro-environment, pro-Palestine."

Sadly, he can't say this in German.

Moments later I meet another young man, Luke. He calls himself liberal, tells me that he is pro-gay marriage, pro-choice and pro-environment, which to him means that climate change is man-made.

Are you also pro-Palestine?

"Yes, I am. How did you know?"

He doesn't speak German either, but his set of beliefs is Germanic.

Let me say something here. If you had asked me before my travels in America if Americans knew about issues such as the Israeli-Palestinian conflict, I'd have said to you: No way.

Well, the little I knew.

I look for the famed German-speakers here, but they are perhaps hiding. The liberals here, if you care to know, don't hide. The young, at least, the ones known as millennials (those born between the early 1980s and the early 2000s), love the light of the sun and would rather not hide. These millennials, I think, also love the idea of being more "liberal" than their parents and are happy to share their newfound left-love with strangers.

In general, North Dakota is a red state, conservative (Republican), but Fargo is "bluish" (leaning Democratic), especially its younger population. This is, at least, what I'm told by the locals.

I walk around, looking for some cultural events, but can't find any impressive ones.

And so I go looking for the true-blooded North Dakotans. State senator Tim Flakoll is having soup at the Würst Bier Hall in downtown Fargo, and he is getting ready to consume a nice-looking sausage on a plate next to his bowl of soup when I show up.

Würst Bier Hall. That's German! At least that.

What does it mean to be a North Dakotan? I ask him, in English, just as he's about to put a spoonful of soup into his mouth. He puts the spoon down and he thinks. A man's gotta think before he answers such a deep question.

After giving it some thought he says: "I think that North Dakotans are not easily described, but I think that one of the things you'd notice about North Dakotans, no matter where you come from, is that they care about the people around them, about their community, and everything else. And it's genuine!"

That's nice.

• • •

North Dakota's real capital is Bismarck. If I understand correctly, the city was named Bismarck almost 150 years ago in honor of German Chancellor Otto von Bismarck, the man who unified a bunch of territories into one country that today we call Germany.

They might not speak German here, but they are big on German roots.

I drive to Bismarck.

Driving is the ultimate American experience. In the American states I have visited so far, excluding New York, I noticed that public transportation is chiefly for the poor, mostly blacks and Spanish. The train system in most of the states is either nonexistent or useless, and this renders the car, the private car, the main transportation tool. With time, you can get attached to your car. I'm not totally there yet, but I suspect that my white companion Malibu feels a bit close to me.

With these thoughts in my head I reach the capitol building in Bismarck.

The North Dakota capitol building looks like an office building, though not a very modern office building. There's nothing spectacular in its design, and it reminds me of a big parking garage in Brooklyn.

It's not nice to say, I know.

In any case, I'm here because I want to meet Wayne Stenehjem, North Dakota's attorney general. Wayne is Norwegian by descent and he's damn proud of it. The ones who founded this state, he proudly tells me, were Norwegians. The Germans say that their ancestors founded this state, but oh boy: they are wrong!

I raise no objection and we move on to talk about justice, crime and other juicy morsels.

Aggravated assaults went down last year, he tells me, but the "areas we are very concerned about are drug arrests." In 2009 there were 2,063 drug arrests, but last year the figure went up to four thousand.

"The kind of offenses we are seeing now are much more complex," he says, and the quantities of drugs offered on the street are much higher. Drug pushers come from "the drug cartels in Mexico and form the motorcycle gangs." This increase is related to the oil boom in North Dakota, which resulted in more people having more money to spend. In addition, the boom added to the male population and now men far outnumber women, hence the state has seen an increase in prostitution.

Basic math, I'd say.

There's also a rise in gang activity in North Dakota, due to an influx of gangs from other states. "We see a huge gang increase in eastern North Dakota," he tells me.

Wayne presents me with some interesting crime statistics: while robberies are up, aggravated assaults are down.

I don't get it. For both of these statistics to be correct, robbers must be kissing and hugging you while they rob you at gunpoint.

I ask him to explain it to me. "Aggravated assault is a different offense," he says. I guess these statistics were issued by the PR department of the State of North Dakota. Only PR people can come up with such logic.

Tomorrow I'll try to see the real people behind the numbers: the prisoners.

As for the remainder of the day, I walk the streets of Bismarck until evening and pay close attention to the flags, to see if they follow the flag rules I learned on Mackinac Island, Michigan.

They do. The flags are up and they are lit.

Back in Chicago, the Jewish community sat in session and decided not to decide about the Iran deal. Meantime, the two senators that the CUFI people tried to meet in DC have just announced their decisions: Senator Chuck Schumer will vote against the deal and Senator Kirsten Gillibrand will vote for it.

I go to my hotel, the Radisson. I spread on the sofa and turn on the TV.

The first Republican presidential debate is being broadcast live on Fox News. It is an important event in this country, I can tell, as every news media discusses it in minute detail. To many of them it's also about how Donald Trump will perform in a debate setting.

What is more interesting, at least to me, is how the candidates eagerly mention their faith in God and in Jesus. And their support for Israel. American support for Israel, financial or otherwise, is one of the issues that these candidates agree on. This is something one will never hear in any election debate in any European country of our day.

One of the senators, Ted Cruz, even declares that he will move the American embassy from Tel Aviv to Jerusalem if he's elected. I have heard this from him before in a private setting in New York, but now he says it to the rest of America.

According to the BBC, the number of people watching this debate is twenty-four million, "a record for a primary contest."

• • •

Morning comes and I drive to the state's penitentiary. It is a long process to get in, not to mention to get the permission to get in, but finally I'm inside.

First, I meet a nice blond lady, Leann Bertsch, the director of the Department of Corrections and Rehabilitation (DOCR). She gives me some numbers. Cost per inmate per year: $39,000. Recidivism rate: 39 percent.

She is a proud German, by the way – an American of German descent, that is.

Shortly she will fly overseas to study how other countries deal with crime and justice. "We incarcerate more people in the United States than the Europeans do; we are much more punitive in this nation," she says.

Why?

"History and culture. It's kind of a whole history. There was some precedent, probably started in the eighties, to get tough on crime, and a lot of money was given to states to really get punitive. We are locking up a lot of people who could be safe in our community, too. In our women's prison, I always say, you could probably release 80 percent of them and not blink an eye; you'll feel just as safe. We are over-incarcerating people."

I thank her, and I start my tour of this prison, a male prison. Walking the corridors of the prison requires earplugs. There are so many doors before I reach the cells, and each iron door makes a deafening sound before an operator opens it, both when it is opening and when closing behind me.

Over half of the prisoners, I'm told while walking, work in the prison. Scale of salaries: lowest paying job is $1.55 a day, highest is $10.00 a day.

A dollar fifty-five a day. Who are they kidding?

Time to meet the people. First I meet two prisoners, a white guy and a Native American. What have you done that brought you here? I ask the white guy, who is doing his three-and-a-half-year jail time here.

"Ask me a different question," he answers.

I rephrase the question: What have they accused you of?

"DUI [driving under the influence of alcohol]."

That's it?

"And escape."

Escape from...?

"Jail."

The other guy, the Native American, says he is here because of "terrorizing and escape."

Terrorizing who?

"My cousin."

Both say that they have pleaded guilty.

• • •

Native Americans make up about 10 percent of the North Dakotan population, Warden Braun tells me, but between 30 percent and 35 percent of this prison population. I'm not sure that this is right, and I will have to check it.

I like Warden Braun. When I first heard his name and title, before seeing him, I imagined a tough, even cruel guy. But now that I'm with him, Warden Braun strikes me as a nice, kind person. He jokes with his imprisoned folks, taps them on the shoulders, and they seem to like him. "I'm lucky to be in this facility," one of the prisoners tells me.

North Dakotans care about the people around them, including those in prison.

Except for the judges of this state, the guys who will sentence you to three and a half years for one DUI. Are they really that cruel? I ask a prison official how come a DUI ends up in three and a half years of jail time.

"He didn't tell you the truth. He is here for a sexual offense," he tells me. The prisoners who are here for sexual offenses are the lowest social level of the prisoner community. "If they are in here for some type of sexual offense, the likelihood of them telling you that is going to be very, very small."

I move on to the toughest part of this prison, its maximum-security section, Administrative Segregation, herein called the segregation unit. This is a prison within a prison, where prisoners don't share cells with others and spend their time in isolation. In the segregation unit a prisoner is inside his cell for twenty-three hours a day. On the twenty-fourth hour the prisoner can exercise in a different cell where there is a bit of sunlight, if the sun is out. This other cell has a little more room to move around in than his own cell, but not much more.

Life is not pretty here.

And it is here that I meet Gerry. Gerry is fifty-five years of age and is smiling when he sees me. You look happy, I say. Are you?

"I'm happy that I'm alive."

Cynthia of Englewood said just the same. What are you here for? I ask.

"Burglary and sexual assault."

This guy does say the "sexual" thing... How many years did you get?

"Twenty years."

How many more years to go before you're out of here?

"Just under ten to go."

He explains to me the reason for the severity of his prison term: "This is not my first rodeo. I got that many years because I've been here before." There's something called a "habitual offender," a repeat offender, and these offenders are sentenced to double the time.

Did you plead guilty?

"Yes. I am guilty."

He was drunk, totally drunk, and he stole videos from a video store, which he realized only when he woke up the next day and noticed the videos at his residence. As for the sex offense: he had sex with a sixteen-year-old girl, consensual sex, but sex with a person of her age is considered rape. For this offense, he was sentenced to ten years in prison.

Gerry works in the prison, in the maximum-security part of it, and it is here that he sees his mission: helping fellow inmates. "I'm tired of my previous life. I've had enough. I turned my life over to Christ, so now I minister as much as I can." It will be years before he sees the sun again, because there are no furloughs for him unless to attend his mom's funeral when she dies. Gerry will not be out of these walls before he's sixty-five years of age.

Ten years for sleeping with a sixteen-year-old. I ask an officer if this is not ridiculous, as there must be thousands of men just in this state who have done the same and walk freely as very respected citizens. "Gerry told you the truth. In my opinion, his jail term is extreme," the officer replies. "I'm not the judge and there's nothing I can do about this."

What will you do when you get out of here? I ask Gerry.

"I'll get to know my children and my grandchildren. I'll live! I'll minister, I'll preach, I'll work. I hope I'll still be physically able to work."

I continue to walk between cells and prisoners.

Prisoners can purchase a TV with a small screen that looks like a tablet, and for a fee of $15 per month can watch cable TV. As I walk past their locked cells I see some of them sitting and staring at moving pictures on these units.

All together there are about eight hundred people incarcerated in the penitentiary. How long is the average prisoner locked in his cell per day? I ask one of the guards.

Those who have a "job" get out of one cell and go to work in other closed rooms in the prison, he tells me. They also get out of their cells for the meals, which they eat together. Those in the segregation unit eat in their cells.

Another opportunity to get out of the cell is for religious ceremonies. Praying in the prison's church, for example. But not all here are Gerry, and not all worship Jesus. The Native Americans have their own space to worship. It's a place that is shaped like a tent, though it's not one.

White supremacists, who have a respected presence here, also claim that they are religious, and they have their own place of worship. What do they believe in? Their religion is Àsatrú and "it is a recognized religion," according to prison officials.

What is Àsatrú? According to Asatru.org, "Long before Christianity came to northern Europe, the people there – our ancestors – had their own religions. One of these was Àsatrú. It was practiced in the lands that are today Scandinavia, England, Germany, France, the Netherlands, and other countries as well. Àsatrú is the original or native religious belief for the peoples who lived in these regions."

Good to believe in something as long as you are in prison. At the supremacists' corner of worship in this prison, a little place, they have a few stones – or something that looks like stones. I wish I could stay long enough to watch the skinheads pray.

It is here, by the way, that I learn something else: the logic in being a "skinhead."

In the old days, white men had long hair. But they had many enemies who wished them cruel deaths and beheaded them when they were captured. The enemies would grab their hair in one hand and behead them with the other. It is why their ancestors, as white supremacist legend goes, chose to shave their heads.

I live and learn.

• • •

If I expected the penitentiary to be populated mostly by blacks, I was wrong. Most prisoners here are white.

The actual breakdown of state prisoners, as I find in a DOCR newsletter called "The Insider," is as follows:

Number of inmates under the authority of North Dakota's DOCR: 1,751. Average inmate age: 36. Male inmates: 1,536. Females: 215. White inmates: 1,158. Blacks: 121. Native Americans: 358. Spanish: 99. Asian: 8. And then come the rest.

In general, I find out, Native Americans consist of about 6 percent of the overall population in North Dakota. People who claim German ancestry: about 50 percent.

There is no classification for "German" inmates, in case you wondered.

If you are into statistics: The largest group of people in all of the United States, in terms of ancestry, is not Irish or English, Spanish or black, but German. As of the latest available statistics, for every Jew in this country there are ten German Americans. How often have you heard of the German Americans? Almost never. But you do hear much about the Jews. Why? Because.

As far as I can tell, no Jew is in this prison at this time.

"When you head west, the prison population will be much different," Warden Braun tells me, which means that it will be a much more violent prison population.

As I leave this penitentiary, digesting what I've just heard and seen, I realize: in the Land of the Free, prisoners abound.

I'm going west. But not to see more prisoners; this visit was depressing enough.

• • •

On my way west I see a sign for a city called Hebron, which is the name of the first Jewish city in history. What the heck is a "Hebron" doing here?

I stop to take a peek. The place looks deserted, and the streets have big potholes. Are there no living souls in this place?

I amble about for a while until I meet Beth, the only moving object among the many potholes. Beth, a Jehovah's Witness, tells me that Hebron is a religious town. Here, she says, there are a number of churches, plus a Jehovah's Witnesses "Kingdom Hall." Ten percent of the population, she shares with me, are Jehovah's Witnesses.

She loves the Kingdom Hall of Hebron. "It's a beautiful Kingdom Hall," she tells me, and her eyes glow above the potholes. "I made the personal decision to be baptized as a Witness when I was a teenager," she informs me. Obviously, she's not the girl Gerry had sex with.

Unlike Christians, a Witness worships Jesus' father, she teaches me, but not Jesus. "When I pray," Beth continues, "I allow my husband to pray aloud, and I pray quietly."

Why?

"We find it proper and respectful for men to pray out loud because they are the headships. The women, us, we are in subjection to man. Not in a demeaning way. The husbands look after us and they make spiritual decisions."

Who did you vote for in the last election for president?

"No one. Jehovah's Witnesses are neutral and they don't take part in elections."

I ask Beth to tell me her opinion about ISIS. ISIS soldiers behead Christians, and anyone else they don't like, whenever they find them.

Beth is a Witness, a member of the Kingdom Hall, and this is her stand on ISIS: "We are neutral about it."

Am I in Switzerland? No, I'm in Hebron. Across the street is the office of the local paper, the *Hebron Herald*. I walk in and meet the paper's owner, Jane Brandt. She shows me different copies of her paper, and, while looking at them, I ask her: Are you pro-life or pro-choice? Jane is willing to answer this question provided I turn off the recorder. It is amazing to watch a Small Town, USA, newspaper person so fearful to share a political or religious view in today's America.

Quite often, when initially approached people won't talk about anything political or religious because, they say, they want to avoid "controversial" issues. Questions such as "Who did you vote for in the last election for president?" are often not answered, and some people get upset when I ask them this question. Others do answer these and similar questions but change their responses 180 degrees the moment they feel comfortable talking with me.

In all cases, the underlying reason for their behavior is fear. Still, Jane surprises me, as this is the first time I have heard it so clear and so straight, and from a press person to boot: I'll tell you my opinion about xyz provided you keep it secret.

Why are so many Americans so afraid to say what they think? Maybe the Free are not that free and the Brave not that brave.

Malibu is behaving extremely well, and we drive into Montana.

Gate Ten

*Native American drunks and rapists have fun at
the local Knife College, and you are paying for it –
The good news: polygamy will soon be legal*

I'VE ALWAYS WANTED TO VISIT MONTANA. I IMAGINE IT AS A STATE OF
strong colors. Don't ask me why. In my imagination Montana is a
state of mountains, horses, sexy young cowgirls, wild cowboys, great
music and tons of tough loves.

It's the perfect place to forget Gerry and all the other inmates.

At the visitors center on the edge of Montana, coming from
North Dakota, I read this: "Montana is famous for its dinosaur fossils." This is not all. It goes on to say, "The oldest dinosaur fossils are
found in rocks of the Jurassic period, which are 155 million years old."

One-hundred-fifty-five-million-year-old dinosaurs; forget the
young girls and horses.

This is not good news for me. Should I avoid this state? I consult
with a loveable old lady who works in the center, and she advises that
I stick around in Montana. There are many cowboys, she promises
me, in Miles City, which is one hundred miles from here. Faster than
a deer, I reach Miles City.

I see casinos, but no cowboys. "The cowboys are in the bars,"
some folks tell me.

Which is the cowboys' favorite bar? I ask.

"The Bison Bar," they say.

At the Bison Bar I see an older couple plus a younger man by the name of Chad, who I think has had too much to drink. He's kind of interesting, though. In reply to a gibe by the older couple, he says to them: "Don't make me blush, I got girls for that." Great line!

Question is, where are the cowboys? "In the ranches," the drinkers reply.

Where are the ranches?

"Go to Doug Martin, he's in Kinsey."

Where's Kinsey? I don't know but I'll try to find it.

• • •

Driving through Miles City, I notice a house with a big Confederate flag next to a normal US flag plus a "Liberty or Death" flag. I'm looking for cowgirls and cowboys and I get dinosaurs and flags. Hopefully, Doug will save the day.

I arrive in Kinsey healthy and happy but I have no idea how to find Doug. No GPS has a "Doug" location.

I keep on driving. As I drive into nowhere I see a man walking on the road's edge with big earphones on his head. Lucky me, he knows Doug, and he directs me to Doug's place.

Doug, wearing a cowboy hat, stares at the approaching Malibu. I'm very happy to meet a cowboy, a real cowboy, but this cowboy doesn't seem to be very happy to meet me. Well, let's be honest here: Why would he be? He sees a Malibu driving into his ranch, and I should be happy that he doesn't greet it with a bullet. I read stories like that in American media.

I get out of the car, and our eyes meet. He takes one look at me and immediately realizes that I didn't come to steal his horses. I'm not the type.

Doug, I quickly see, has more than just horses; he has bulls too. Actually, more bulls than horses. He should be called bullboy.

First things first. Doug tells me that he is not a rancher but a farmer.

Doug has more news for me: Very few individuals actually own a ranch or a farm. Most of the people working on ranches are "hired hands," and they work for huge companies. "The Koch Brothers have hundreds of thousands of acres," he says by way of explanation.

If he's right, and he has no reason to lie to me, then the cowboys of the movies don't exist in real life. In the movies they own the land and the cattle, but in reality they are employees of some Koch Brothers, sweating much and earning little. The few who are real cowboys, most of them have inherited the land and the animals, Doug tells me.

Doug makes his living from a business he owns; the farm he maintains as a hobby. On his farm he trains cattle and man in the art of rodeo, and that's why he has more bulls than horses. When we advance closer to his animals, I see two female students riding two horses, desperately trying to catch a bull with rope lassos. "I don't raise beef cattle. I raise cattle with horns and I raise cattle that run," is how he puts it.

I watch Doug and his students at work. It's amazing to see the horses running to chase the bulls, as if the bulls were their biggest enemies. The horses do this because they are trained to do so, which makes me wonder if we humans are not exactly the same.

Doug is also a man of faith and is very interested in politics. He is "definitely pro-life," thinks that climate change "has been happening for a million years and will happen for a million years more," and he is pro-Israel. "When America turns its back on Israel, we are done as a country. We are getting pretty close to it," Doug warns me.

But before America disappears, I depart from Doug and drive another couple of miles and spot another ranch, or a farm; I'm not sure which. I drive in and soon am greeted by a few dogs and then a lady. "My brother is a cowboy," she tells me, "but there aren't many of them left. The big corporations and technology make cowboys obsolete. There's no need for cowboys on horses to check on cows, which cowboys used to do. Today you have four-wheelers to do the horses' job."

In just a few years, I now think, Montana's visitors center will have a big poster that will tell the story of the cowboy fossils, celebrating a people that once upon a time lived in Montana.

It is sad to watch a fading, dying culture. But life goes on. And I drive on.

• • •

Pressing west, I see a sign for a place called Lame Deer. What could a place called Lame Deer be? Probably a mental institution or a cannabis-friendly hotel. I drive in. Should be interesting.

Guess what? It's a reservation. I wanted cowboys, I get Indians.

While the cowboys are disappearing, the Indians stick around.

Imagine Chevy naming my car Lame Deer instead of Malibu. They would go bankrupt in less than an hour. But the Indians can come up with any lame excuse for a name and they make it. How do they do it?

In an attempt to find out I go to meet Winfield S. Russell, vice president of the Northern Cheyenne Tribe. I like him from the first moment I lay my eyes on him. He tells me that his tribe owns 444,000 acres.

I've been to reservations before, but none this big. Here you could build a half million Soaring Eagle casinos. How many people live here? I ask Winfield.

"Five thousand five hundred," he answers. That's over eighty acres per Indian, child or adult. The fascinating thing about this is that neither of us explodes in laughter at this very moment.

What's totally not funny here is the crime rate. Lame Deer has a very high crime rate, Winfield tells me, especially in the drugs department. "Most of the people here have a drug problem," he informs me.

How many people speak the Cheyenne language?

"About three hundred, and it's slowly deteriorating," meaning that the number of speakers will one day soon hover just above zero. This place, he adds, also suffers from acute poverty. If I had half a million acres I wouldn't be poor, I'd be a Koch Brother. But in Lame Deer everything's different.

Given the fact that the language is dying, that crime is high, that poverty is acute and that the people spend their days drinking, which I observed while walking in, why not get out of this reservation business altogether and integrate into American life? I ask him.

"We have our own sovereignty; we have our own land; we take care of our own people," he answers.

Why not join the melting pot of America?

"We have our own way of life. We have tribal traditional law, and we still have our sovereignty; we have our own government. We have our own tribal law-and-order code. If you drink liquor, if you are intoxicated, you get arrested for that!"

You have a prison here?

"We have a jail here."

How many people are in jail?

"I'd say about, in a month, for intoxication, 150 to 500 in jail."

How long do they stay in your jail?

"It depends."

On what?

"Usually a night."

You have five hundred criminals, I mean those who got caught; is that the reason to have a sovereign state?

"No, I don't think so."

So, why have a sovereign state?

This he cannot answer, except for saying that other tribes have reservations and so should his tribe. I like this Winfield, but I don't get him.

"Notice," read the signs on walls of public buildings here. "The use of loud and abusive language will not be tolerated on these premises. Section 7-7-5 of the Northern Cheyenne Law and Order Code defines such activities as disorderly conduct."

They have their own law books here, and Winfield proudly tells me that "I served my country. I was in the Marine Corps. I served in Vietnam."

And he tells me something else: "Seventy to 80 percent here are unemployed; they get assistance from the federal government."

Winfield says all these things but he's not happy with the picture he's painting for me, and so he tries his best to add some cheerful color to the portrait. Not all is bad, after all, he now says to me. Lame Deer has a college, and there, he wants me to know, residents study the ancient language of their ancestors. Would I like to attend a class and see for myself?

We drive over to Chief Dull Knife College. What a great name for a college! And, yes, there's a class here for the Cheyenne language.

I join the other students. The assignment for today's lesson: translate Elvis Presley's song titles into Cheyenne.

The class is divided into groups, and each group is assigned to translate some titles.

For example: "Love Me Tender," "Heartbreak Hotel," "Love Me," "I Forgot to Remember to Forget." Fifteen students attend the class. The youngest is forty years of age; all the others are past retirement age.

Not one young soul.

Outside the class, in the hall, I read the following: "Attention! The use of loud, abusive language and/or physical violence on the Chief Dull Knife College Campus or at College sponsored activities, shall be considered assault and will NOT be tolerated."

I guess there are some problems of language in this reservation.

Here's another public notice on the wall: "ATTENTION! All sex offenders must come into the Office of Adult Probation and update all pictures, physical address and file information A.S.A.P."

I leave the reservation and go to Malibu. I think I should keep going west to Washington State, where it's legal to buy marijuana and all kinds of cannabis goodies. I need that stuff!

• • •

Before I drive, I sit inside Malibu and try to collect my thoughts. What have I seen thus far in America? I ask myself.

- Native American spirituality is a prime candidate for next year's Nobel Prize in the fiction category.
- When one black dies, cry. When many die, ignore.
- Cowboys and cowgirls live in Jurassic Park.
- Whites flee, blacks conquer.

– American cultural institutions are escapism labs.

– Jews like to hang on a cross.

– Smoking is a crime against humanity.

– In a changing climate, Palestinians shine.

– Jesus is fun.

– Hezballah is great.

– Expressing your political views is a dangerous activity in the Land of the Free.

– The Home of the Brave is a baseball stadium.

– One hundred guns per two people is not enough.

– Yoga is what Jews do in their temples.

– Blacks kill blacks because that's nigga culture.

– Knife is a name of a college.

– Quakers love silence and Palestine.

– My fat fingers will break my iPad.

There is more that I learned in the past couple of months, but I stop thinking.

I light up an Indonesian cigar and watch the smoke stream out of my mouth. There will be a $250 fine if the rental people catch me smoking in the car. Fortunately, the Spanish employees who gave me this car don't enter Indian reservations and will never catch me smoking.

• • •

Before I inhale some cannabis into my system, I decide to stick around a little longer in the Fossil State. Montana, which is rich in oil deposits, has recently gone through a financial boom due to "fracking," a newly developed oil exploration technique.

I want to meet people who are in the oil business. Preferably rich, and better yet, very rich. And in less than twenty-four hours, after I connect with somebody who knows somebody who knows somebody, I get to meet a multimillionaire by the name of Carter Stewart. You don't have to ask whether Carter is red or blue; you get to know what he is by paying a visit to his bathroom.

Yeah.

How?

The rolls of toilet paper have the image of Obama printed on them.

I saw something similar in Ukraine; there, the toilet paper carried the image of the Russian leader, Vladimir Putin.

In any case, and once I have paid nature its due, Carter talks. First, he talks about America: "We have watched our freedom erode for the last thirty years, and little by little some of our individual freedoms are being taken away."

Give me an example.

"Okay, I'll give you an example. If you find a sunken ship or a treasure out on a federal land, you don't get to keep it; the federal government keeps it. It used to be that you, as an individual, would get to keep it."

Abrogated freedoms or not, Carter owns three guns. He also has a (fake) million-dollar bill on his desk with a picture of Obama in the "dead president" portrait. In addition, the slogan "In God We Trust" is here delivered, "In Obama We Trust."

Multimillionaires can be funny people.

Has freedom of expression also been curtailed in the last thirty years?

"It has been, by the politically correct crowd – the people who say, 'You can't say this word, or you can't say that word.'"

Which word are we talking about?

"I don't want to use the word."

Use it!

"No, I'm not gonna use it. You know exactly what word I'm talking about, the one that refers to black people."

Are you talking about the *nigger* word?

"Yes. But that's just one example."

He gives me another example: the Confederate flag. "I can understand why some people don't want to have that symbol. But if some people want to put it up, to remember their heritage, because their ancestors fought and died in that war, why take it away from them?"

Carter, as you might have guessed by now, is pro-life, against gay marriage, against the Iran deal, pro-Israel "all the way" and believes that "there's no such thing as climate change."

"I'm a geologist," he says. "Geology means the study of the earth. I've studied the earth since I started going to college, and I still study the earth, on a daily basis. So, I know that thing is as phony as can be."

• • •

I think we'd better be talking about oil markets, not politics.

Why did the oil market fall so sharply?

"Saudi Arabia flooded the market about a year ago."

Why did the Saudis do it?

"They wanted to regain a 5 percent market share they had lost. But even by their own accord, now they say it wasn't a bright idea. The price of their export now is 50 percent of what it was. It was a bonehead move on their part. They are trying to put the pressure on us and drive us out of business."

How much are you worth?

He tells me he is worth about half of what he was worth this time last year, but that he really doesn't know how much he's worth now.

How much were you worth last year?

"I'd say about $150 million."

So, your net worth now is seventy-five million?

"Probably."

You lost $75 million?

"Probably."

Because of the decline in the price of oil?

"Yes."

Are you worried?

"I'm worried about the short term, because we are now having to take all of our money and give it back to the bank, because we are leveraged. We do what we can do to make it, to pay the bank every month, and we keep working on trying to sell different assets."

What's the worst that can happen to you? How much lower could your seventy-five million go?

"It can always go to nothing, but I don't think it's gonna because we still have assets that bring in money."

Paint for me the worst picture. "The worst picture is that oil goes down to ten dollars a barrel again, or nine dollars a barrel."

If that happens, what will you do?

"I'm a pretty talented guy; I'll think of something."

Are you worried?

"I am. I think about it every night, you know. I think about it every day, about solving the problems every day. It's part of working."

Do you lose sleep over it?

"No."

Give me an estimate of much you think you will be worth ten years from now.

"Half a billion."

Did you grow up with money?

"No. Not whatsoever. I buried my dad with my own money, with my last $2,500."

Carter presents himself as a man with much self-confidence, ever sure that what he believes in is the only truth. But, first of all, he is a businessman.

"There's a lot of wealth in the ground out there. When the price goes down everybody quits, a lot of leases come open, and this actually creates opportunity. I was talking to one of my friends about the price of oil and he says, 'Well, it's all the big Jewish firms on Wall Street that are basically shorting all the oil companies and shorting the price of oil and driving it down.'"

You think that this is really what's happening?

"I think that possibly this is what is happening. They have driven the price down again."

Being pro-Israel, how strange, does not necessarily mean lack of anti-Semitism. You can love Israel and still think that there are a bunch of Jews out there who control world markets and world finance.

I think of Abe Foxman and of what he told me: "Americans are prejudiced."

An idea comes to my mind. I obviously need a break from the liberals, the conservatives, the ever-fearing whites, the gangs, the Jews, the Jehovah's Witnesses, the anti-Semites, the Indians, and all those in between. Why, then, don't I go to Yellowstone National Park?

I've heard that the park is a fascinating place, but I don't know much about it.

Montana's office of tourism defines Yellowstone National Park as "the best idea America has ever had." This national park is America's first national park, and, according to Montana's tourism office, it is also "the world's first national park."

Let's go!

• • •

Getting to Yellowstone takes some driving. But what driving! I take the Beartooth All-American Road. What is an All-American road? The tourism officials define it thusly:

> Designated an All-American Road in 2002, the Beartooth Highway has been described by former CBS correspondent Charles Kuralt as "the most beautiful drive in America." Reaching heights of nearly 11,000 feet, this 53.7-mile, 3 hour drive offers skytop views of snowcapped peaks, glaciers, alpine lakes and plateaus. Seasonal.

More or less, as far as I experience it, they got it right. It does take forever to drive, because of sharp turns, narrow roads and low speed limits, but this is indeed a most beautiful drive. It's driving and nature at their best. The weather changes drastically, falling more than fifty degrees once you reach the top, and it is awesome! The mountains are wonderful, and the place is practically unsettled except for animals.

In general, Montana is a huge state but has very few people. I think we could settle here all the refugees of Syria, Libya, Sudan, Palestine, Afghanistan and practically every other conflict area the world over, and there would still be enough empty land in Montana for all its surviving cowboys.

Yellowstone Park itself, once you are in it, is a bit of a letdown. But two and a half hours into the ride in the park I reach "the Grand Canyon of the Yellowstone."

Imagine if a master artist, the same guy from Lake Superior, had taken a big swath of rocky area, torn it to huge pieces, formed previously unknown shapes from the huge rocks and then painted them masterfully – how would you react? This work of art is otherworldly: naked rocks, very deep and very high, in various formations; shapes and colors paying homage to streaming waters far below, giving the impression of life and death combined, at once heavenly and earthly.

For Bible followers, this awesome imagery is evidence of God's brilliant imagination; for believers in Evolution, it is a testimony to the brutality and beauty of nature.

The Austrian Alps, my former beloved, are eclipsed by this beauty.

Sorry, Austria.

Ahead of me I see cars parked at every available spot and people amassed on every hill in sight, some equipped with long-lens cameras and binoculars, all facing a point far away. Some have parked their cars and vans on the hills and are standing on top of their vehicles for a better view. What is there on the other side to see? A bear, I'm told. Have these people never seen a bear before?

Well, there is a story attached to this frenzy on the hills. Last week a sixty-three-year-old hiker was attacked by a grizzly bear in Yellowstone, and his body, partially eaten, was found by a park ranger at the scene. Is this the same bear? The people want to know. Is this the brother of that bear? Its offspring? Nobody knows, but everybody wants to see this very bear.

To me, the sight that's more interesting is the mob trying to catch a glimpse of the bear that might have eaten a man.

This is also America. I keep moving.

Until I reach Mud Volcano, which is another wonder to behold. Colored liquids spring forth from the belly of the earth. Near the volcano, buffaloes roam, some sauntering toward Malibu, but luckily they don't consume her.

More interesting sites lie ahead.

Geysers. There are three hundred of them in this park, I learn, and they are feasts for the soul, eye and heart.

At first, they remind me of New York streets: a hole in the ground and a hot white steam bursting from the subway trucks beneath. Only there's no subway here. In addition, it's not just steam but bursts of boiling liquid that come gushing out and up. No, this is not New York, this is Wyoming. (Yellowstone is partly in Montana and mostly in Wyoming.)

This here, let me tell you, is America's real melting pot!

Imagine Berlin and Warsaw during World War II, with all the explosions and clouds of smoke, only nobody is dying here and the clouds are not smoke but steam and water. It is Earth at its liveliest interaction with itself, telling of the wrath of the earth beneath our feet. Moving, yelling, laughing, screaming, crying, bursting and all-out dancing.

I spend eight hours in the park – Malibu looks beautiful in Yellowstone, by the way – and in the ninth hour I drive back to the "real" world.

• • •

I reach downtown Bozeman and check out the city. Bozeman is a cool city with really cool, posh stores for people who have the urgent need to transfer cash from their savings accounts into the pockets of the mountain people.

There are also many students here, from the local Montana State University, which gives Bozeman a cultural edge.

I meet Todd, for example. Todd, a man worried about climate change, is into nature: marijuana and hashish. He is actually on a mission to make them legal in the state.

And he is anti-smoking. Cigarettes no, joints yes. He is what you would call a "progressive liberal."

"People should not go to prison for cannabis," he pleads with me, as if I were Montana's chief justice and could do something about it.

Todd has other issues on his mind besides weed. He is, he tells me, pro-choice, pro-environment, pro-gay, and pro-Palestine. Nice to know.

Of the millennials I met in North Dakota and Montana, both red states, many of them held more leftist views than the older generation. Is this the general tendency of the young? I ask Todd.

Todd responds that this is indeed the case. "People are just starting to realize that we have been lied to for a really long time, and the younger generation, I think, is more in tune with that, and realizing that most things you see on television are lies or fabricated. That's what I think."

As I'm about to leave Montana for good I ask myself: Will I never, ever see a cowboy with my very own eyes? Perhaps I should give it a little stronger push, maybe even check with the NSA folks, or some other nerds, and see if somebody out there can come up with something.

I get a tip from a top-secret source, and I follow it.

• • •

I drive on. And am rewarded. After driving over endless lonesome roads, some unfinished, I make myself comfortable at Mike's ranch. Mike takes me for a walk on his 2,500-acre ranch and chews tobacco continuously as he explains the ranch to me, spitting every third or fourth step of the way.

Is he the personification of a cowboy? Maybe. Who knows?

Mike is a "Christian, not of any established church. I go to church once a year, on Christmas," and absolutely does not like the "son of a bitch" Obama. He wears a cowboy hat and is firmly against gun control laws. "You don't control your gun, you hit nothing," is how he phrases it.

You need a PhD in philosophy to understand cowboys. Mike is neither Republican nor Democrat. "Don't start me talking about politics."

Sometimes I'm deaf, like now. Are you pro-choice or pro-life? I ask him. "Pro-life."

Gay marriage? "I'm a Christian!"

Pro-Israel or pro-Palestine? "I think they should take those people and put them back in Germany. They have been fighting there since day one, so they should go back."

"Those people" are the Jews? "Yes."

Tell me: Shouldn't we do the same thing with the Americans? Many of them came here from Germany and took the land from the people who had lived here before them. Why not send both the Jews and the Americans back to Germany?

This pisses Mike off and he spits three more times than usual. "There's no room for them all in Germany," he says after spitting yet again.

His cows are about three miles from here, in a sixty-five-thousand-acre piece of land leased from the federal government by him and by a number of other people, and he rides his horses there on a daily basis, to check on the cows and put out salt blocks for the animals.

But he barely makes a living from his cows. It takes five hundred to seven hundred cows to make a living for a family, he tells me, and he has only 150 cows. How does he survive on his ranch? He is leasing part of his land, he's working for other ranchers, he trains horses for others, and he also works as a plumber and a welder. And part of the ranch is rented out as a guesthouse for tourists by other members of his family.

Nonetheless, whatever his financial difficulties, this man wears his hat with pride. He is a cowboy!

He invites me to dinner at the guesthouse, and he introduces me to the other diners.

Interesting folks. Here's a Jewish couple from California – two Jews who, for a fee, feel cowboy. These two non-spitting cowboys have money, and they sponsor Palestinian movies. That's what they tell me. And then they correct themselves; they support, they now say, any movie that is critical of Israel.

Another couple, from Italy, support nobody.

Neither does Mike. Spitting Mike, a hard-working man, illustrates to me the difficulties of being a cowboy. It's easy to put on a cowboy hat and get busy listening to some great country music, but being one is a totally different story.

Maybe it's a good idea, after all, to send the Americans to Germany. The Indians will have more acres, and more of them will be able to sing Elvis Presley's songs in perfect Indian.

That'll be the day.

• • •

I leave the cowboy and enter reality: Malibu. And this Malibu drives to Missoula, on its way to Seattle. I take a little rest in Missoula.

I go to a bar and ask for a brandy. They don't ask what kind of brandy I want and give me Christian Brothers, the one I had in Chicago. It's one country, and we are all Christian brothers.

No Jews here, thank God; they are busy in California looking for some Palestinian movies to sponsor.

Right next to me sits an interesting man named Pat Williams, who introduces himself as a "former congressman from Montana. I represented the whole state, and I served in the Congress for eighteen years." These days he teaches at the University of Montana.

Can you explain to me why there are so many American flags almost everywhere I drive?

"Americans love to show their patriotism. I think that the Americans who fly their flag are nationalistic. One could take that as bad or good, but I think they are being nationalistic."

Why is America so patriotic?

"Probably because of America's military experience. Two wars, a number of minor wars. Some lost, some won, but a lot of Americans fought, some got wounded, and some died, and it made them patriotic."

Are you talking about the Vietnam and Korean wars?

"Vietnam, Korea, Panama, for heaven's sake, and safeguarding Europe through NATO. Very expensive, very."

Pat is pro-choice, pro-gay marriage and pro-Palestine. While serving in Congress he was pro-Israel, he tells me, but since he has become a professor he's changed his mind. Let him.

Are you also pro-polygamy?

"No."

Why not? I'm pro-gay marriage and I'm pro-polygamy. Mature people should be able to decide how they want to marry and whom. This is a human rights issue. A basic human right.

"A family with one man, a wife married to one man has been a cornerstone in the American – "

Now you are talking like those Americans who are against gay marriage; they say the same thing.

"No."

Yes! You are talking like –

"I'm fine with one woman and one man, one woman with one woman, one man with one man."

Why not have –

"Because I'm not used to it!"

So what? If I have two women who want to marry me, or if there's a woman who has two men who want to marry her, we should have a right, just like gays!

Congressman Pat is getting a bit lost here. But he's a Democrat, and any statement that seems to invalidate gay rights is worse than rape. And so, he quickly changes his mind.

"Right," he says.

Are you now pro-polygamy?

"Yeah, I can do that."

Can I make this statement: "Congressman Pat is pro-polygamy"?

"Yes."

Fear will take the Brave to places they never knew existed.

Professor Pat teaches "history of the national parks and wilderness" at the University of Montana. One day, I hope, I'll do the same. I'll be a professor of Yellowstone Park polygamy ceremonies.

Life's good!

Tomorrow I'm leaving Montana.

I like the people of Montana. They are welcoming, friendly and they have gorgeous mountains. Surprisingly, to me, these Rocky Mountain people know about foreign affairs issues no less than New Yorkers. Their knowledge doesn't amount to much, I admit, but New Yorkers don't know one iota more than them.

West of Montana is Idaho, a state I'm not sure that I pronounce right.

I'll stop there tomorrow.

Gate Eleven

A drunk mayor chases ugly girls and lives to tell the tale

I HAVE BEEN TO THE CENTER OF THE UNIVERSE. WHERE IS IT? WALLACE, Idaho.

To be a bit more exact, it's right at the intersection of Bank and Sixth. There it is written, right in the middle of the intersection: Center of the Universe. Who decided that this is indeed the universe's center?

Rich, who knows everything there is to know about the area, says that six guys at a nearby bar originated the idea. Their philosophical theory went like this: "If something can't not be proven to exist, it could just as well exist."

After this bar decision, Rich tells me, the mayor of Wallace made a proclamation, which was approved by the city council. And now, for all legal purposes, this is the center of the universe.

By listening to the locals, I learn how to pronounce Idaho. When I pronounce it, I think it's a funny name.

Idaho, a passing wind whispers in my ears, has many funny people.

Like Mac Pooler, the mayor of the city of Kellogg. His Honor tells me about himself: "I was born in Kellogg, where I went to school. I went two years to college, and I didn't graduate. I excelled in beer drinking, playing football, and chasing ugly girls. When I left school, my blood alcohol was higher than my grade-point average. But I didn't have to pay for school because I had a scholarship. So I got drafted into the army, I come out and I came back to Kellogg. I had the opportunity to be the mayor of Kellogg, the city I grew up in, where the people knew me as I grew up."

He's funny, I think. Let me find out what this man is made of. The big issues in America, over and over, are abortions and gay rights. Are you pro-choice or –

"I don't take political stands. Those are mine to keep."

Is your response part of America's free speech, free expression, freedom and liberty?

"That's a good question. There are two things you don't argue in the United States, religion and politics, because you'll either get slapped or shot. That's my philosophy. I don't want to go there. It's my choice, as a citizen, not to argue politics."

This funny man, like so many Americans, is driven by fear. I can't blame him for being who he is.

We talk more, more and more, and he says to me that the USA "has gone from a moderate country to a liberal country. The liberal people are tickled to death; they are glad it went finally to the left. You have three sides in our country: the moderates, usually the Republicans, the independents, and on the left side you have the loonies, the Democrats."

Yep, that's life. When you're patient and stick around with people, most often they will open up to you eventually.

Where are the young people going, right or left? I ask him. "Left."

Why? "Because 94 percent of the professors in colleges are left; they are liberals. Over 80 percent of [public] education is taught by liberals. So they [students] get the liberal side more. TV stations, except for Fox News, are left."

It is at this point that Mac is finally ready to share his opinions about abortions and gay rights. Abortions: "I don't think the government should get involved in telling a woman what to do." Gay rights: "They can do whatever the hell they want as long as they leave me alone."

America is getting involved in many international conflicts, either by putting troops on the ground or firing missiles from the sky. Why?

"You want to know my opinion on that? We have no goddamn business being over there."

Why is it that American governments keep doing this?

"Because we got a bunch of idiots out there. We stick our noses in places we shouldn't be, and once we are there we don't know how to get out."

That said, he has one exception: Israel. He's pro-Israel. Ella, his nine-year-old granddaughter, comes by to say hello to her grandpa.

Tell me, Ella, what's the best thing in Idaho? I ask her.

"Freedom," she says.

And I think: This is how an American is formed, almost from birth. *Papa, Mama, Grandpa, freedom*: these are the first words he or she learns.

As I am about to leave this funny, warm mayor, he tells me: "You go west to Washington, that's where we put all our loonies."

• • •

On the way to the "loonies" in Washington state, I am told that the Jewish Federation of Chicago has just backtracked on its former stand, and that its board came to a decision to oppose the Iran deal. What made them change their mind? Perhaps another salmon.

On the other hand, the *Hollywood Reporter* writes that "98 Prominent Hollywood Jews Back Iran Nuclear Deal in Open Letter." To those who don't understand the importance of this news item: moviemakers are the biggest mavens in nuclear physics and international law. Retired Abe Foxman must be reading this and exploding in laughter.

Iran deal or not, wildfires rage ahead of me as I drive in the direction of the "loonies." I stop to meet Jason Kirchner of the US Forest Service in Coeur d'Alene, Idaho, and he tells me that "this is the worst fire season in north Idaho since 1926, quite possibly the worst since 1910."

Is it because of "global warming"?

"No way to say."

Based on the weather forecast, he predicts that the wildfires will go on for a few more weeks.

Wow!

I walk back to the car, and as I keep driving I smell the fires. I turn my radio on, to whatever station it sets itself. I listen in. Today's topic on this station: Jesus, the Rapture and the Second Coming. The State of Israel, the voice says, is a solid proof that Jesus is on his way.

This is what they say, not me; I just listen.

I enter Washington State, and the landscape is pretty boring. As I pass Ellensburg, though, the landscape gets more and more beautiful by the mile. I like it.

I turn off the radio and just drive.

I have to find out what America is made of besides Mike, Mac, Pat, Lame Deer, and the ninety-eight of Hollywood. I'm in the State of the Loonies; let's get to know them personally!

Gate Twelve

There's one excellent American restaurant every thousand miles

SEATTLE, WASHINGTON.

I choose a downtown hotel, a Sheraton, so that I can let Malibu rest and use my feet the way they were intended. Once Malibu is taken care of, I approach the lady at the front desk and ask her the most urgent question there is: Why is this city called Seattle?

"The city is named after Chief Seattle."

Who is he?

"An Indian."

Ah. When was he among the living? "I don't know."

This American habit of naming streets and cities for the people their ancestors murdered is something I don't really get. Imagine Germany getting into this habit. Would be fun. Berlin would be called Abraham and Hamburg would be named Sarah.

Anything to see in this city? I ask the lady.

"Go down, about fifteen minutes from here, and you'll see food carts where young Indian men get their lunch. You have to go now, because lunchtime is almost over."

What are they doing there?

"Seattle is the headquarters of Amazon; they own many buildings here, and they employ many Indians."

Oh, good. She is not talking about Native Americans; she is talking about real Indians, people who have come here from India to work. I walk over to see the starving Indians.

Downtown Seattle is gorgeous. The skyscrapers are different from those in New York; here somebody considered design before going to construction.

Walking the streets of Seattle, I am reminded of Europe. There is some resemblance to Hamburg here, I think, especially the shops, the overall street architecture, and of course the waters – Elliott Bay, in this case. Even the train trundling down the tracks above my head at this moment is stylish, worlds apart from the "American" dusty steel tracks of Chicago. I also love the streetcars here; they are gorgeous.

I keep walking. As I get closer and closer to where the food trucks are supposed to be and don't see them, I suspect that I might be late. But I keep walking anyway. Who knows? Maybe I'll get to meet a descendant of Chief Seattle, which will be well worth my time.

Unfortunately, instead of starving Indian crowds I encounter two well-fed Americans. Is Amazon anywhere near? I ask them.

"Almost every building here is Amazon," the lady replies.

Are you working for Amazon?

"Luckily not!"

Why luckily?

"Didn't you read the article in the *New York Times*?"

A few days ago the *Times* ran a long article about Amazon, which I actually read. In the article the paper reported on mistreated Amazon employees bursting into tears at their desks, plus other juicy tidbits.

I bid the two Americans well and keep walking until I see an Indian guy. Where are the Indians and their food? I ask him.

I think, though I can't promise, that this guy would have shot me if he had had a gun on him. He is very upset.

"What Indians? There are no Indians here!"

Where are you from?

"India."

I move on.

Yes, that's a loonie.

Three Americans, each wearing an Amazon ID, pass by. Excuse me, I ask them, could you direct me to the eating Indians? They think I'm a mental case. What eating Indians?

I have to express myself better, I see. And I do. I explain to them exactly what I'm looking for.

"Oh, they! Too late. The food trucks are gone by this time," one of them says to me.

How many Indians work for Amazon?

They look at each other, each determining who might be willing to answer first. What are you doing, guys? I ask. Are you afraid to talk because of one stupid article?

One of them, the tallest and fattest, replies: "We are more sensitive these days, that's true, but not because we believe that we have been exposed. Honestly, I can tell you: I've been working for Amazon three years now and I have not seen one person crying at his desk. That article had many flaws."

How many Indians are working for Amazon?

"I don't know."

Guess. Give me a wild guess.

He wouldn't. And neither of the other two would. They are the average Americans, and they have fears. Is this the Land of the Fearful?

Twenty feet down the road I meet an Indian couple, both working for Amazon. How many Indians are working for Amazon? I ask them.

"Four percent," the lady says.

I heard that at least 40 percent of Amazon's employees are Indian! I say to them. I didn't really hear this, but I just try a number.

"Surely not. Maybe 20 percent," says the man.

How about 30?

"Twenty to 25," the lady now says.

She is a classic loonie, no doubt.

In general, if you give people enough time to talk, I have noticed, they will contradict themselves. Is there much value to public opinion surveys? I guess it depends on the issue.

Bottom line: the number of Indians working for Amazon is a top military secret.

• • •

I keep on walking. It's good to walk.

Downtown Seattle showcases a more diverse crowd than I've managed to see in the past few weeks. For example, blacks. Not many blacks, at least not today, and those I do see are mostly homeless, drugged or both.

And then I get to meet Greg, a nice-looking gay guy who is in love with a lawyer. Are you married? I ask him, as gay marriage is winning more and more American hearts.

"No, my partner is not ready."

His partner, the lawyer, has an aversion to legal documents and obligations. Let the straights do that.

Greg tells me that Seattle residents spend their lives pretending that they are happy and relaxed, but that underneath this façade they are extremely tense people. Living in Seattle, he says to me, is very expensive, and people work very hard just to survive.

• • •

The next day, as I comb the metropolis here in a state that has made "recreational" marijuana consumption legal, I see many homeless people, more than I have seen since leaving New York. Some of the homeless seem drugged. They must have alcohol and weed, LSD and heroin, and whatever else, all mixed up in their bodies. Most are white.

Later this evening the 5th Avenue Theatre will present the Broadway musical *Matilda*, I read on a poster I happen to pass.

I have no clue what this show is about, but I like the name Matilda, and I make up my mind to watch it tonight. Yes, true, I'm totally disappointed with American theater, but I still want to give it a chance.

For food I go to a restaurant called Palace Kitchen. In the State of the Loonies, you never know, they might have good chefs.

I sit down and get a menu. Every word on the menu is lowercase except for "Palace Kitchen." Either these people are very cool, or they are totally drugged.

Whatever the case, I order a dish called "fried washington sweet corn" from the appetizer list. The description of this dish is: "crispy shallots, parmesan, spicy lemon mayo." Price: 14.5. Why the fifty cents? Because it looks more "exact" this way.

In about twenty minutes my appetizer arrives. It is worth every penny, including the fifty cents.

Feeling good, I move on to the main dish. I order "grilled rare albacore tuna," which comes with "yellow new tomatoes, rattlesnake beans, soft boiled egg, toasted garlic vinaigrette." Price: 32. No fifty cents here.

It takes about thirty minutes for this portion to arrive. And it is Delicious, with a capital D. Each and every bite is full of divine flavor, prepared by a heavenly chef. Really. The "yellow new tomatoes," which are actually red, are the best tomatoes I've ever tasted. Never, ever did I think that tomatoes could taste better than ice cream, but they do. In Seattle.

For dessert I order "kentucky bourbon cake." Don't ask me to explain this one; just come over and try. Cost? 9.5.

Though this place does not define itself and its kitchen, the word *French* is hiding in every bite. This is French at its best. Finding good food in America is not an easy task. This is my lucky day.

• • •

I walk over to the theater and get to my seat the moment the curtain rises. The title role is played by a Filipina actress, and there are more blacks on the stage than in the audience. From the get-go, *Matilda* works wonders, transforming the stage into a world of magic. The show, about a little girl in love with books who is belittled by her parents, is superb, inspiring and magnificent. The choreography, the music, the writing, the lights, the set design, the directing, the dancing – all top class.

I'm having a really good day today: great food, great show. And both in America!

During intermission I check out who is behind this show. Oh Lordy Lord, it's a British import. Why can't Americans come up with such delightful shows? Perhaps if Americans had less fear they would write better plays.

• • •

Recreational marijuana is legal, and marijuana smokers are seen as "cool," but cigarette smokers are classified as lepers or worse. Walk the streets of Seattle and you will find No Smoking signs all over, even on benches on the sidewalk.

So I smoke while standing. Between puffs I am approached by drugged young people who, one after the other, recite the same line: "Excuse me: Can you spare fifty cents?"

Seattle has many rich people, many outstanding corporations, and parades of luxury cars roaming its streets, but those who have fallen through its golden cracks have no hope. People who call themselves "liberal" almost always pride themselves as people who care for the poor and the weak. But here it's different; liberalism here is limited to those who can afford it.

Earlier this month, activists of a group called Black Lives Matter (BLM) interrupted a speech by Vermont senator Bernie Sanders, running for the Democratic presidential candidacy against Hillary Clinton. Bernie's supporters, who, like him, are the most liberal and progressive in American politics, booed the black activists. Later on, one of the BLM activists said: "I was going to tell Bernie how racist this city is, filled with its [so-called] progressives, but you did it for me," and accused the audience of practicing "white supremacist liberalism," according to the *Seattle Times*.

This accusation, sad to say, rings true when walking Seattle streets and watching its poor in this stylish city. "Progressive"? No way!

The only problem with BLM is this: They get involved only when whites are in the middle. If blacks kill blacks, which is a leading cause of black deaths in America, black lives don't matter. Why? Because.

How liberal is Seattle? A look at the Seattle opera offers a hint. Seattle's opera, in case you didn't know, is proud as hell of its greatest achievement: Richard Wagner. In its publications, Seattle Opera proudly defines its history thusly: "The company is recognized internationally for the quality of its productions and as the pre-eminent presenter of Wagner's opera in the United States."

Even its mission statement boasts of its love of Wagner. "By continuing our emphasis on the work of Richard Wagner and by achieving national and international recognition for the quality of all our programming, Seattle Opera commits itself to advancing the cultural life of the Pacific Northwest through education and performance."

I personally have no problem with Wagner, even though Wagner was Adolf Hitler's and the Nazis' most beloved composer. But taking this history into account, I find it strange to see Seattle Opera's fascination with Wagner, given that it is a public cultural organization, which should exhibit extra sensitivities to some minority groups, such as the Jewish community.

To many Jews, "Wagner" connotes glorification of the Nazi period, a time when many of their ancestors ended life in crematoriums. Why does Seattle Opera not take such feelings into account? Perhaps its management is composed of people suffering from "white supremacist liberalism" disease.

Seattle, with its massive homelessness, fails the most important test of real liberalism.

• • •

It is time, don't you think, to get myself a joint or two. Why have I procrastinated up to now? Move, fat boy! I say to yours truly. And move I do.

I find the stores that sell the stuff and go there. But I'm blocked by a guard, a fat black man, at the entrance. The fat man now asks for my ID card.

"Entrance is allowed only to people who are twenty-one years old or older."

Good lord! That's a compliment worth a thousand joints! I show him my driver's license, and he lets me in.

There are different joints here and I ask the saleslady to give me the most popular one. She does, and I buy it.

I walk out and light up. I inhale, deeper than deep. Again. Again. Again. Puff after puff, drag after drag. In a short while I'm flying; I feel lighter than I've ever been. Like a little bee. Worth the eight bucks that I paid for it, I think.

But not for long.

Soon enough, how sad, this bee grows and it turns into a little bird, the bird turns into an eagle, the eagle into a lamb, the lamb into a deer, the deer into a bear and the bear into an elephant. I feel heavy, confused, and I sink into total dizziness. I can't tell the difference between Wagner and Moses.

I must go to sleep, but my hotel room is quite far from here. Malibu is not with me, and there are no taxis anywhere, at least not that I can tell. With my last energy I board a public bus, where many a black rides.

My head spins; I lose the ability to speak. I try, but my tongue doesn't function anymore. How come I can't speak? Have I turned into a fish?

I don't know.

Can you spare fifty cents, hey you?

• • •

My head clear, I head to Seattle's Capitol Hill neighborhood. Fun place. First off, the major intersections here are decked out in LGBT colors. Could any city be more welcoming than this?

This Seattle, let me be clear here, is the very definition of liberalism.

I walk a few blocks and then I see an "LGBT visitors center." Beautiful. Gorgeous.

Greg, walking out of the center, tells me that "outsiders say that we are not friendly, that we don't take the time to talk to people from outside Seattle."

Is that true?

"I talk to you, don't I?"

Are you liberal?

"Absolutely."

Pro-Israel or pro-Palestine?

"Palestine. Definitely. I would love to talk more with you but I don't have time, really. I have to go."

He goes.

And I keep on walking, past aggressive homeless people drugged to their very core. I walk more.

Here is a young man sleeping on the sidewalk, next to a scrap of cardboard on which he has written the following: "Too ugly to prostitute. Too nice to steal! Anything helps."

He is lying next to a No War sign. This is a Seattleite homeless man, after all.

A few steps ahead is a young girl who will draw your face for a fee, or will sell you her self-portrait for a fee. How much? Whatever you want to pay. She's homeless, and she needs cash. She's a lively girl, her name is Latisha, and she is nineteen years of age.

How did you get to be homeless?

"I was kicked out from my house when I was fourteen."

Why?

"Because my mom is crazy, absolutely insane. But I'm fine."

She even went to college, University of Kansas.

How many years did you study there, and what did you study?

"Political science, for one year."

One year only? What happened?

"The first week I went to this party and this guy, really drunk, he took me to his dorm room, and I slept all day. It affected me all year; I didn't go to any of my classes; I just slept all day. Yeah. It's fucked. I was fucked up for a year. Eventually I woke up and I realized I couldn't do college anymore. The kid who did that to me was in my class, and I couldn't handle it. It was killing me. I packed up all my stuff in my car. I stopped drinking, stopped doing drugs. I came out to the West Coast and now I'm here! I like it here. I [have been] here for months. It is a really cool place. They offer a lot of help for homeless people and stuff, like there's the Orion Center. And I get food stamps."

How much do you get in food stamps?

"A hundred dollars."

One hundred per week?

"Month."

One hundred dollars for one month?

"Yeah. This month it's all gone. I sell pictures all day to make some money."

How much money do you make a day?

"Ten bucks a day."

You get free food?

"Breakfast, lunch and dinner I get for free at the Orion Center. With the ten dollars that I make I can buy more food or gas. Sometimes I buy cigarettes and I walk around the drunk people and I sell them for a dollar each. I get twenty dollars for one pack of cigarettes. Yeah."

That's creative!

"Yeah!"

Can't you sleep at the homeless center?

"No. I mean, you call before six p.m. and there is a chance you might get one of the twenty beds for the night, but you almost never get in. You know?"

The homeless shelter has room for only twenty people?

"Yeah. It's a shelter for kids, twenty-five years and under. That's the rule."

How many shelters like this exist here?

"Two youth shelters. The Orion is the good one, fantastic. You can come for three hours a day, you can shower, you can do laundry, you get free food, they give a bunch of clothes, shoes. Great. Really helpful. The other shelter feels like a mental hospital when you go in. There are just crazy people over there. They are rocking back and forth like shit. And violent."

With all her problems, Latisha is positive. "I'll vote for Bernie," she tells me, speaking of the Vermont senator. "We will get free education and I'll go to school again."

Latisha, who is bisexual, is a liberal. So she tells me. Very liberal. If you were wondering: Latisha is pro-Palestine.

• • •

I keep on walking. Right ahead of me, in between one Indian eatery and another, there is a "fashion" store, where you can buy a Palestinian scarf ("Pali," as some Europeans call it) for five bucks. Seattle's got them all.

For example, Qatar. Qatar is a Seattle man born in Somalia who earns his living by driving a cab.

Qatar, who arrived in the USA as a refugee, speaks: "Seattle is a liberal city. They don't like me here because I'm black, but they don't show it. In Dallas, I was there, they are conservatives and they show you that they don't like you.

"That's the difference between conservatives and liberals. Here, where the people are liberals, they show you a friendly face, but it's not real; they are not real friends. Seattle is a liberal city; they don't hate anybody, and they don't like anybody. For them, it's all about money. I don't mind about the whites here, because they don't bother me, but I don't like the African Americans."

Why?

"I'm from Somalia and African Americans say that I'm not black."

But you are! You are very black!

"I don't have a big nose like the African Americans and they say that I'm not black because of my small nose. Where are you from, are you from Britain?"

No, from Germany.

"Do you like Adolf Hitler?"

I haven't made up my mind about him yet. How about you?

"I like him. I think he did good things."

Because he killed the Jews?

"Yes."

Are there Jews in Seattle?

"Yes."

Are they good or bad?

"Bad."

You know them?

"Yes."

And you know that they are bad?

"Yes."

Explain!

"They live by themselves; they help each other; they own every-thing. They own Uber; they own Starbucks; they own Facebook; they own Google."

Do they also own Apple?

"Yeah."

Do they also own Coca Cola?

"Yes!"

What else?

"They own Microsoft. Bill Gates is Jewish."

Is he?

"Yeah. The Jews also own McDonald's, Taco Bell. Diamonds. Everything. And they don't help anybody who is not Jewish. That's why Hitler killed them. In the United States there's no Hitler and this is a problem, because nobody will kill them."

So, what will happen?

"God knows. President Obama tried to fight the Jews, take their money by raising taxes on them, but they are smarter than him. They have the money, and they rule. America is not a country, a nation. America is a corporation. Everybody cares for his own interest and that's it."

I bid him farewell and am ready to say goodbye to this city. I learned enough here, more than I wanted to know. Let the people here have their Wagner, their Hitler, their Palestine and their can-nabis. I'm ready to get outta here. As far away as possible.

How far? Far.

In a few days, Barack Obama is flying to Alaska. Before him, Secretary of State John Kerry is scheduled to arrive there. If Alaska is good enough for them, it should be good for me as well.

Goodbye, Malibu. I return the car to the rental company and take a flight to Anchorage, Alaska.

Let me see the leaders of this country up close.

Gate Thirteen

*Journalists are not allowed to urinate unless
accompanied by young escorts*

IN ANCHORAGE, ALASKA, YOU NEED A CAR TO MOVE AROUND, AND I RENT A
Ford Fiesta ES. This is the smallest car I've driven so far, but it was
the only one I found on the lot.

The president and his secretary of state are coming here to
discuss climate change in an international conference organized by
the State Department, entitled "Conference on Global Leadership
in the Arctic: Cooperation, Innovation, Engagement and Resilience
(GLACIER)." In less grandiose wording, this is a conference about
combating climate change.

In an article by Alaska Senator Dan Sullivan published today
in the *Alaska Dispatch News*, the senator writes: "When President
Obama visits, I hope he sees Alaska for what it is: both a symbol of
the very best in the American character and spirit, but also a real
place, with real people."

Maybe so, maybe not. One thing I learn moments after I land in
Anchorage is this: not all Alaskans are happy to see Obama coming,
or, more precisely, many Alaskans would prefer he fly somewhere
else. The reason? When the president is here, private planes will
be under severe flying restrictions, and to Alaskans this is undue
hardship; they like to move from one place to another in their little

planes. Many places in Alaska are accessible only by plane, and when Obama arrives many Alaskans will be stuck.

Even worse, the president's scheduled arrival coincides with the start of the moose hunting season, when the good folks of Alaska fly their planes to the best hunting spots, but now they've got Obama in their way. As for me, I don't plan to hunt any moose.

I eat salmon at a restaurant called Simon & Seafort's, where I share a table with three Alaskan residents – private plane owners and licensed pilots. I'm interested to know what they think of GLACIER and climate change. After talking with people in the northern continental USA, some of whom I mentioned in previous pages, I found that almost all those who are into the climate change issue are also into Palestine. What's the relationship between climate change and Palestine? Nothing, is the short answer. I don't know, is the long one.

The fish is not bad, by the way. It costs two arms and two legs, but what can I do? I sit with rich people, and they like expensive restaurants. One of the people at the table, Chris, seems to be the richest of them. He is in the finance business, he hunts, he flies and he owns a lot of property. And he is a thinker, to top it all.

Alaska, he tells me, is the freest of all the US states. In Alaska, he says, and the others agree, people exercise freedom more than any other American. How come? Well, it's the private planes. Here in Alaska, you can park your plane practically anywhere you want: near a beach, on top of a hill, in the depth of a valley, wherever, excluding residential areas. In short: the state is your private plane parking lot.

That's freedom. That's liberty.

Why is it, I ask Chris once I'm done with the fish, that big American planes fly to foreign countries, such as Libya, Iraq, Afghanistan, etcetera and etcetera, and bomb them out of existence?

"You have to understand America. We built this country on an idea, the idea of freedom, and if there are countries in the world which are not treating their citizens well, it is our obligation to go there and fix the problem."

Who gave you this right?

"I didn't say 'right,' I said 'obligation.'"

Who gave you the moral superiority to justify flying to another country, another culture, and killing its people just because they do not follow the same rules that your culture does?

Chris is getting very upset at me. More than just upset. He is mad. He calls the waitress, asks for the bill and gives her his credit card.

In an instant she is back with the bill, and the card.

"I pay for the table, it's over $300, for one reason," he says while signing the check, "so that I can tell you what I think of you." He puts the card back in his pocket, lays his hands on the bill and says to me: "You are full of shit, and you'll do yourself a favor if you leave Alaska as soon as possible."

At this, he ceremoniously leaves the table. This Chris, in case you were wondering, is also a "loonie," a conservative loonie.

Another person at the table now says to me: "I hope you understand what you just did. If you plan to stay in Alaska, don't be surprised if you get into some serious problems. Chris knows everybody here. He is a very powerful man and he can hurt you."

I learn a new meaning to the words *freedom* and *liberty*.

I look at Chris's retreating figure and a thought comes to me: What Chris has just done is no different than what the Western world has been doing in the Middle East in recent years. Flush with cash and muscles, they tell the people of the East that they are full of shit, that they should leave the area at once, and then they bomb them.

Climate change. Is it really happening? If I am to trust the weather specialists of our day, it is happening and it is endangering the entire planet. The weather specialists also say that tomorrow morning it will be rainy in Anchorage. Will this come to pass?

Let's wait for tomorrow and see.

• • •

Tomorrow has come. Is it raining? No. Is it cloudy? It's mostly sunny. Is it possible that those specialists, who can't predict the weather for the next day, are capable of predicting the weather in fifty years? It is. Everything is possible in America.

This reminds me: A few days ago the stock market took a nosedive, shedding gains made over many previous months, and some Evangelical pastors "prophesized" that the stock market would promptly crash. It did not. The stock market is actually doing pretty well, thank you.

Personally, I wish I could take a stand on climate change. Everybody does, and I look like the biggest fool in the United States these days because I don't take a stand. On the other hand, less than a century ago if you didn't kill a Jew you looked bad, because almost everybody did. Before that, in this very country, if you didn't have a black slave you also looked bad. And not that long ago, almost everybody was sure that gays were psychos.

• • •

Climate change or not, I'd like to see the glaciers. I'm in Alaska, after all! I drive to Whittier, which is about sixty miles from Anchorage, to join a boat excursion to see the glaciers. I need to check the glaciers' conditions: Are they icy? Are they melting? Is anything cooking?

I embark on a tour boat, also known as a "cruise ship," and am ready for my encounter with the glaciers.

On this ship, they serve lunch at predetermined tables. At my table there are four Mormons from Utah; over at the neighboring table are two intellectuals from New Mexico. Anything the Mormons believe in, the intellectuals believe in its very opposite, which is really refreshing to witness. The Mormons believe that Americans are great and wonderful, and the intellectuals believe that Americans are selfish creatures motivated by money and acute narcissism. Forget the glaciers. These people are a delight!

Most of the other people on this trip are Asian tourists, and they are effusively anticipating the prospect of seeing glaciers soon. It is only when these Asians raise their voices in a language that is incomprehensible to me, shouting excited consonants and the loudest of vowels, that I realize we've reached the glaciers.

I walk out to the deck and look at the glaciers. A glacier, defined by Merriam-Webster's dictionary as "a large body of ice moving slowly down a slope or valley or spreading outward on a land surface," is indeed what my eyes see: an icy white mass on top of brown mountains. The ice is thick, really thick, and at times huge chunks of it drop into the water below. Is this what they call climate change? What do I know? I don't.

I look up close at the glaciers. Bluish colors emanate from the face of the ice. Some of the glaciers in the path of our cruise are so gorgeous that for a moment I mistake them for giant diamonds. Then the ship turns around, heading back to land.

The good thing is this: I'm enjoying the company here, and we still have some time to spend together. The Mormons tell me that Jesus Christ came to the United States, or whatever it was called then, immediately after he was resurrected. That's two thousand years ago.

The intellectuals at the other table totally reject the Mormons' story. They are offended by it. The intellectuals, a man and a woman who are in a relationship since about Jesus' time, are not married and think that marriage is just a stupid paper, but they strongly advocate for gay marriage.

Which reminds me: the gay marriage issue played big in the recent mayoral election in Anchorage. In the heat of the mayoral battle one of the contenders said: "I support the idea of adults being able to choose who they have a relationship with. Father and son should be allowed to marry, if they're both consenting adults."

Despite the stupidity of such a sentence, this guy eventually won the mayoral race. His name is Ethan Berkowitz. I think I should meet him once this trip is over. And, indeed, when I'm back on dry land I go to see him.

• • •

Like Rahm Emanuel, Ethan Berkowitz is Jewish. Unlike Rahm, Ethan has no armed policeman seated in the reception area, just a smiling secretary and some other employees. Mayor Ethan Berkowitz is very busy these days. The GLACIER conference is opening shortly, and many His Highnesses and Her Excellencies are showing up. They include: His Highness Barack Obama, the Honorable John F. Kerry, His Excellency Tang Guoqiang of China, His Excellency Kristian Jensen of Denmark, His Excellency Gunnar Bragi Sveinsson of Iceland, Her Excellency Kazuko Shiraishi of Japan, the Honorable Henryka Moscicka-Dendys of Poland, Her Excellency Margot Wallström of Sweden and many others. They are Ethan's guests, yet he has found the time to sit down with me and schmooze about such abstract topics as being Jewish in Alaska. I am grateful.

Ethan was born in San Francisco and has lived in Alaska for the past twenty-five years. What brought you to Alaska? I ask him.

"I worked down at the Antarctic; I shoveled snow; I drove people around; I unloaded planes and ships. I live up in the Arctic now. I can tell my mother I made my way up in the world! That's what I tell her!"

What made you come here?

"I worked for a judge, down at the Antarctic, and I wanted to have another good adventure before I settled down and grew up. Not having grown up, I haven't gone back home yet..."

Are you still a baby?

"There is a twelve-year-old in all of us."

Tell me some of your Alaska adventures.

"You get to see a country that you wouldn't see anywhere else. There's nothing quite like seeing the Northern Lights or hearing the sound of extremely dry snow as you walk across it. Those are profound. Or sharing meals with people who grew up in Native cultures."

You can do that in Michigan.

"You can't have muktuk [an Eskimo delicacy made of whale skin] in Michigan."

You can have paktak (a word I just made up) in Michigan!

"Maybe!"

Do you think that people relate to you differently because you are Jewish?

He pauses here. He starts to say a word or two, stops, starts again, stops, starts and stops. Then, finally, he says: "I don't think most people think about that." But then, a few moments later, he says: "I think that anti-Semitism exists."

At times, he tells me, he hears people say about him that "he is not like us."

Are these words coming from people on the right side of politics?

"Yes. It's a code, code words. I hear it."

How often have you heard these code words?

"In every campaign I have been part of."

What's the story of anti-Semitism in Alaska?

"We have a lot of the militants here, the right-wing militants."

Percentage-wise, how many are they?

"I don't know."

Guess.

"There are pockets of it. Not here in Anchorage, but in other parts of the state."

Big pockets?

"Significant."

Did you become more Jewish or less Jewish in Alaska?

"This is really an interesting question." After a pause he says that being in Alaska "has strengthened my Jewish identity. Here, we Jews are the Frozen Chosen."

• • •

Many an Alaskan tells me that they are in Alaska because of its pristine natural beauty. You have to take a flight above the glaciers, they say. They're local; they should know.

I hook up with a local company called Rust's Flying Service and I join them for the next flight out. The plane I board is a small, amphibious craft known as a floatplane. This plane cruises on water and flies in the air.

The pilot, Bruce, is a pilots' pilot. His papa was a pilot, his children are pilots and his wife is too. I sit on the seat next to him, where copilots sit in planes that use them, and he takes off. "Copilot controls have been removed," the sign in front of me says. Thank goodness; I wouldn't know what to do if something went wrong.

The plane starts cruising on the waters, like a boat, which is kind of cool. And then, when Bruce gets clearance, we fly. "One in five Alaskans is a pilot," he says as we reach an altitude of thirteen hundred feet. This is not the normal altitude on commercial airplanes.

Cruising at thirteen hundred feet will get nobody anywhere on a passenger flight.

Personally, I prefer this height; at least I can see something. Bruce points to the left, where there's a white structure that looks from this distance like a Russian Orthodox church or a mosque. Must be a church, I think. Russia sold Alaska to the Americans many, many years ago, and it stands to reason that they were praying here before they left.

"It's a mosque," Bruce corrects me. How did a mosque get here? Did we fly so fast that we've reached Saudi Arabia? Nope. Did Muslims from the hot Middle East come by to cool off? Not exactly. Nobody prays at that mosque, Bruce says.

I ask him if we could drop by for a quick prayer, so that the mosque won't feel lonely, but he says no. The area where the mosque is, he informs me, is a US military installation. It's an army base where American soldiers practice warfare in Islamic countries.

Could somebody please replace the copilot controls? If they were active I'd direct the plane to the mosque, but Bruce won't hear of it. He's a one-dimension man: glaciers. "All the glaciers in Alaska are shrinking," he says, and soon enough we approach our first glacier.

Bruce lowers the altitude. We are now about six hundred feet above the ground, and the visibility of what's below us is excellent. We are flying above the Knik Glacier, which Bruce says is "like an ice river."

The ice exhibit under my feet, below this plane, is a mesmerizing sight. I can't take my eyes off this glacier. It is a master work of art in ice. It's a sculpture, a painting, a being that has no equal. It's one huge exhibit, with no beginning and no end, of infinite beauty. It's wavy, it's straight, it shines in angelic white, and it has a heavenly soul. Think of being surrounded by glowing white ice of every conceivable shape. It is so amazingly grandiose in its beauty, having myriad layers in it and above it, that no camera can capture it. Believe me, I tried.

Bruce keeps on flying; at times he pilots the plane rightwards, then leftwards, back and forth, just because he loves it. He missed his profession; he should have been a dancer. And then he dances his way to another glacier. I wish I could live here, among the glaciers.

For some reason the glaciers take me back to my childhood, when I studied the Bible and the story of how the world came to be. I'm not religious anymore, but for a moment there I can see the Wind of God flying next to me, above these whitest and bluest of glaciers.

So unreal!

Bruce points to a particular glacier, of whatever name, and says that it receded quite a number of yards just in the last few weeks. Is that due to climate change? Bruce, a devout Alaskan pilot, is not a man in love with sound bites, of either the left or of the right. "Some say it's due to climate change, some say it's a natural cycle," he replies. He doesn't know who is right.

"We don't have enough records to answer this."

I'm not the only dumb-dumb in the world. What a relief!

• • •

When I get up the next morning I make it my duty to read the news. Tomorrow, according to the *Washington Post*, President Obama "will announce the renaming of Mount McKinley, honoring the 25th president, to Mount Denali, an Athabascan name used by generations of Alaska Natives that means 'the great one.'" Americans love their Indians. Especially the dead ones.

According to the weather forecast, the temperature in Anchorage will soon reach thirty-nine degrees. In New York, where I started this journey, the temperature will rise to ninety-one today. I'm so happy I'm in Alaska.

• • •

Good morning. The GLACIER conference, hosted by the US Department of State, is opening in a few minutes at Anchorage's Dena'ina Civic and Convention Center. Dignitaries, domestic and foreign, are about to convene in order to solve the world's problems. On today's schedule are speeches by United States President Barack Obama and US Secretary of State John F. Kerry. The opening statement at this prestigious conference will, naturally, be delivered by the most important person in attendance: Mr. Lee Stephan, the "President and First Chief" of the Traditional Tribal Council of Eklutna, Native Village.

Next to speak will be the Honorable Ethan Berkowitz, followed by some other distinguished speakers; last to speak at the early morning session will be the Honorable John F. Kerry. The conference will close at end of the day with "remarks by the President of the United States."

At 9:15 a.m. attendees are motioned to be quiet. They comply. At 9:19, Kerry and the dignitaries enter. The audience members rise.

The First Chief speaks. "In your honor I have, eh, try to speak my language. I never learned it, but I'm going give it a shot," he says, and proceeds to say a few words in the Native language, which are probably all the words he knows. The First Chief quickly moves to speak in English again, and he thanks President Obama for the honor of opening this distinguished conference.

Will the second speaker, the Honorable Ethan, speak in Hebrew? No. Instead he talks about the diversity of Alaska's people and remarks that "we live the climate change every day." Once upon a time, he says, "sell air conditioners to Alaskans" was the punchline of a joke, but today it's reality. Before concluding, he utters a word in a Native language, proudly transforming himself from a Jew into a Native.

I need a break. I get up from my seat, take three steps, and a lady approaches me, asking what I need. Toilet, I say.

Follow me, she says. She takes me around the conference hall, from one end to the other, and then out all the way to the restroom.

She shows me to the door of the men's room and waits there. Once I'm done she escorts me back to my seat.

Two seats next to me is an Alaskan journalist, a red-haired beauty who identifies herself as a "married gay," and she wants to get out. She gets off her seat and walks toward the exit door, only to be stopped by security. They tell her that she cannot leave the conference hall. Period.

Yes, nobody is allowed to leave this place during sessions. We are trapped inside. We have no choice but to listen to the speakers, who, one after the other, prophesy the end of world as we know it unless we take deliberate actions to stop climate change. If we don't take action, we are warned, wildfires will increase, glaciers will melt, villages and towns will disappear, temperatures will rise to African levels, and all white folks will become black. Something like that.

And then John F. Kerry speaks.

He lets us know that everywhere he travels "leaders and average folks talk to me about the impacts of climate change," and that he is "so grateful for such a display of interest by so many countries coming here today to be part of this discussion." How often does Kerry talk to "average folks"? I'm not sure, but I know what will happen to them when they want to pee while he talks to others.

For all Kerry's big talk, this conference is not well attended; many seats here are empty. Still, Kerry seems to enjoy the stage. "Villages in Alaska are already being battered by the storms and some have had to move, or will.... Houses and other buildings are literally collapsing into rubble. Already this is happening," he says.

Following his speech, sessions break out in different rooms. I go to one of them. Escorted, of course.

Slowly but surely I start to get used to being escorted. Most escorts are young Alaskan women or American military men in civilian clothes. They share with me their big love for Alaska and some other intimate stories, but all stop mid-story at the exact moment we arrive at my next destination, be it a toilet or another session.

My newest destination for the moment is a session about the dangers our world is facing, with emphasis on Alaskan Natives whose villages are either being eroded at this very moment or are about to erode. Pictures of all kinds of villages with Native-sounding names are projected on the walls. And they are effective. By showing real people, and not just strange-consonant scientific terms, the message comes across much clearer. It's a climate change message about people, people who will be drowned or otherwise disappear if we don't stop the glacier erosion.

I'm impressed.

Downstairs, after being escorted by yet another young girl, I meet some Alaskans of the white kind. How many Native villagers live in Alaska? I ask one such Alaskan.

"Do you mean off-the-road villages?"

Yes, the Natives.

"My WAG is about 125,000 people. But that's just a WAG."

What's WAG?

"Wild-ass guess."

Got it. And how many of them are at risk of losing their homes?

Well, this she doesn't know. Actually, no one I approach at this conference does.

What everyone knows, on the other hand, is this: there is no smoking anywhere in the building, including the balcony. Usually it's okay to smoke on the balcony, but today it's a security risk. What does a cigarette have to do with security? I don't know, and nobody will share with me the sophisticated relationship between homeland security and Marlboro.

I go to the pressroom, and there I see three big screens: the middle one is displaying a session taking place upstairs, on the left CNN is playing and on the right screen is MSNBC, both favorite networks of the left side of politics. No Fox News here. Conservatives, I guess, are not welcome.

I want to smoke a cigarette and am told that in between sessions, when there are no speakers, I am allowed to go out.

I do.

Outside I see about two hundred people, standing ready to welcome Obama when his motorcade passes by, some holding signs that declare their love for him. Among them are a grandmother and her grandchildren, Justin and Amelia. I ask the two kids if they love Obama and why. "Yes. He is the president," Justin says.

Any other reason?

Yes. The president makes good laws, the kid says. His grandma is not impressed. She tries to whisper better reasons in his ears. I tell her that I'm interested in Justin's and Amelia's opinions and that it would be really great and cool if she let them have their own say.

Justin is pleased by my comment and is ready to explain what laws the president has legislated. "The law that people have to stop at stop signs," he says.

Grandma is not happy. And she shows it, with sour facial expressions.

Justin wants to please his grandma and pulls off another good law: "Boys and girls can marry." A discussion follows between the two children as to the meaning of this law, and then they get back to me and explain that two girls can marry each other and also two boys.

Grandma is very happy.

Justin knows another law made by the president, and he shares it with me. The president, he says, is changing the name of Mount McKinley to Mount Denali. A big smile appears on grandma's face.

Why is the president changing the name to Denali? I ask him.

"Because he likes the name," he answers, and Amelia concurs.

Grandma is not at all happy. The fact that Denali was Indian and McKinley white, which is the idea behind the change of names, is totally lost on these kids. But they love Obama for coming up with the name "Denali." I like it too. I like the name Denali much more than McKinley.

I go back to attend the conference.

• • •

As time passes I find out that the day after tomorrow Kerry will be in Philadelphia to deliver a major speech about the Iran deal. A busy man, this secretary.

Escorted by a nineteen-year-old Alaskan beauty I make my way up to the third floor, where the president is to give a speech in about an hour. There I meet a man named Dr. Matthew Sturm. Matthew has an exhibition of ice – all kinds of it – with signs next to them: "Touch me." He hopes, he says to me, that President Obama will pass by him and touch the ice. One ice sample, black in color, is thirty thousand years old, he says.

I ask Dr. Matthew who is right: the conservatives who don't believe in climate change or the liberals who do? He tells me that the proof is in front of my eyes: this thirty-thousand-year-old piece of ice proves that climate change has been going on for many, many years. In addition, he chides, conservative business owners have climate change contingency plans; they talk big, but they do small.

Perhaps he doesn't know, but what he says is also said by many conservatives. They say that climate change is a natural process that has been going on for thousands of years, long before people started burning fossil fuels, but they don't believe in "climate change" in the way that this administration, and many European countries, do, meaning that it's mostly man-made and that it can be reversed.

Be that as it may, "climate change" has taken on a whole new meaning in today's culture war: you are either pro-climate change or anti-climate change. And, for whatever reason, liberals believe in climate change and conservatives don't.

I still don't know who's right and who's wrong. All I know is this: President Obama is about to arrive.

I try to enter the hall in which he'll be speaking, but am told that I cannot. Why not? Reporters are not allowed in the main hall. Who said? That's the instruction. I protest. I was invited here by White House officials for the sole purpose of attending Obama's speech, I argue, and won't take no for an answer.

Not knowing what to do with me, one escort negotiates with another escort, then two more escorts get involved, and then another official. Nobody knows what to do. Until, miracle of miracles, yet another official comes in with a clarification: I'm welcome to join the session, but I first must go downstairs and only then come up again with some other reporters.

Down and up, up and down. That's why this building has escalators – to use them!

It is possible, I don't know, that this is exactly the way America has been negotiating the Iran deal for the past few years.

In any case, I go down and out. To smoke.

Outside I see the president's motorcade, somewhere between twenty and thirty cars, as it slowly makes its way to the building. Part of the entourage, a person in the know tells me in a soft voice, consists of a bunch of "White House reporters" and an ambulance. Why an ambulance? Just in case. Why are the cars moving so slowly? "This is Anchorage; they are looking for a parking place." Good to have some funny people around.

Cigarette smoked, I enter the building again. The guards already know me and laugh every time they screen me in.

I get an escort and we go upstairs.

At a quarter to the hour, everybody's quiet. It's amazing how people will shut up when they think a president is about to enter. A few minutes pass, and then John Kerry goes to the podium to introduce the president. Between nuclear bombs and freezing glaciers, this man finds the time to say lines such as: "Ladies and gentlemen, the President of the United States of America, Barack Obama!"

On cue, Barack appears. "Thank you to the many Alaskans," he says, "Alaska Natives and other indigenous peoples of the Arctic." Americans, as we all know by now, love their Natives. Obama proceeds to business. "Our understanding of climate change advances each day," he says. "Human activity is disrupting the climate, in many ways faster than we previously thought."

There are two teleprompters next to him, one on the right and one on the left, which make it easy for him to speak about climates, winds and storms as a man learned in the science of glaciers, icebergs, emissions, geology, chemistry, biology and a host of other sciences.

I have seen Obama before, when he was still a presidential candidate. He was a young, agile man then. Now, as he starts preparing for life after the White House, he seems to have grown quite a bit older. He doesn't move much, save for his head, which turns back and forth from the right prompter to the left. He seems tired.

Surprisingly, some in the American media, for example NBC news, depict this speech as "a forceful address." Perhaps those reporters smoked a joint before coming here, a legal activity in this state.

In any case, what Obama lacks in stagecraft, at least today, he makes up for with scary prophesies and forecasts. "People will suffer. Economies will suffer. Entire nations will find themselves under severe, severe problems. More drought, more floods, rising sea levels, greater migration, more refugees, more scarcity, more conflict," unless we take action to stop climate change.

Is this a scare tactic? Maybe yes, maybe no.

On one occasion he does rise to the task of oratory. It happens when he utters this line: "Those who want to ignore the science are increasingly alone; they are on their own shrinking island." Applause immediately follows.

As is often the case with Obama, he presents himself as a man above all others. "Any leader who refuses to take this issue seriously or treats it like a joke is not fit to lead," he says, as if he is the only one worthy of the "leader" title. He ends his remarks in a way almost no European leader ever will. "May God bless all of you and your countries."

Now that I've gotten a closer look at America's leaders, have I learned anything?

Yes. First and foremost, they are politicians. As I listened to President Obama I couldn't stop thinking of Illinois's Thirteenth District. Is it conceivable that a man who doesn't care about one district, the district that first voted him in, would care for the entire world? Is it possible for a man who doesn't give a hoot about the people living today to care so deeply for those living tomorrow?

Maybe Obama the person does care, but as a "leader" he lacks the strength to lead the people out of their misery. Maybe, just maybe, he is a guy who is not fit to lead.

Whatever the case, for me the most interesting discovery at this conference is the treatment of the reporters. What's the story here? An older military man in attendance, who says he has worked with more than one president, tells me that the Obama administration is very much about "control." This administration, he says, wants to control the media and keep it tight.

Wasn't President George W. Bush the same? "No way!"

President Bill Clinton? "You must be kidding! Not including President Obama, presidents are very lax with the media. You would never be escorted to the toilet! This administration is different. This administration wants to control everything, and it does." And it succeeds.

As the conference ends for the day and we all leave the building, a group of Christian singers awaits us on the other side of the street, urging us to believe in Jesus. But I have had enough preaching for one day, and I head to a local bar.

Believe it or not, instead of ordering a shot of Christian Brothers, I order coffee.

Next to me sit a number of people who have come from Washington, DC, as part of the president's visit to Alaska. All are government employees, some of higher rank than the others, and all are into beer or wine. It's good to talk with government officials while they drink.

The highest of ranks in this cadre of drinkers is a lovely lady who speaks her mind, and I will not name her. This is what she has to say:

"The Obama administration, from the perspective of people like me, a government employee, is one of the worst. The people of this administration came in without any background or experience in governing and they didn't know what they were doing. They had ideas, big ideas, but they lacked the knowledge to execute them. We, government employees, know how government operates. Policies need to be managed, executed, and the money must be there to have it done.

"Why do we support Israel? We support Israel because of the Jews in this country. The Jews in this country give money to politicians, and the politicians have to do what the Jews want them to do. Everybody in Hollywood is Jewish, and they gave Obama the money to run. He won, he became president, and he brought in the people he knew: smart young people, but with no experience in governing. New politicians don't understand that they can't do anything if they don't have the people around them who are capable of executing their policies. I remember how they came in and all they wanted to do was to 'discuss' what should be done; they thought they were in a university."

Why does the "Jew" thing keep popping up? I order a Belgian beer. I drink and drink. Glass emptied, I leave.

Where should I go from here? Perhaps California. California has many liberals, the kind of people who believe in climate change. Maybe I'll get smarter there and will understand these people better.

Gate Fourteen

Sexy whites like black whores

WHERE SHOULD I STOP FIRST IN CALIFORNIA? LET'S SEE IF ANYTHING'S cooking there that grabs my attention. Here's what I read in the *San Francisco Business Times*: "UC Berkeley launches Saudi-funded Philanthropy University."

Say what?

A little explanation follows: "University of California, Berkeley, and its Haas School of Business are launching an online 'Philanthropy University' to help folks in the nonprofit realm with finance, fund-raising, strategy, leadership and other challenges."

As far as I know Saudis, they are interested in charity as much as I'm interested in forestry. But life offers its surprises, and maybe one day I will discover an interest in forestry.

Whatever their reason, I'm intrigued by this Berkeley university. I've heard much about UC Berkeley through the years, and it's time I get to know it and find me a charitable Saudi or two.

It's early afternoon when I arrive at the campus. Oh my God, what I see! An endless stream of people moving around countless small tables, everybody trying to convince everybody else to join this or that particular club. What's happening here? I ask a few students.

"Tabling," they answer. Berkeley, they explain, has about fifteen hundred different clubs, and each club wants members. Some of the clubs are just for fun, such as health clubs, but others are more serious: "Muslim Student Association," "Queer Business and Leadership," an atheist club, a bunch of Catholic clubs; here is one for Palestine, and quite a distance off is a Jewish one.

There is even a Republican club here, which happens to be one of the biggest clubs at Berkeley. I thought that Berkeley was liberal, so how come the Republican club here is one of the biggest? I ask a young Republican.

"Republicans in Berkeley feel constantly attacked and they want to be together, for protection," he replies.

Are you pro-choice or pro-life?

"I have dedicated much thought to this issue and I came up with a simple idea: abortion tax. You want to have an abortion? No problem, but it will cost you."

Walking around the students, a huge herd of young flesh, I notice that almost every second person here is Asian. As for blacks, there are very, very few; you can hardly see them here. The blacks are in Germantown and in Englewood.

There is no smoking anywhere in this campus, even in the streets. Berkeley is huge in size, and nobody lights up. When I do, people look at me as if I were a rapist-in-waiting. As long as they don't approach me, I have no reason to deny it. With time, as I want to feel a part of them, I stop lighting up as well. Let me be a Berkeley guy.

I keep walking, like a good, healthy man.

Here are some Jewish students. Berkeley has the largest number of Nobel laureates of any university, they share with me, and it's an honor to study here.

How does it feel to be Jewish here?

"It's not easy," one of them says.

What do you mean?

"For me it's tough, because Israel is important for me and most Berkeley students are pro-Palestinian. When I share positive thoughts about Israel, they move a distance from me. But for most

Jewish students here, either those who don't get involved in politics or those who are pro-Palestine, it's okay."

Some Jewish students, I hear, don't get politically involved for fear that they will be viewed badly by the other students. How are the professors? I ask a young lady.

"Nine out of ten are against Israel and for the Palestinians."

Do you regret choosing this university?

"No! Berkeley is a great university!"

If you had children, would you advise them to study here?

"Yes!"

I can't say that I fully understand her. To get a better grasp of this prestigious university, I go to chat with the boss of all bosses, Nicholas Dirks, who is UC Berkeley's chancellor.

• • •

Nicholas Dirks, as his name implies, is of German descent. Do you have German characteristics? I ask him.

"How would you characterize German?"

Whatever people say about them, you know: exactness, honesty, a little racist…

Sitting by Nicholas is Berkeley's spokesperson, an American Jew by the name of Dan. And this American Jew bursts into loud laughter when he hears this. Nicholas laughs as well, and says: "I don't want to go there, you know. This can only get me in trouble!"

It's great if you get in trouble, at least for me!

"Yeah. And I get fired!"

As the laughter subsides, Nicholas says: "I am obsessively punctual."

Are you also direct with people, telling them exactly what you think?

"Yes."

Am I fat or not?

"You are not fat at all! You could use a little more exercise, but that's true for all of us."

Laughter again. And when this subsides, I move on. Yesterday, at the "tabling," it seemed to me that about half of UC Berkeley's students are Asian. Is that really so? What's the percentage of Asian students at Berkeley?

"Close to 40 percent," Dan interrupts. "Asians are the single largest group."

What's the number for blacks? I ask Nicholas, ignoring Dan.

"Three percent," says Nicholas.

How come Berkeley has so many Asians and so few blacks?

"This morning we announced a new African American initiative, and one of our hopes is to dramatically increase the percentage of African American students in our student body."

Just this morning! Did you announce it in my honor?

"Yes, absolutely! It's for you!"

Let me ask you: Berkeley is known, at least in some circles, as being very much anti-Israel. Is this true?

"Actually, I don't know quite where that impression came about."

You know that such an impression exists –

"I don't hear many complaints from Jewish students about that."

I spoke with some Jewish students and I was told that it's tough here. Some Jewish students even told me that they don't get involved politically on campus because they don't want to be singled out by other students. Are you aware of any of this?

"No," he replies, and then immediately corrects himself: "I am aware of some of it, but we have reached out to Jewish students and we want to make sure that they get involved as they wish to. We have done a survey, in fact, across the Jewish student community and we've found that there's a high level of satisfaction with their life at Berkeley."

I know nothing about Berkeley. What I said now to you is what the students said to me. They said, for example, that in their estimate nine out of ten professors are against Israel.

It is at this point that Dan, the Jew, interrupts me. He is upset that I raise this issue. Had he known that I would raise this issue he would have made sure that I would not be sitting here now with the chancellor.

He goes on and on, defending Berkeley's name over and over. I let him blow off some steam and then ask Nicholas: Is it true that nine out of ten lecturers here are anti-Israel?

"First of all, I'd have no way of knowing. We don't actually survey what the political views of professors are. I mean, we have a commitment to academic freedom, very deep at this university, and so we don't have any political litmus test for any political position. The important thing is that all our faculty, and they are among the most highly reputed faculty of any university in the world, pass the most stringent test of disciplinary performance. Whether they were hired in political science or in anthropology, or whatever, they are the top of their profession."

I change topics and ask Nicholas if academia shapes public thinking on issues such as human rights and other social issues.

"The relationship of the university to any of these things, I think, has been critical." As he sees it, universities have also in the past had a "major cultural and political impact on the United States."

When walking around Berkeley I noticed fewer flags than in most other cities that I have been to thus far. Is Berkeley less patriotic than other cities? Are the people here anti-American, anti-government?

"Heavens, no!"

Are you proud to be an American?

"Absolutely!"

Before I leave, Dan tells me that he would like to talk with me in private. We sit down for a little talk and Dan says that according to a survey done by the university "90 percent of the Jewish students say that they feel welcome and respected on this campus." If this is true, this is the first time in four thousand years that 90 percent of Jews agree on any given topic.

• • •

California requires driving. If you want to go from one place to another, you gotta drive. If you use public transportation, you will spend a lifetime at the bus stop.

I rent again. This time, like Berkeley's admissions people, I settle on an Asian car, the Japanese Nissan Versa Note. I get my body into the driver's seat and turn on the machine. This Japanese, let me tell you, handles itself much more smoothly than my previous cars, and driving it is a sheer delight.

The question is: Where should I drive from here? A little history might help.

The decision to create the United Nations was made in no other place than the United States. To be more exact: California. To be even more exact: San Francisco. Many years ago, long before smoking was outlawed, the charter of the United Nations was signed in San Francisco. To be specific: June 26, 1945. Three years later, this United Nations adopted the Universal Declaration of Human Rights, a declaration that is a major part of today's Western thinking.

I think I should make my acquaintance with San Francisco.

I reach San Francisco via the Golden Gate Bridge. I used to think that the Brooklyn Bridge in New York was the finest of the world's bridges. No way, Jose! This Golden Gate Bridge is majestic in comparison, a bridge that seems to never end. But it does, after 1.7 miles.

As I drive I notice all the Spanish names in this part of America, San this and San that. This part of America used to be a Spanish colony and its people celebrate the colonizers. Sorry, Indians. You should be happy that the president named a mountain in your honor; that's more than enough.

Driving in San Francisco, let me tell you, comes with a price: San Francisco's drivers. They are creatures whose vocabularies are missing one word: patience. I'm new to the city and I want to take in the view, and so I drive a little slow. Oh boy, these people hate it! They honk their horns as if World War III had just erupted. Cool it, folks!

San Francisco, may I share another detail with you, has a little problem, an old elephant that won't leave the room: homeless people, mostly black. It is sad to see the many poor, black poor, in this rich country.

I give up driving here. I park the car near my hotel, which is downtown, and go for a walk. There are many similarities between this city and Manhattan: constant traffic, privileged rich and a high cost of living. I meet people who pay $3,000 a month for a one-bedroom apartment, not including household expenses such as utilities.

At the base of my hotel, a four-star hotel, homeless black people are gearing up for a night's sleep. My hotel is near Union Square, a major shopping area, and the stench of urine fills the air. The sidewalks are shockingly dirty, reminding me of the poorest towns in the Third World.

Is this America? Finely dressed people, the kind you would encounter at high-class charity events, pass by but fail to notice the poor lying by their feet. The only poor they do see are the prostitutes, who are picked up by some of them and taken into nearby hotels. San Francisco, as seen here, is home to two kinds of people: the rich and the homeless.

I go up to my hotel room and turn the TV on. The TV unit is exquisitely beautiful. I love its design, color, look, feel and its overall appeal. But then comes content. Not one of the channels offers anything remotely interesting. How can so many channels be so boring?

Who writes this awful stuff? We are in an age, a thought creeps into my mind, of genius packagers and retarded writers.

I go to sleep. My dreams are usually more intriguing than what I can expect to find on the screen.

• • •

Early the next morning I read the news. This comes from the *New York Times*: "Austrian officials said that 6,500 migrants, many of them from Syria, had reached Austria by Saturday afternoon, and at least 2,200 were already on their way to Germany."

Wonderful Austrians. They sell their Glock pistols to American stores so that gangs in Minneapolis and other parts of the United States can kill each other with ease, but within their own borders they are so great and so humane. Elsewhere I read that Germany will accept 800,000 refugees this year, most of them Syrians, and perhaps even more.

Did I mention the Germans are extreme? America agreed to take ten thousand refugees, but Germany is shooting for a million.

For Germans, this is a great boost for their image. Long despised for the horrors that their country inflicted on Jews and others during World War II, Germans have a constant, dire need to be absolved. In reality, almost everybody out there loves the Germans, but the Germans are not sure that this is deeply rooted and fear that everyone else could turn against them at any second. They have not yet convinced the world, they think, how great they really are.

Enter the Syrians. The civil war in Syria, which has produced countless refugees roaming the earth in search of shelter, is a golden opportunity for the Germans to show the world that they care for others and that they are a great nation, and better than any other. The whole world lets the refugees drop dead in the sand or drown at sea, but Germany, only Germany, shows compassion. People worldwide take notice, and everybody with a heart praises the Germans.

Germany is also one of the biggest weapons manufacturers in the world, but almost nobody is paying attention to this little detail right now.

Frankly, I'm happy I'm not in Germany these days. Last time the people in Germany felt so good about themselves, during the years of the Reich, it didn't end up nicely.

In a funny way, the only ones who remember those years are some Syrian refugees. They are the ones who, upon reaching Germany, had this polite request: Could you show me to the Adolf Hitler museum? In their minds, the Germans are great because they killed so many Jews in the last century, and they, the refugees, want to show their appreciation to their German hosts by honoring the Führer.

I go downstairs to have a smoke. A young black lady carrying an iPhone approaches me. "Hey, baby," she asks, "want to hang out?"

Thanks, I tell her; not now. She moves on to the next baby.

I take another puff out of my cigarette, and two black ladies approach me. "Hi, Sexy. Want to have good time?" one of them asks.

Next time, my dears.

I pray that this not be the fate of the Syrian refugees in Germany. It is quite easy to open the gates of your country to foreigners, but it's a totally different story once they are in. It will take years upon years of love and dedication to help the refugees forget the dark past and march, ever so cautiously and patiently, toward a brighter future. Is Germany built for it? This sexy man doesn't know.

• • •

I go to the Castro District, also known as the Castro. Built by German, Irish and Scandinavian immigrants well over a century ago, over the years it has turned into something else altogether. Referred to by some as "the gayest spot on earth," the Castro is a neighborhood known worldwide for its gay residents and its gay activism.

Once I, Sexy, arrive, my eyes catch sight of naked people roaming around, parading their genitals for all to see. It's an interesting sight to behold: young and old in the nude, surrounded by people with various signs which read, in part: "Gay 4 Pay is Okay," "Free Hugs, Cheap Sex," "Stop the War on Whores," "My Body, My Rules" and "My Friends Are Sex Workers." One man, dressed like some sort of priest and calling himself Sister Merry Peter, walks around with a Whole Foods bag and collects money, while in the background various speakers charge the audience with lofty messages.

Whole Foods is a nationwide chain of grocery stores that has earned the "liberal" badge. I'm not sure why; perhaps due to the store's policy of supplying only paper, not plastic bags, because plastic is bad for the environment.

Who are you? I ask the "priest."

"I am a sister of perpetual indulgence. We are an international order of queer nuns who work to liberate the community from shame and guilt and to help everyone find their own unique joy."

Do you believe in the Virgin Mary?

"Honey, there are so many Virgin Marys and I don't have time to believe in all of them."

Do you believe in the Son of God?

"Of course I do, my darling! I meet him every Tuesday on the corner for coffee, and usually we spend our time bitching about what happened the night before, and that whore Virgin Mary. She was a long-suffering mother."

I love this sister!

Why are these people here, these priests and nudists? A few days ago the Department of Homeland Security, a government body tasked with protecting America from terror attacks and other breaches of public security, shut down a website called rentboy.com and arrested its operators.

Rentboy, which was in operation for about two decades, specialized in matching gay escorts and their rich male clients. Why the US government decided to close them down, and why now, is anybody's guess. My guess is this: young, attractive males emit too many dangerous gasses into the atmosphere. The gathering here, a demonstration, is aimed at getting the website back on and its operators cleared of all charges.

No matter what the government thinks, I like the Castro. The people here are spirited souls and, like many persecuted minorities, these gays have developed a great sense of humor – and I adore it. Yes, not every gay is funny, but collectively they have created a "fun" environment, which is absolutely refreshing.

Within minutes, I join the fun. I pick up some of the handmade posters and fly them high and higher. Standing near me is a lady who calls herself "slut." I talk with her a bit, and she explains to me the act of prostitution in legal terms, as if I really care to know. "Penal Code 647b," she says, is the law against prostitution in California.

"At first, prostitution was illegal on the basis of solicitation," but later on the government expanded the law to include agreeing to prostitution. She goes on and on and on, detailing the history of law and of prostitution, how they relate and don't relate, and a whole host of other issues. She is, no doubt, the most intellectual prostitute in history.

Gypsy, a forty-six-year-old mother of three, walks around in full nudity and tells me that she is here "in support of this demonstration for the rights of the sex workers. They deserve to be treated just like anyone else and should not be treated as criminals."

Are you personally part of the sex industry?

"I used to be. I used to be a stripper as well. And I shoot pornography."

Are you lesbian?

"No. Straight as a board."

On the other side of the street is Mr. Pam. Needless to say, being that this is the Castro, Mr. Pam is in reality a woman, known among the faithful as Gay Porn Mama. She is a bit overweight, ever smiling, and she tells me that "I'm a proud and passionate gay pornographer." She was raised Catholic, and still is, because "you can never really escape Catholicism."

How was your first porno movie? How did it feel? "Amazing!"

What's more fun, gay or lesbian films?

"With boys, you know when it ends. They ejaculate and it's done. With girls, I don't know when it's ending."

How about straight porn?

"I've never shot straight porn because I like watching it."

Ah, so you are bisexual. Why not shoot straight sex?

"It would be too distracting. I would want to jump in! I would get jealous!"

I finally found myself some liberals, the real deal. I like these Americans!

Across the street is a gas station, where they charge $3.89 per gallon. In Wisconsin I paid $2.29 a gallon. When I point this out to the people here, nobody is upset. As far as they are concerned, the government and businesses can charge whatever they want as long as they, the people, will be able to rent a boy by the hour.

What else is new today? Another in a series of Jewish lawmakers, Democratic National Committee chairwoman Debbie Wasserman Schultz, announced that she would support the Iran deal.

The Iran deal is likely to have enough support in Congress that soon it will probably be a reality. Rentboy is a security risk – Iran is not. Pastor John of CUFI should relax and come down here to have some fun. We have a priest here, why not a pastor?

• • •

My Versa likes to move – that's why she is a car. Today she takes me to Palo Alto, California. Goodbye San Francisco, hello Palo Alto.

I park and walk around to acquaint myself with the people and the place.

The late Steve Jobs, founder of the Apple company, lived in this neighborhood before he passed away – which tells me about the kind of people living here. There are some very nice houses in this Palo Alto, which I can view only from the outside. Some of these houses, I'm told, go for as little as $10 million apiece.

And it is here in Palo Alto that I meet two Stanford students: she has a PhD in engineering, and he will get his PhD next year. Both are cool. Very cool. "If you are educated, if you are a scientist," the male says, "you would no doubt be a progressive liberal." The female agrees. Both – what a big shocker – believe in climate change and are pro-Palestine.

I drive to Stanford University. I want to see where they raise such educated, scientific people. What a gorgeous place! A great park, beautiful buildings and – how grateful I am – no stench of urine. Fabulous!

Unlike Berkeley, Stanford has not started the semester yet. I try to enter some of the buildings, but only the ghosts respond. An exception is Stanford's Hillel chapter, the Taube Hillel House. Hillel is a Jewish student organization, and I guess the Jews like to work a bit harder than the others.

I walk in. A lady sits next to a desk, and behind her is a puppy lying in a cage. It's some kind of German dog, and she says that a similar dog used to chase Jews in World War II. She loves her dog and she brings him to work so that he is not home alone.

With her in the room are a few students, all Jews. Is this chapter reddish or bluish? I ask them.

Oops. It's a forbidden question around here, and all present, besides the Nazi dog, immediately feel uncomfortable.

These are the real Frozen Chosen. Only under repeated questioning, and afraid that yours truly will send dogs to chase them if they don't reply, do they say that in the past Hillel had hosted leftist speakers and that they do not recall any instance of a right-leaning speaker showing up here.

So, you are blue. Right?

They are offended by this question and, fearful that I'll ask more, they all leave.

I leave as well and try to find some other creatures around here. Next to a fraternity house with a funny name, I meet some students, none Jewish, and they tell me that I can ask them any question I want as long as I promise that at the end of the conversation there will be some beer.

That's the spirit. I love it! But where the hell am I going to get beer?

Top of the news today in major American media: 1. Germany will spend $6.7 billion on the refugees. 2. A Palestinian woman in the West Bank died at the hand of Israelis.

• • •

California is blue, and San Francisco is bluer than blue, but Republican presidential candidate and retired neurosurgeon Ben Carson will appear tomorrow in San Francisco. I am curious to hear him.

I drive to the Commonwealth Club of California, which is "the nation's oldest and largest public affairs forum," according to its literature, to hear and see the man in person. What is a nice guy like you doing in a race like this? the moderator, a local journalist, asks Ben.

"Well that's a very good question," Ben replies. He tells us that following a certain National Prayer Breakfast, "there were so many people clamoring for me to run for president, which I thought was kind of a ridiculous idea, but I kept running into particularly elderly

Americans who would tell me they had given up on America and they were just waiting to die," and so he decided to run.

I have no idea what he's talking about, but he talks. He tells us about his life. "My mother was trying to get me to wear something I didn't want to wear, I picked up a hammer, went to hit her in the head with it. Fortunately, my brother caught it from behind. Other than that, I was a pretty good kid."

I think he and Shanta would get along well, as both love hammers.

Ben has no charisma, and even when he says the most stupid line it falls flat. When this man talks, sorry to say, I find myself fighting hard not to fall asleep. If he becomes president, I'll become a neurosurgeon.

I am ready to leave California. Where should I go next?

I pick Hawaii, a state with a unique American history: the attack on Pearl Harbor.

I drop off my Versa at the airport and take a flight to Hawaii. On the plane I read that Senator Richard Blumenthal of Connecticut, who is Jewish, announced his support for the Iran deal, effectively ensuring that this deal will not be rejected by the Senate. In other words: the Iran deal is now a certainty. Do I care? No. Nobody on his way to Hawaii cares about Iranians. It's Hawaii!

Gate Fifteen

Smoking is permitted while standing in the
middle of the road in moving traffic

HAWAII, THE REMOTEST GROUP OF ISLANDS IN THE WORLD AND THE wettest dream of surfers and of honeymooners, waits for her lost son, me, to enter into her womb.

Hawaii, by the way, is the youngest American state. It became the United States' fiftieth state only in 1959. And I can't wait to see the young lady. I'm to land at Hawaii's busiest and most populous island, Oahu, and my first destination is the Waikiki section of the capitol city, Honolulu. Waikiki is where most Hawaii tourists end up and where most of Oahu's hotels and shopping centers wait to please the esteemed guests.

I follow the crowd.

My first impression as I get out of the belly of the plane and breathe the air of this tropical island is that Hawaii is not America. There's this "aloha" all over, a word that's not exactly English. Second impression: Hawaii is not a state but a bakery. It's hot here, it's humid; it's a nuclear melting pot.

Hawaii, I hear, has the bluest of bloods and is thoroughly democratic. Its elected officials, senators and members of Congress, and its governor and lieutenant governor are all Democrats. Hey, Barack Obama was born here.

243

Hawaii, I'm also told by people at the airport, is about 40 percent Asian. What déjà vu! Am I in UC Berkeley land?

Whatever the case, I rent a Nissan Versa Note again. In Asia, be Asian.

I turn the AC on and cool off. So good! Maybe that's why people come all the way to Hawaii.

I drive a bit but after a while, as happens with all good things, the ride comes to an end and when I reach the hotel I get out of Versa. I hope it's a good hotel. Good or not, it's very liberal. Progressive liberal. As proof of its ultra-liberal tendencies, the stern lady at the front desk forces me to sign that I'm well aware that if I smoke in my room or on the balcony I will be charged $425.

I walk out to have a cigarette on the beach, which is across the street. I forgot that I'm in an all-liberal state. There are huge No Smoking signs every few steps along the beach and the sidewalk that runs parallel to it.

I follow the signs, in hope that they end somewhere, but they don't. I cross the street, and there are more No Smoking signs next to anything that was built by man, such as hotels and stores. I must be a safe distance from each and any of them if I want to smoke, the signs say.

Having studied mathematics, I decide to measure the exact location of legally permissible smoking areas in Waikiki. It takes a long study, and after much sweat and multiple measurements I have the answer: legally permissible smoking areas are exactly in the middle of the street, in between lanes, in moving traffic. What's the logic in it? Hawaii wants all smokers dead before they light up.

I choose life and I light up on the sidewalk, right by a bloody red No Smoking sign. Some righteous nonsmokers tell me that I'm in a no-smoking zone and I tell them: No speak English, speak Romanian. They leave me alone. Suckers.

• • •

Pearl Harbor.

Hawaii has a unique place in the hearts of Americans. It is in this state that America was attacked by a foreign power, a rare occurrence in the country's history. It happened on December 7, 1941, when Japan attacked the US naval base at Pearl Harbor, a short ride from here.

I ask my Versa if she will be willing to take me there, given the conflict of interests, but the Japanese says yes.

During the attack a number of US battleships sank and their sailors died on the spot. The USS *Arizona*, one of those ships, was not raised from the sea and to this day it is the last resting place of over one thousand American sailors.

As might be expected, a museum has cropped up in the area. I walk in and join a group of tourists for a ride on a ferry to the monument built above these sailors' remains. A park ranger, formerly with the navy, greets us. "Any questions?" he asks.

Yes, I say. Since when is this part of the world America?

"Hawaii became a state in 1959. Before that, at the time of the Japanese attack, it was a US Territory."

How did it become a territory?

"This is a complicated issue."

Give it to me simple.

"Hawaii was taken by the US illegally. There used to be a monarchy here, but America overthrew the monarchy, put the Hawaiian queen under arrest, and that was it."

Go slow, my friend. Tell me the whole story!

"I suggest you go to the Iolani Palace to learn more."

I do.

• • •

Iolani Palace was actually destroyed, which means that what I see here is a restored palace, a replica. Iolani Palace is a beautiful place regardless, and it tells a history.

Here's the Cliff Notes version. Once upon a time there was a kingdom called the Kingdom of Hawaii. One day good, white Christian missionaries came by to share Jesus with the Hawaiians and, one thing leading to the other, lots of blood was spilled and the American State of Hawaii was born.

Here I also learn of the Queen's Letter of Protest, in which the queen of Hawaii resigned under protest in order to avoid the spilling of more blood, hoping against all hope that the throne would soon be restored. But this did not happen. What was restored is this building, this museum.

Yet it is here that a sense of history overwhelms me and a picture takes shape in front of my eyes: the United States annexed this island because, as the Air Force guy in the Irish pub in New York told me, "because we can."

Fast-forward a century plus and you are in the present. In today's Hawaii the descendants of the butchers, those who in cold blood murdered people and obliterated their culture, proclaim utmost love for the original culture that once stood proud here. They say a thousand alohas a day in hotels and shopping malls, all for the sake of making huge profits off their ancestors' crimes.

And they know it. In 1993 the US Congress (Public Law 103-150) apologized to the Hawaiian people for the illegal acts done by the American government in regard to Hawaii. The resolution passed both the House and the Senate and was signed into law by President Bill Clinton. The resolution states in part:

> The Congress…apologizes to Native Hawaiians on behalf of the people of the United States for the overthrow of the Kingdom of Hawaii on January 17, 1893, with the participation of agents and citizens of the United States, and the deprivation of the rights of Native Hawaiians to self-determination.

In other words: the United States admits that it had illegally seized this land. Is the United States planning to withdraw from Hawaii? The answer comes at the end of the resolution: "Nothing in this Joint

Resolution is intended to serve as a settlement of any claims against the United States." I love Bill! Such a fine touch!

Outside the palace I see a man named Kalani, a homeless Hawaiian, and he rages against America. Justice will come one day, he tells me, and America will repent for its crime of annexing this island.

When will this happen?

"Next year!"

Yep, of course.

• • •

The largest shopping mall in Honolulu, I'm told, is the Ala Moana Center. I drive there. On my first few steps into the mall I pass a number of kiosks, which are strategically located in the passages and corridors leading to regular stores. Quite a number of these kiosks, as in many other malls in the United States, are operated by young Israelis who will sell you everything no breathing human needs. Here in Hawaii they sell skirts that turn into shirts, underwear that turns into dresses, Dead Sea oils that will turn you into a teenager and perfumes made from diamonds.

Japanese tourists love these *shmontses*. I usually ignore these Israelis, but somehow now I feel like stopping for a moment. Are you getting rich here? I ask an Israeli lady who is in her seventh year in Hawaii.

"This is a very complex and complicated question," she answers me and, sadly, she has no time to talk. She's busy with an old Japanese lady who, I think, wants to become a young Chinese.

Most of these young Israelis are right-wingers. They believe that Israel should fight as hard as possible against the Palestinians, while they sell diamond perfumes in Hawaii. Overall, these Israelis strike me as a bunch of Ali Baba's thieves. It is quite likely that their Dead Sea products come from Bangladesh.

• • •

Hawaii is at its most stunning outside the tourist areas. I drive for days on the island of Oahu and can't get enough of its beauty. But it's not until my last evening in Hawaii that I get a fuller, much more realistic picture of life in this state. A local resident, who happens to be an Orthodox Jew, asks me if I'd like to go with him on a ride, away from the Japanese buyers and far from the island's diamond perfumes, to see the real face of Honolulu. "It's gonna be tough," he says.

Let's go, I say.

Orthodox Jews, unlike most of their non-Orthodox brethren, are people who are proud of being Jewish, and they have enough room in their psyches to care about other people as well. Not that all Orthodox Jews care, just as it wouldn't be true to say that all non-Orthodox don't care, but those who care among the Orthodox don't just pay lip service when they talk of those who are less fortunate than themselves. They don't have to play this game, because they don't care what other people think of them to start with. For them, "poor" does not mean some "Palestinian" out there on the other side of the planet, but real poor living next to them.

We drive in the direction of the non-Palestinian poor of Hawaii. It's a ride to hell. The hellish site is a city within a city, a state within a state, a reality within a reality. It's called an "encampment." This encampment, my guide tells me, is just one of a number of encampments in Hawaii.

What's an encampment? I let my eyes answer. Lines of tents, one after another, on both sides of the road, packed with people who have no home, no address, no future and hardly a life. Here are the voiceless and the forgotten: American citizens, seniors and infants, men and women, all members of the Red Zone Society of America.

I make my acquaintance with some of them, and they break my heart. Here are little kids, and here are old people. Some are less than one year of age, and some are quite old, but all are deep into homelessness and most will likely never get out of it.

The current American president, who was raised on this island and loves to vacation in it, did not come to the world the way these kids did. He went to a private school in a nice part of town, while these kids go to no school. Their school, so to speak, is a life amidst piles of garbage.

Here's a man, born in American Samoa, who identifies himself as "Mad Dog." I ask him to explain to me what my eyes see, but he tells me what they don't: "No white people here."

Whites, he tells me, don't even pass by here. And if they happened to pass by, for whatever reason, they don't stop to chat. Mad Dog is touched by the simple act of my standing next to him, touching him, shaking his hand and wanting to hear him out.

"I'm not a homeless," he says, with the little pride that is still in him. "I am a houseless."

First and foremost, he faults himself. Pointing at a bottle of beer, from which he drinks, he says: "I wouldn't be here if not for this."

How much do you drink?

"Two packs of eighteen."

Thirty-six bottles a day! How do you get the money for it? And how can you drink so much?

Emotionally taken by the mere fact that I show interest in him and in his life, he tells me his story. For starters, he got out of prison just recently. In Oklahoma.

To make a long story short, the authorities in Hawaii prefer to save money on imprisoned people and they contract out-of-state private prison companies – yes, those exist in America – to "host" their prisoners.

The way this works is very interesting. When a man – or a woman – gets a prison term, the authorities dress him up nicely, put him on a commercial plane, and fly him to a prison of their choice, depending on which private prison they have a contract with, and the prisoner serves his time there. When he is released, the authorities dress him nicely once more and fly him back. The private prison business, by the way, is one of the fastest-growing businesses in the country.

What crime did you commit?

"Selling dope."

You served your sentence and you are back in Hawaii. Are you back into selling dope?

"You drink beer with me, ah?"

I will.

He gives me a bottle.

There are between five hundred and one thousand people living in tents from Ala Moana Boulevard to the ocean and the JABSOM medical school nearby, depending on how many the authorities have been able to kick out of here in the last sweep. Yes, they do this here. From time to time the authorities, who want to make sure that no tourist encounters the poor, come and make a "sweep," during which they push the people out and sweep their tents away.

Number of children here today: between fifty and seventy. Mad Dog spends an awful lot on beer, but he doesn't drink by himself. He gives free bottles to others in this encampment, as he has just done with me.

Are you a proud American? I ask Mad Dog.

"I love America, but I'm not proud to be an American. In America you can be the biggest criminal, but you will be acquitted in court if you have money for a good lawyer."

Are you happy that Barack Obama is America's president?

"I'm happy that a brown man made it to be a president."

Do you think he cares about you?

Somehow, I don't know why, this question touches a chord in him. He doesn't talk. He pauses. He looks around, up, and then at me. He is emotional now. "You honored me by being here and I won't lie to you," he says before answering this last question. And then he does: "That motherfucker doesn't care a fuck about me."

Mad Dog's wife comes by and pats him on his shoulders. She loves him. I look at them and at the little kids strolling by. I want to cry.

I hug the man, as tight as I can – and I leave.

The United States of America, and the European and the Asian rich who by vacationing here perpetuate the homeless catastrophe, never looked so bad to me as they do at this very moment. Sorry. If not for them, no sweeps would be made here and housing on the island would be affordable. But do they care? No. They want a shirt that turns into a skirt. Period.

Some tourists celebrate their wedding anniversaries here. They would do better to celebrate the funeral of their spirit.

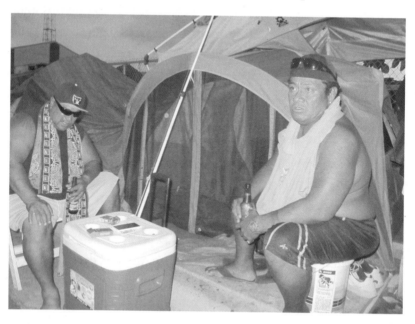

• • •

Before the night is over – what a strange day, today – I meet a Jewish professor, a transplant to Hawaii from California, in a local non-touristic restaurant outside of Waikiki. Smart, sharp, well-versed and knowledgeable, she speaks about her life as if she were talking about another person, not herself.

Year after year, she tells me, those in charge at her university in California tried to force her to lecture on Yom Kippur, the holiest day on the Jewish calendar, and a day when most Jews take off work. So she moved to Hawaii, where she is teaching at a local university, and on Yom Kippur she'll take off.

"Hawaii is the least anti-Semitic state in the Union," she says. Not that they terribly love Jews here, but for Hawaiians the Jews are just another kind of "whites," whom they collectively refer to as *haole*, meaning a person without soul.

What an improvement!

As the clock keeps moving and we get one fish dish after another, I ask her: Is it true that Berkeley's professors are anti-Jewish or anti-Israel?

As far as she remembers, she tells me, there are nine professors there who have expressed anti-Jewish or anti-Israel views. Chancellor Nicholas Dirks, take notice!

Some of the intellectuals I met think that this year is the hottest on record, and they were all too happy to share this piece of information with me. This lady is an intellectual like them but she does not strike me as a progressive liberal, and so I'm interested to know what she thinks.

"The climate records that we have," she says, "are limited, telling us a small fraction of the whole story. For example, quite a few years ago there was a spell of extremely hot weather in California, and it was followed by a very cold spell. We don't know what caused it then and we don't know what causes it now. We don't have enough data.

'Climate change' today is a religion, and like the existence of God you cannot prove it and you cannot disprove it. It's all a matter of faith."

Aloha.

• • •

An email:

> Friend,
>
> I just made it to Simi Valley, California for tonight's GOP (Republican) debate and, like so many folks here, I couldn't be more excited for these Republicans to get up on that stage and tell us what they really feel. I mean, I can say so much about how bad their policies are, but there's nothing more convincing than hearing it straight from the horse's mouth.
>
> Debbie Wasserman Schultz
> Chair, Democratic National Committee

These two groups, the Democrats and the Republicans, really hate each other.

And I go to Utah to see America's most ridiculed: the Mormons. I leave behind the ninety-one-degree weather of Honolulu and fly to the forty-six-degree Salt Lake City. The weather should have been much warmer, since climate change does not stop in Alaska or Hawaii, but in the state of the Mormons the weather is more cautious in playing its tricky games.

Gate Sixteen

The most beautiful teenagers are Mormon

FIRST THING I NOTICE IS THAT SALT LAKE CITY IS MOST LIKELY NOT BLUE. THE evidence is right there at the airport terminal: people can smoke inside the building, in designated areas. This is something that in New York you can only dream of.

This is not New York. This is another world. Mormons. Joseph Smith. Polygamy. *The Book of Mormon*. These are just some of the sound bites associated with this city and this state. Sixty-two percent of the people in this state are Mormons. Who are the Mormons? I go out to look for them.

A stroll around Temple Square and its vicinity in downtown Salt Lake City reveals the most beautiful young girls in the most modest of dresses, the handsomest young boys with the most heavenly of smiles, the cleanest of parking garages worldwide, the finest of flowers on any street anywhere, the nicest of buildings, the most welcoming of shopping malls – and all this I've gleaned in my first ten minutes.

These perfect people are Mormons. The buildings and the properties belong to them. Who are the Mormons? The Mormons, the smiling beauties tell me, are Christians. As simple as that.

Not Mormons?

Mormons, they say, is just a nickname.

What's the real name?

Latter-day Saints. These young beauties, I must admit, indeed look like saints, like the beautiful saints in the Sistine Chapel in Vatican City. The only difference between them is that there the beauties are painted on the walls; here they are in the flesh.

Have I entered the Islamic paradise with its motherlode of sexy virgins? I wish. This is not Arabia; this is Utah.

These young, the beautiful and the handsome, come in every color. What you could call diversity.

Which makes me think. In virtually every state I've been to thus far, people bragged about the "diversity" in their state, but none included "Mormons" in the list of their diverse groups. In fact, for many a year America's most elite cultural figures have poked fun at the Mormons in a way in which none would even dream to treat Muslims, for example. Witness America's theatrical shows, such as the satirical *The Book of Mormon* or Tony Kushner's *Angels in America*, that present Mormonism in the worst light possible.

There's a word for them: hypocrites.

In any case, the beauties here direct me to halls and buildings, to books and missionaries, where I am treated like a king in the hope that I, too, become a man nicknamed Mormon. "Mormon" is derived from the name of an angel named Moroni who one day came to visit a nineteenth-century American by the name of Joseph Smith and led him to golden plates buried in the earth, upon which were written in Reformed Egyptian the book that Joseph later translated, set down and called *Book of Mormon*.

That's the story, the official story. What's "Reformed Egyptian"? Nobody knows. In what temple or museum may one take a look at the golden plates? None. Why? Because the angel took them with him.

Similar to Jesus and his grave. You can't see it, because it's not there.

Joseph Smith, born in 1805 and assassinated in 1844, is the founder of the Mormon religion, which today, according to Church sources, numbers fifteen million followers. This American-founded religion has more members than there are Jews.

Well, not exactly. For the most part, Mormons are direct descendants of Ephraim, son of Joseph from the biblical account of the twelve tribes of Israel, while the Jews are mostly the descendants of the tribe of Judah, the brother of Joseph. In short, both Jew and

Mormon come from the biblical Abraham, Joseph's and Judah's great-grandpa, who happened to be the first Jew of history. In other words, Mormons and Jews are Israelites, meaning that both are Jewish.

How do I know that Mormons have anything to do with Ephraim? Well, they write it. Here's an example, from a 1923 publication called *The Improvement Era*: "The great majority of those who become members of the Church are literal descendants of Abraham through Ephraim, son of Joseph."

And now it's time to go over some basics. Mormons are members of the Church of Jesus Christ of Latter-day Saints (LDS), and the LDS in Utah has a PR department, whose people assigned two members of their team to teach me much about these Israelites. Jesus Christ, they inform me, appeared in the Americas after his resurrection. Love it! No Christian alive or dead has ever come up with a more convincing reason as to why Jesus had to be resurrected. Until Joseph Smith. And he came up with this idea in his twenties.

Like Jesus, this founder of religion was quite young when he changed the world.

• • •

As Christianity is kind of Judaism Plus, Mormonism is Christianity Plus. These "plusses" change a religion from A to Z, but it's important not to forget their roots.

Mormons don't believe in the Trinity, the PR pros also tell me, and they don't pray to Jesus. They believe, as they explain to me, that God the father, God the son and God the Holy Ghost are separate beings.

The Trinity, if you were not raised on it, doesn't make much sense. And Mormonism, in many ways, "fixes" and "improves" those parts that are illogical or problematic in Christianity, just as Christianity has tried to do with Judaism, for example, by replacing God's destroyed temple in Jerusalem with the Son of God.

Another Mormon improvement on Christianity is "proxy baptism," meaning posthumous baptism. How does it work?

It is explained to me by various believers in the antechamber of the Salt Lake Temple, while I stand facing a scale model of the Temple structure. Down below the Temple, the baptismal bath stands over twelve oxen, symbolizing the twelve tribes of Israel. There, a living person assumes the identity of a dead person and, fully clothed, jumps into the bath and turns the dead person into a Mormon. Something like that.

I want to see it taking place in practice but I'm not allowed to enter the Temple proper. To be more exact: no one is allowed into the Temple unless they have a "recommend" card. I have a Visa card, but the guards, dressed all in white like doctors in lab coats, do not accept Visa. They want Recommend. How could I get such a card? Well, I have to become Mormon first, and then have a distinguished member of the community recommend me.

I try to get the PR folks to recommend me, except the guards seem not to believe that PR people have the credentials to undertake anything sacred.

To those who believe in Jesus, proxy baptism is actually a great idea. Most Christians believe that people who have not been baptized in life will not enter paradise, which is a very cruel idea. Think of the dead infants or people who, let's say, died on their way to be baptized. Isn't this cruel?

Thank heaven for Mormons!

It is for this reason that Mormons have invested millions upon millions of dollars in genealogy centers around the globe: to baptize the dead. You see, to baptize the dead you have to know their names. And for this, you need computers with loads of data.

For the most part, non-Mormons don't have an issue with such centers, but there are exceptions. Jews, for example.

Historically, Jews have been murdered in greater numbers than most other peoples. In just the last century, six million of them were slaughtered in a mere few years. Which, as you might guess, is a good reason to keep many Mormons very, very busy.

And indeed, for many years the Mormons quarreled with the Jews over the Mormons' practice of baptizing Jewish victims of the Holocaust, effectively Mormonizing millions of dead Jews. But after a long-lasting dispute with American Jewish organizations, LDS gave its word that no proxy baptism would ever take place again.

Do they keep their word? Maybe yes, maybe no.

I schlep the polished LDS PR people to the Family History Library across the street from Temple Square. There, I have been told, records of deceased people and the dates of their baptisms can be found. As we walk in, an LDS attendant shows me to a chair in a room packed with computers. I sit down and type the name of my deceased great-grandfather, a founder of a Hasidic dynasty in Poland. Believe it or not, the Mormons baptized him.

The faces of the two PR people turn white, but I'm not here to torture them. I turn to them, stretch my hand out and say: Shake, please, the hand of your Mormon brother.

If I had to sum up my experiences today, they would be very simple: the Mormons are Jews, and I am a Mormon.

The funniest element of this summation is that each one of us, as far as I know, is fully sober. The only drink I've had today is Diet Coke; Mormons are not allowed to have any alcohol, not to mention coffee, tea, cola, tobacco or cannabis.

• • •

Outside, there is a bank called Zions Bank. It originated, like everything here, with Joseph Smith, who one day decided that Zion actually refers to America.

How did he get the idea that Zion should be in America? Mormons, you should first know, believe in the Bible, in which the word *Zion* appears more than one hundred times. (That's where you get *Zionist* from.) Zion is in Israel, but Joseph Smith had a different idea in mind. Zion is not in the Middle East – Zion is here.

Based on Mormon writings, it seems that Joseph Smith mistranslated the word *Zion* to mean "the pure in heart," and Mormons are pure in heart, as everybody knows. And they are in America.

Bingo.

His translation, sorry, is not even close. But Joseph Smith is far from being the only one guilty of mistranslation. Mistranslations of Hebrew occur also in the New Testament, and to date billions of people do not know it.

Are the Mormons Christian? At the core of Mormon faith and doctrine, which the Mormons would rather not share with strangers, is this one-liner, composed many years ago by the fifth Mormon prophet, Lorenzo Snow: "As man is, God once was; as God is, man may become." This idea, that God was once a man, makes Mormonism unique in the monotheistic world, though it is figuratively similar to the Christian notion of Son of God in the form of man.

Whatever the case, I ask the PR people if they could connect me with someone higher up in the church hierarchy. They say that, very sadly and unfortunately, nobody higher up is available for the foreseeable future. In PR lingo, this means: "Over my dead body!" They really, really don't want me to see any higher-ups.

Why? Because this is what PR is about: hide the higher-ups from the probing eyes of journalists. More or less what my smoking partner told me in Chicago.

Between you and me, the LDS establishment reminds me of the Obama administration. Both attach me to beautiful ladies and handsome men, and both try to make sure that every step I make is supervised.

As far as I see it, PR is America's biggest disease; and the better a PR team is, the worse the outcome. Faced with well-oiled PR machinery such as that of this hugely successful religion, or of the White House, I do my best to circumvent the system.

And so I finagle my way into the office of William Atkins, LDS legal genius. What I want to know is just a little detail. Jews have been telling me that Mormons strongly support Israel, yet the Mormon Church keeps quiet about it. I want to know what the real story is.

William's official title is associate general counsel, and he was the one who delivered the Church's response to the Supreme Court's decision to allow gay marriage: "I think you're going to see a rapid development in erosion of religious freedoms," he said in a speech at Brigham Young University. Will William be as clear about Israel?

Being that we are both Jewish, or Mormon, I ask William why it is that the Mormons do not publicly support their Jewish sibling, Israel.

William answers that, as a matter of policy, the Church does not get involved in anything political.

You believe in the Bible, I remind him, and in the Bible it is written that God has given the Holy Land to the Jews. Correct or incorrect?

William, legal genius that he is, disagrees. First, he declares that "I love the Palestinians as people as much as I love the Israelis." This done, he answers my question: "No. The Holy Land was given by God to the twelve tribes."

The Jews come from the twelve tribes, right?

"*One* of the tribes!"

Well, that includes the Jews. No?

"Israelites!"

For him, I assume, this means that the "Holy Land" belongs to some kind of "Israelites" but not to the Jews. And so I point out to him that the name "Jews" actually appears in the Bible, for example in the Book of Esther, and that from the Bible's perspective "Israelites" and "Jews" are the same.

His initial response is: "Hmmm." Then there is a pause. And then he says: "The promises of the Holy Land were given to the House of Israel!"

Of the twelve tribes, ten were lost to history and only about two remain. Wouldn't you say? You, the Mormons, who come from the tribe of Ephraim, and the Jews, who come from the tribe of Judah. That's why they are called "Jews." And so, the Holy Land then belongs to the Mormons and the Jews but not to the Arabs. Isn't this so?

"The Jews are *co*-owners!"

When the other tribes reappear, if they do, they will be welcome to join, but as of now only the Jews, and the Mormons, remain of the twelve tribes. Right?

It is only at this point that this higher-up succumbs: "Yes. Legally God gave the land to the Jews."

Then, from a biblical perspective, the land does not belong to the Palestinians.

"No."

Why, then, will the Mormon Church not take a stand on this issue?

"Because some people don't believe that the current State of Israel represents the prophetic Jewish tribes."

Forget that. Theologically speaking, who should inherit the land?

"The theological answer: the Jews. But you can't take that and project it on politics."

Why not? Is the Mormon Church afraid to stand on the side of God?

It is here that William shows his genius. Of course, he says, God has given the land to the Jews, and this is also part of the Mormon faith, but LDS won't take a stand on the issue because the Church doesn't want to say that the "present government of Israel represents the Jewish people."

Forget the government; the government does not represent anybody. My question was, and is, about the people. Would LDS say in public that the "present people now living in Israel" – and I'm referring to the Jews here – live in a land that belongs to them? William has no answer. Not now. He says he'll get back to me. When will he get back to me? As far as I can tell, it will be at least one day after my great-grandfather rises from the dead as a Mormon.

So, here's my message to the Jews: If you believe that in time of need you can rely on the Mormons, forget it. But, for the record, the Mormons have no plans to demand the land. Their founder, Joseph Smith, took Zion with him to America.

As I am about to depart from William, he makes sure that I don't leave his office empty-handed. He gives me a typewritten book that details the history of his family from 1883 to 1967, and which includes poems and family pictures.

How sweet! Here's how one poem starts: "It was wonderful to wonder / In the place we called the Flat. T'was a little bit of heaven, / For a child with an old straw hat." A lovely man, this William!

• • •

I go to a service in a Mormon church, called a "ward," and watch in amusement as adult participants fill out attendance sheets. This church keeps its believers tight!

What's in the news today? Back at my hotel room, at the DoubleTree hotel, I turn on the TV, select CNN, and there I see the rebroadcast of the second Republican presidential debate. I didn't watch it while it took place, so I watch it now. Guess which word pops up over and over?

Israel.

As if these candidates were running for office in Jerusalem.

For whatever reason, "Israel" is deep on the mind of many Americans, as is the case with too many Europeans. Why is this? Ask Dr. Sigmund Freud. And if you meet him, if he's resurrected like Jesus Christ and Elvis Presley, I have another question that I would like you to ask him: Why is it that almost all of those who say that they believe in climate change are also pro-Palestine?

I keep hearing this from people, this bizarre relationship between the Israeli-Palestinian conflict and climate change, and am amazed every time anew.

In any case, Salt Lake City is beautiful but Moab is much nicer. Not that I have seen it yet; I'm just repeating here what some guy told me earlier today. What's in Moab? I asked him.

"The Arches Park right next to it," he answered.

He seemed like someone who knows what he's talking about, and I decide to trust him. I rent a car (yes, Versa again) and drive with the new Japanese to Moab.

•••

The ride from Salt Lake City to Moab is one of the loveliest I've driven in this country.

It's not the first time I've said this, right? It's a beautiful country, my dear, and I'm taken by it.

I drive past breathtaking red mountains, and then, right outside Moab, I enter the Arches National Park. Here's how the National Park Service describes the place, which it calls "a red rock wonderland":

> Discover a landscape of contrasting colors, landforms and textures unlike any other in the world...hundreds of soaring pinnacles, massive fins and giant balanced rocks. This red rock wonderland will amaze you with its formations, refresh you with its trails and inspire you with its sunsets.

What can I say? This is one of the few times that I've caught a government agency telling it like it is.

The Arches National Park is uplifting at almost every step. Driving and walking through it, one gets the impression that this country is a very ancient country. And indeed, it took untold number of years for these formations to take shape.

As I pass by them, they strike me as ancient archeological sites. Here, for example, is a "structure" that seems to be either a castle or a fortress, built well before the dinosaurs roamed the earth.

Some of the sandstone formations remind me of Middle Eastern landscapes. But this is not the Middle East. This is America. One hell of a gorgeous country, exceedingly rich in natural beauty. I have no more words. Get your ass up here to see it with your own eyes.

I keep on driving in this land of America, until I reach Dead Horse Point.

What a marvelous display of nature, this time in totally different form, captures my gaze! Here are huge chunks of earth in various shapes, not like fortresses but more like immense pieces of earth playing poker with each other.

Dazzling! It looks as if the earth opened, ages in the past, and its parts have shifted in all directions over the intervening centuries.

It may as well be called Mount Change.

• • •

The Hawaii professor is taking a day off tomorrow. It's Yom Kippur. What should I do on Yom Kippur? I have been to Mormon services in a ward, a Quaker meeting, and to Christian services; isn't it time I go to a Jewish service?

A person I hardly know (I only met her once before) invites me to come to Aspen, Colorado, a neighboring state to Utah. She's Jewish and she knows where the Jews are having their services.

Let's go to Colorado, Versa!

Gate Seventeen

If you were born on Easter Sunday, you can resurrect the dead

THE LANDSCAPES THAT I LEAVE BEHIND ME RESEMBLED ANCIENT architectural genius; the landscapes here, as I drive in Colorado, resemble paintings made by a master. As I arrive in Aspen it is just before the start of Yom Kippur, which begins after sundown.

Aspen's Jews are some of the most successful of American Jews, living in one of America's most desired locations: Aspen, the destination of the rich and famous. Naturally, I go to the largest Jewish congregation in Aspen, where the services on this day take place at the five-hundred-seat Harris Concert Hall, a place far nicer-looking than Chief Dull Knife College.

Well, these are Jews, not Indians.

And what Jews! Most of them are about the same age as Jesus would be, had he not been hung on a cross and were still alive. Young Jews are not here. Not that they are afraid to be outside after sunset; Aspen, Colorado is not Englewood, Illinois. Aspen is exactly 180 degrees from Englewood. But young Jews, what shocking news, are not interested in anything Jewish. They are off melting in a pot somewhere, in some hot American bakery.

Honestly, now that I'm here attending the service, I see you can't blame the young Jews. The service, in a word, sucks. The rabbi delivers a sermon about another rabbi who survived the death camps during the Holocaust, followed by a music selection that most likely originated in a concentration camp. And then, as if that were not enough, the rabbi thanks Germany for helping the Syrian refugees and for housing some of them in former concentration camps (which Germany is obviously doing).

All in all, this is a perfect funeral service for America's Judaism. I watch this service, which contains very few Jewish motifs, and wonder why these old people bothered to come here. There's very little of anything "Jewish" to this service. Like the Indians, very few here know their ancestors' language, in this case Hebrew, and the whole thing is so melted down that there is nothing to see and very little to hear. It's all empty of any meaning.

There is a comparable "melting" phenomenon between the German Americans and these Jews, with one difference: the Germans completed the melting cycle ages ago, and most of them no longer bother to be Germanic. The Jews are still in the process of eliminating their culture, but soon they will get there.

And until they are totally melted, some Americans will continue to be obsessed with them.

Especially the media. The American news magazine *Salon*, for example, published an article today in which it accuses the Israeli army of "cowardly brutality," claiming that an Israeli soldier squashed a Palestinian kid, and then it goes on to compare Israel to Nazi Germany in all but name.

At this particular date in history, when every day thousands of Arabs are murdered, violated, lose their homes and are abused by other Arabs in the ever-turbulent Middle East, it is interesting to read this story of one Arab kid supposedly suffering at the hands of one Jew. Ten, twenty years ago an article like this would have been published in a KKK magazine.

The times they are a-changin', as the Bob Dylan song goes.

• • •

The next day, I go to see nature. Luckily, nature is the one entity in America that is not forced into a melting pot to evaporate. I drive in the direction of the Maroon Bells, two peaks in the Elk Mountains, which are about a dozen miles from the city of Aspen.

The ride up into the mountainous area facing the Maroon Bells is nature in its most masterful display of color: green, red, yellow, brown, maroon, turquoise, gold, white, gray and pink – and this is just a short list of the colors on display here. Below the Bells is a multicolored body of water: glitzy green, blue, brown, silver and variations of all of them. I've never seen anything like it.

Ahead of me I see salt-like layers of snow on top of the Maroon Bells, so called because of the mountains' color and shape. The Bells are surrounded by a magical landscape of colors and shapes.

When the wind rustles the golden leaves of the aspen trees, which are abundant here, the effect is a dazzling display of glitter. These aspen trees have very thin leaves, and the softest of winds is enough for them to quake. The effect of shimmering gold is a real beauty that you won't see even in paradise. This sight is marijuana for the soul. Bring your asses right here, young Jews, and see how beautiful it is when you don't melt.

• • •

Unlike me, who's giving up on the Jews here, Pope Francis is not giving up on his Christians. He is in the USA and he is preaching, as loud as anybody will hear him. What is he preaching about? You guessed it: climate change. I have no opinion about climate change, as I've said, but if the pope preaches it I know that I must doubt it even more.

I drive on, in the direction of Denver, and choose the scenic roads. The drive in the mountains, totally surrounded by yellow and gold trees, is one of the greatest pleasures one could have while alive and driving. It's a dreamy ride, and again I am taken by the beauty of this land.

I stop on the road, near a motel by the name of Topaz Lodge, where I see four people sitting on chairs, busily inhaling nicotine into their system. They feast on a huge pizza pie that, they tell me, they got three traffic lights down the road for $8.99.

A steal.

They introduce themselves to me as "mountain movers." The mountain up the road, mostly made of rock, is being dynamited in order to build a new highway. Their job is to haul the falling rocks out of the way. "We are moving earth from a mountain to a quarry," they tell me, quite proud of their achievements.

"If an intellectual was assigned to do our job," they tell me, "he wouldn't last a single day." Not even one of them believes in "climate change." To be more exact: they all believe that the climate always changes. This very place, they explain to me, used to be all ice "a million years ago."

In addition, all are staunch supporters of Israel.

Jerome, one of the four, tells me that President Obama should go back to where he was born. Where is that?

"Africa or Indonesia, but certainly not Hawaii."

There are a few million people in this land who strongly believe that Obama was not born in the USA and is not a real American. They can't prove it, but lack of proof has never stopped anybody, be they mountain movers or Berkeley intellectuals.

• • •

Morning comes and I go to Moe's Broadway Bagel in Denver. I get a cheese-and-egg bagel, sit at the table on the sidewalk and read the news.

The Speaker of the House, John A. Boehner, announced yesterday that he would resign his post by the end of next month. Reason? The Republican Party is bitterly divided between its moderates and its super-conservative Tea Party, and he is tired of the infighting.

The differences between the two camps are many. One of the immediate ticking bombs is this: The Tea guys threaten to shut the government down unless they can pass a resolution to defund the women's health organization Planned Parenthood, which aids women seeking abortions. If they can't get their wish, they say, they won't approve the upcoming fiscal budget and the US government will be forced to shut down.

I face a much a bigger problem than John. My cheese-and-egg bagel is totally lacking salt and pepper and has absolutely no taste. Can nobody in this land learn how to make an egg sandwich, god-damn it?

I'm on the 16th Street Mall, which is one long pedestrian strip, and I observe the people passing by. Nine out of ten are dressed in the lousiest clothes one could imagine in the worst of nightmares. I get into a conversation with some of them and find out that they are not from here. They have come to Denver for the Great American Beer Festival, which is taking place a few blocks away.

They also tell me that sixty thousand people attend the festival, which sounds to me like a perfect opportunity to get free beer. I walk there.

As I enter, I'm given a small glass to use in the various stands of the breweries presented here for beer tastings. "If you break or lose the glass there will be no replacement," the man who gives me the glass says in earnest. How am I going to keep a glass in my hands for the next ten hours?

Not to worry. For five bucks I can get a cup-holder necklace, a pocket with strings that go around the neck, and the glass will hang safely below my mouth. I get one. On it there is this line: "X-Com-municated Mormon Drinking Team." Below is some solemn advice: "Finish your beer… There are sober Mormons in Utah."

A little politics in a huge beer joint. Nobody around here sells cup holders with "Muslim Drinking Team" on them. Give it to the Mormons.

I make the rounds, drink here and there, this and that, and try to talk non-Mormon politics with a young man who has been drinking more than his head allows. I say to myself: It would be interesting to hear what a drunk American really thinks on the issues.

First, I ask him if he's red or blue. I get nowhere. Even as drunk as this man is, he knows what lines not to cross. "I draw a red line when it comes to politics," he says to me. Oh God, even drunks are scared to talk politics in the Land of the Free!

For your information: the beer I like the most here is the Dos-vidanya, an oak bourbon barrel-aged beer, 12.5 percent ABV, which has a very rich taste. Simply excellent.

Cheers!

• • •

Moments after I leave the festival I get an email from my good friend, Barack Obama. Subject: "We could meet this fall, Tuvia."

He writes:

Tuvia —

I remember my first day as a community organizer like it was yesterday. I was handed a long list of neighborhood residents, and for the next three weeks, I went door-to-door to meet with every one of them.

And so on and on, tales and more tales. I wonder what he's talking about. Hasn't the NSA already informed him that the residents of his district will deny every single word he writes?

Bottom line: what President Obama really wants comes at the bottom of his email – a contribution, anywhere between $15 and $1,000, and if I please would prefer to make it a "monthly recurring contribution," this would be very, very welcome.

President Obama can brag all he wants about the blacks and the Spanish of Illinois and how much he cares about them. But even he wouldn't say that at any point he had taken care of the blacks of Colorado.

Maybe I should meet them. There's a black megachurch in Denver, I discover, and it's called Potter's House. Come Sunday, I go there.

The church offers two services in their three-thousand-seat hall, and I come for the second service. A startlingly talented fat lady, aided by an all-black choir, sings: "You have removed my shame. You take me as I am."

The congregants, on their feet, sing along. And what singing this is! The lead singer, who fires up the audience a thousand times stronger than any American politician alive, delivers her notes far higher than any American aircraft has ever reached. Every piece of brick, stone and iron in the building shakes at the sound of her voice, and you can almost see angels dancing at her feet. What I witness here is a powerful orgy between man and God. Really.

Oscar of Chicago: You should come here and join these people!

These black people have the capacity to shake the skies with their singing, a task no white person has yet accomplished, to the best of my knowledge. Their singing smells of freed souls, their passion is mountains high, and their presence is a display of immense strength.

This is not Aspen. The worshipers here are not American Jews. The devotion, sincerity, passion, pride and happiness I see here is unmatched. This black church stands tall in total opposition to the doom and gloom I found in black 'hoods. If only these people knew the strength they possess.

My luck, there's a guest speaker. She is a white lady who loves to sing and shout. "Praise the Lord in His house, He will fix your house," she shouts and proceeds with screaming promises of health and wealth to these people. In case anybody had doubted her capacity to deliver, she adds: "I was born on Easter Sunday and I have resurrection power. Don't push me, I can dynamite."

She is trying hard to act "black," but totally lacks the spirit that comes so easily to the people in attendance here. After repeated screams and shouts, she offers a prayer to Jesus: "Wash me in your blood." Why did they invite her?

The senior pastor of this megachurch is Rev. Dr. E. Christopher Hill, a black pastor. When he is at the podium he is a sheer delight.

At times he yells from the podium to individual members of this huge audience.

"Hey, Sis," he says to a lady who tells him she's from Omaha. "Are there blacks in Omaha?" Everybody is laughing. I want to see what this man is made of. And on the morrow I go to visit him privately in his office.

• • •

Today the parking lot is almost empty, but there are many guards somewhere around here. I notice them as I enter the church's property, when they come out of their hidden holes to check who I am. In this church, I guess, they don't want to meet the same fate as the AME church in Charleston.

When I enter the building I see a bunch of posters in the lobby announcing a forthcoming trip to Israel. I keep walking.

"Pastor Chris," as the reverend is known here, embraces me when I enter his office. He is all smiles, full of energy, and his face is shining. No wonder thousands of people follow him. To start, I share with him my findings so far: America is divided, racism is all over, and those who speak in the name of "diversity" don't really know blacks. Is this correct? I ask him.

"Very much so," he answers without a second's hesitation.

I have been to 'hoods and have seen the poverty there, as well as the utter criminality that screams from every corner – the doom and gloom of Black America. But then, here in your church: fun, amazingly spiritual, enormous energy – more positive and spiritual than any white church out there. The exact opposite of the 'hood. Could you explain to me these two opposites of Black America? How could people be so down on one side and so up on the other? Are they not the same people?

"Church for us is an escape. Church is the place where we can be ourselves. I've got high officials in the church that are public officials.

One of my members has thirty thousand employees. They cry in the church. Here they are free. In our church, this is a place where we don't have to be white. This is the place where we don't have to be a minority in America's melting pot. Historically, all of our liberation movements came out of the church. The church for us is the freest place that we have, because we are not supported or underwritten by the white power structure."

Very nice. But what makes black churches so much more spirited than white churches?

"See, the black preacher, during slavery, he would go to the whites' church. He would sit in the back, or stay outside the window, hear the sermon and then go back to the slaves and preach the same sermon fifteen thousand times better!"

How so?

"Because they [blacks] would hear it differently. The story of the Hebrew slaves in Egypt has a whole other meaning to an African American. Because we have chains in common. Segregation. Living in a ghetto, as we would call it. We are naming it [the ghetto] from something that we have extracted from Jewish experience in Europe. There're so many similarities between the Old Testament scriptures and our experience that show up in our worship. We are African Americans."

This is an explanation of the greatness in black churches. How do you explain the other side of the coin: the 'hood, the gangsters, the high rate of murder in the black community?

It takes Pastor Chris some time to answer this. Schools in black neighborhoods, he says, "are inferior. In America we build prisons based on third-grade test scores. So, if the test scores in the area are bad we know we need more prisons. The prison system now is being traded on Wall Street, for 'prison futures.' We are a commodity. The police, the social worker, the prosecutor, the judge, the clerk – everybody is getting paid off of the institutionalizing of the black people. And so, it's better for the system for us to be institutionalized than for us to be educated."

Americans elected a half black to be their president, one who talks and walks like whites. Will Americans elect a real black leader, who talks like the blacks do?

"Do I see America electing a black president in my lifetime? No."

Is "diversity" just a smokescreen?

"Absolutely. America is deeply racist."

If you were to define "America" in one sentence, what would it be?

"Chris Rock described America, from a black perspective, the best I've ever heard it: 'America is like the uncle who put you through college but he molested you.' That's how we access America. This is the best country in the world, but it molested us. It broke families apart. They sold our mothers on blocks. They raped our daughters. And we are the result of this."

That's history. How would you define America now?

"It's not history; it's still there. I can still be pulled over by the police, choked to death on camera, and no one would go to jail. Today. Today I can be shot to death in my church by a young white kid who sees me as a threat to his women. Today! This is America. America has not progressed."

I progress, driving-wise. Where to? I'm not sure, and so I drive east. Evening comes and I cross into Kansas. It's damn cold here, and the strong winds blow at my face mercilessly. That's a climate change.

Gate Eighteen

Ten thousand people come together to scream at the same time

IT IS FOGGY THIS MORNING IN GOODLAND, KANSAS. TIME IS EIGHT IN THE morning, but my iPhone says it's nine, because it thinks that Goodland is in a different time zone; iPhone is wrong, sorry.

What's new today? Today I read the *Salina Journal*. Nothing is new, except that "Kansas's rate of adult obesity in 2014 was 31.3 percent." Obviously, I'm in the right place.

In lieu of exciting news, I read the letters to the *Journal*. Let me see what people in Kansas are thinking about these days. Here goes, a letter from a lady named Carolyn Underwood:

> In regard to trying to get to heaven, one can never try hard enough. Jesus made it so simple: Simply believe that Jesus is the son of God, that he died for your sins and rose again. Ask him for forgiveness and give him your life. It's called grace.

Let's see if the *New York Times* has anything better to say. Here goes: "Scientists reported on Monday definitive signs of liquid water on the surface of present-day Mars, a finding that will fuel speculation that life, if it ever arose there, could persist to now."

This sounds quite interesting and it raises the questions: Does climate change affect Mars as well, and are no-smoking regulations also in effect there? Even more intriguing will be to find out if the creatures of Mars are red or blue, black or white, pro-Israel or pro-Palestine, and if they have a Jesus or Buddha of their own. Do they have Indian reservations there?

As for me, I'd like to get in touch with the ladies of Mars. I hope that political correctness has not reached Mars yet and that I can at least look at them. I go to sleep dreaming of Martian ladies.

• • •

The next morning, I reach Colby. I like driving around in this state of Kansas, which is located almost exactly at the center of the United States. The landscape is very different, not the one I got used to in some other states. There are no mountains around, not a trace of them. This kind of landscape is called "prairie."

And Colby has a prairie museum. The very idea that there is an actual museum that calls itself Prairie Museum intrigues me, and I stop by.

By the way, I never knew that there were so many museums in the United States. Every little town has a museum. I don't know why. Maybe the "diverse" people are dying to find their roots.

There are three visitors in the museum when I arrive. That's it. Here, I guess, I will get personal attention. I approach the two ladies at the reception area. Before they start telling me all they know about prairies, I ask them a simpler question: Could you tell me, please, what are the distinguishing qualities of a Kansan?

"A Kansan is a person who is tough, stubborn, generous, friendly and has a stick-to-it-iveness attitude," one of the ladies says.

Stick-to-it-iveness. I like it! Are these stick-to-it-iveness people red or blue?

"Everybody here is Republican, except for me. My parents are Republican, my husband is a Republican, but I'm a Democrat."

Why?

"Because Democrats care for the people and Republicans don't!"

At this, the other lady interferes: "Does the president care for the people?"

"It's not his fault that the government doesn't care for people. There are too many people in government, and he can't control them."

Let me understand you: if a Republican president gets nothing done it's his fault, but if a Democratic president gets nothing done it's somebody else's fault. Is that so?

"Yes."

Is this logic part of the Kansan stick-to-it-iveness attitude?

"Yes!"

Do you have children?

"Yes."

Are they red or blue?

"I don't know."

Her son, twenty-nine years of age, lives nearby. I ask her: May I ask him?

"No."

Isn't it time you know what your son thinks?

"No!"

On to the museum.

● ● ●

This museum offers some interesting stories about the people who first lived or passed by here. Here's one story about the Blue Brothers, who passed by here on their way to Denver, seeking gold:

> The Blue Brothers and a few others made the mistake of leaving the Platte River road for a shortcut into Denver. When Daniel and his two brothers ran out of food and water, they survived only by cannibalism. An Arapaho found Daniel, the sole survivor, and took him into his tipi to nurse the lost, starving gold seeker back to physical and mental health.

It's a short story that tells of a huge history – the history of America and of the early Americans. It took blood, sweat, disease, starvation, determination, imagination and an immense drive for gold to create this huge country. It wasn't easy.

Outside the museum's main building stand homes from the period. For example: "The Sod House" and "The Eeller House." You can go into these houses, which are exact replicas of the original ones, to experience them for yourself. No guide or guard walks with you, and nobody tells you what this or that object is. You have to figure it out all on your own. Which I try to do.

I feel like I am walking back in time, a hundred or two hundred years in the past, and I discover America in a way I never thought I would: Europe. Almost everything in these houses smells, looks and feels like Old Europe.

Yes, the people who founded this country were not from Mars. They were European. Full-blooded Europeans. I did know this before, but I had never felt it. Today I do.

It's time to read more. "Most immigrants," one of the signs in the other part of the museum reads, "were American born of European descent with German heritage predominating."

Naturally I want to have a better "prairie" experience, and so I take my car for a drive along the dirt roads. I hope that the rental company will never find out what roads I've driven with this Versa.

How does it feel to drive on these roads? Heaven! I drive in and out of fields, rarely encountering another car, but often I'm blocked by cows. I feel like a pioneer and hope that nobody will eat me.

After an hour or two of driving aimlessly into the past I get to Castle Rock. This is a wonder of nature; in the midst of the flat surface known as Kansas is a tall rock "mountain." By itself. A lonely rock. How did it get here? I am not sure, but I guess that this rock is a true Kansan with a stick-to-it-iveness attitude. It is here, for whatever reason, and it ain't moving.

The *Washington Post* reports that "the US has six executions scheduled over the next nine days." Why is America still practicing this cruel punishment? Perhaps because of some stick-to-itiveness mentality.

• • •

Kansas's largest city is Wichita, and Ms. Versa takes me there. The Foo Fighters will perform later this evening at the

local Intrust Bank Arena, and I'm in the mood for a concert. What a name for an arena: Intrust Bank. Like the Cadillac theater.

I'm not the only one looking for tunes; over ten thousand people have shown up seeking the same.

At the appointed hour, Gary Clark Jr. and band open the concert. They are loud – and that's all they have to offer: noise. The lyrics are indecipherable, except for a select few.

Next time American troops invade somewhere they should bring this Gary with them. The enemies would run in fear.

Luckily, this opening ends its loud nothingness before eight o'clock. At about eight, lights go up in the house. Nothing is happening. But the Wichita young are happy. They walk in and out with yet another Budweiser or Miller, and they are happy. How can they drink this stuff? These beers are horrible. Lights go down at 8:39 p.m.

The Foo Fighters appear on stage and the real performance finally starts. The audience roars. The Foos are loud, louder than Gary. And they project blinding strobes into the eyes of those in the audience. The people of We the People love it. The Foos scream and their loudspeakers shake the house. If a tank passed by shooting all of us, no one would hear it.

Occasionally this band gets inspired and it comes up with a tune or two that shows some promise – but anything good quickly fades into another scream. The words, the so-called lyrics, don't have any particular meaning. At least not as far as my ears perceive them. The lead singer, Dave Grohl, loves to use the word *fuck* and gets a high screaming *motherfuckers* at the top of his lungs. The audience love it and they scream the word as ear-splitting as ear-splitting can be.

This back-and-forth screaming between stage and audience soon develops into a shouting match: Who will be louder?

Cost of tickets: thirty-five to seventy-five dollars, before buying anything to eat, drink or remember the event by. Is it worth it? To the people here, it is.

I think I should come back to this arena when the Wichita Thunder hockey team plays here. The Intrust Bank Arena is their home base.

Thunder. Another humble name for a sport team.

The arena is not the only address in Wichita for concerts. Another one, quite smaller, is the Orpheum, where a Christian group, Third Day, appears on the very next night.

I go to see them. I need music and I won't give up.

Third Day is not Foo Fighters. For one thing, they prefer *God* and *Jesus* to *fuck* and *motherfucker*. Additionally, each of their songs has a tune, the words are audible and there is a message. The lyrics flash above the stage, big and clear:

"Now I'm glad. / You died upon the cross / You are my Jesus who loves me." And glad they indeed are.

What's happening here is not a church service, even if it might look like one. This is a concert. Seats cost money. Average price: thirty-four dollars. The people in the audience, about twelve hundred of them, raise their hands to the Holy Spirit as they sing, and they love every moment of it. They are so happy that Jesus died on a cross! He did it for them, because he loves them. And they love to be loved. "I have decided to follow Jesus, no turning back," they sing.

In a way, what I see here is the essence of American Christianity: fun and super-narcissism. In old Christianity, of the European model, the story of Jesus is a tragic tale of God's death on a cross – like any good old European opera. But not to these Americans; to them the story of Jesus is a story with a happy ending. He died for me! He loves me! Life's good.

• • •

The *Wichita Eagle* reports that "a gunman opened fire inside a classroom at a rural Oregon community college Thursday, killing at least nine people before dying in a shootout with police, authorities said. One survivor said he demanded his victims state their religion before he started shooting."

The religion he was targeting, according to various news reports, was Christianity. He asked the students for their religion and to those who told him they were Christian, he said: "Good, because you're a Christian, you're going to see God in just about one second," and then shot them in the head.

Nine people, the same number that Dylann Roof killed in the black church in Charleston, but in two days nobody will remember this shooting. Why? Because the dead here are not blacks, and no white is afraid that blacks will go rioting in the streets.

• • •

I get into my white Japanese and drive, mostly on scenic roads. When I spot a lone house in the prairie, in an otherwise never-ending empty landscape, I drive in. I'm curious to see how they live. But no human being shows any sign of life, only dogs. They bark, they jump around my car, dreaming of some fresh meat, and I realize that I must get out of there.

I back up slowly, making sure I don't drive over the dogs, when suddenly I hear a scratching sound; I must have bumped into an unseen object in the back. I continue to carefully drive out, and when I am a safe distance from the dogs I get out of the car to check if any damage has been done to the Japanese.

Yes.

In the olden days cars used to have steel bumpers, but those days are long gone. This Versa has no bumper, and the damage done to it will probably require replacing two major parts of the car's exterior. Something like a hip replacement. What is this Japanese made out of? Paper? Thank heaven I have insurance.

I drive to a nearby branch of my rental company, Enterprise, and they suggest I replace the car. They don't have any cars available at the moment, but they say that Tulsa, Oklahoma, still has plenty of cars available. I drive there and the Tulsa people show me around their lot and say that I can take any car I want, any size, for no additional cost. They want to make me happy.

That's called service, an American concept. Really. This I know from my years in New York. The customer is a king.

I scan the cars and I spot an American mini SUV, a Chevrolet Captiva, and we immediately connect. Love at first sight. Don't ask me to explain this. There's gay marriage, and there's car marriage. Mine is car marriage.

Gate Nineteen

You can have a blast beating up Iraqis with frozen fish

TULSA, OKLAHOMA. I AM, LO AND BEHOLD, IN THE HEART OF THE BIBLE BELT. But first things first: I need a hotel and I need food. Hopefully, downtown Tulsa has got them both.

I'm nice to Siri – I don't use the *f* word – and she directs me well. I get a hotel downtown, Courtyard by Marriot, and next to it there's an Italian restaurant.

The diners here strike me as well-to-do folks. If I'm not mistaken they have just come from, or are going to, a Wagner opera; I don't know what time it is. I am directed to my table and I order coffee. Got to wake up!

And here I want to make one point very clear: I don't drink American coffee for pleasure. American coffee tastes like water mixed with asphalt. But, fortunately, it contains caffeine – which is why I drink it. You would think that after invading various Arab countries, Americans would have learned a little bit about coffee, but no.

I can't blame them for their lack of taste buds, honestly. This country started with the English, creatures known for great manners and dull palettes.

About five minutes after I start sipping my black medicine, an older white couple walk in. Dressed in the style of the educated and the moneyed, they march to their table. They are planning to have a quiet and romantic evening at the city's center and, understandably, they couldn't have imagined that a man like me would change their plans.

I do. The coffee really stinks, and I am really bored. To make a long story short, instead of eating they are talking to me. I'm a noodge. I was born that way.

Tell me about Oklahoma, I ask them. By the expression on their faces I can tell that they are not sure if I'm a human being or a UFO. But the lady opens her mouth. Oklahoma, the lady tells me, has a very high rate of death by suicide and the highest number of women in prison. This sounds very reasonable to me: if a state puts its females in jail, the men are bound to be quite depressed.

I love listening to stories like this, as they enrich the imagination cells in my brain.

Really.

And then both the lady and the gentleman, Nancy and Bruce, talk to me about America in general. They tell me, for example, that "we" treated the Indians very, very badly and that we are very, very sorry for it.

Now, this gets me going. The story with the Indians, whatever it was, took place a couple of centuries ago, long before either Nancy or Bruce were conceived. How did they get the "we" into this story?

I pose this question to them, but they see nothing wrong with the phrase. "We" means Americans.

And you are "sorry" about it?

Definitely, they both say.

To illustrate to them the absurdity of it, at least from my perspective, I tell them that I am a German and that I really, really, really don't feel bad about what "we" did to the Jews because I was not even born at that time. And, in addition, I'm very proud to be German because "we" are the only ones who treat Syrians so very nicely.

I wish some of my German detractors – I have a number of them – had heard me say this. It would have been so much fun to watch the expressions on their faces! I look at the couple next to me and I give them a smile, one of my stupid smiles, just for the fun of it.

They are not smiling. And to get the smile off my face, the lovely lady challenges me: "Can blacks in Germany vote in the general election? They can vote here, but can they do it in Germany?"

Now, this is very interesting. I tell her that we don't have blacks in Germany. Period. We are all white, blond and tall.

Tulsa, they tell me, is diverse. And America is too. And it's so great, really great – says Nancy – to be in such a diverse country as the United States of America.

I tell them that I enjoy very much, very, very much, the non-diversity of my beloved Germany.

"What, you don't like diversity?" Nancy asks. "How can you live in a country without – "

I cut her off. Be honest! Isn't this "diversity" thing just a lip service invented not long ago? Did it exist when you got married?

No, it did not. "Diversity," as far as Bruce remembers, became part of the American lingo only about fifteen years ago, at the most.

If you were wondering: Nancy and Bruce believe in climate change and prefer the Palestinians to the Israelis. They are, in short, Wagner people.

I take another sip of my asphalt mix and go to the Courtyard to sleep.

Before I close my eyes I think about "diversity." Who, I ask myself, came up with it fifteen years ago? A professor at Nicholas's UC Berkeley? A journalist? Enterprise?

I fall asleep and I dream of buffalos. Don't ask.

• • •

Night goes, morning comes, and downstairs I see Bill, a black guy, and he's in the mood for talking. "Just about every day somebody gets killed here. Gangs all over. Kids who want to be rich in a day, lazy kids who want all the money but don't want to work for it."

Who are those kids?

"Blacks and Spanish. They kill for territory." He means locations to sell drugs.

Not whites?

"The whites are the big guys, the guys who live in the big houses. They have no names. They give the drugs to the black kids to sell on the street."

How often are the shootings?

"Every day."

What happened to "values" in the black community?

"Gone."

Are there no leaders in the black or Spanish communities?

"What leaders?"

I don't know what to say to him, so I say: pastors.

"My classmate, he became a pastor. Now he's in the pen, at the Big Mac."

For what?

"Raping a little girl. They waited till she gave birth, checked the DNA and it was him, he was the father. He won't survive the Big Mac."

What's the Big Mac?

"That's the name of the pen, in McAlester. It's a famous prison, toughest in the country." It is officially known as Oklahoma State Penitentiary.

Why do you think that the pastor won't survive?

"If you are in prison for bank robbery you'll make it okay, no problem. But if you are in prison for rape, especially of young girls, it's the inmates who will take care of you!"

Rape you?

"That's one thing."

And the guards wouldn't stop it?

"The guards, they are the same like the inmates. Only if you bribe them they'll protect you."

Nancy and Bruce don't know stories like that of Bill's friend, which is only one of many happening here in this state and in this country. They love blacks, but from a distance. They don't approach blacks, and they don't talk to them. If they did, they wouldn't ask ridiculous questions about blacks' voting rights in Germany – as if life is just about voting.

What they like is the idea of having blacks around, because this makes them feel "diverse." They like to be served by blacks, for example. I don't call myself "diverse," and I befriend blacks the same way I do whites. I find the blacks warmer than the whites and I enjoy their company. Love of the other is not an idea; it's life itself.

• • •

The Tulsa State Fair is taking place a short ride from here, and I go there. There I see, for example, a pig by the name of Peppa and her fifteen piggies, which were born just a few hours ago. The piglets are very busy trying to suck food from their mama. They are independent, at this tender age of just a few hours, to the point of fighting each other for another lick of mama. It takes human babies years before they reach such independence.

I hook up with a guy, a rich white guy, and he tells me that the Donald is the best man in America. Donald Trump is not really a nice man, I tell the guy. Years back, he tried to force tenants out of buildings that he bought in New York so that he could renovate and sell their apartments at much higher rates. He behaved like the worst of slumlords, which is how he made it big in real estate. He threatened tenants with imminent demolitions, he drastically decreased essential services to them, he instructed employees to obtain information about their private lives and sex habits – in short: there was no stopping him. How could you support such a candidate?

"If Donald did it, there's nothing wrong with it," he responds.

• • •

There's a megachurch in town called Church on the Move. I go to church. Again...

The parking lot outside the church is huge, with endless rows of cars. When I finally park and get out of the car – my car is the nicest on this lot, let me tell you! – I can hear the service through the loudspeakers, something about Jesus giving his life for you and me.

Lovely.

I go to the men's room and while I'm urinating I hear about Jesus' blood and some other goodies. Yes, this church has speakers in the toilets, so that none of us will miss a single word uttered on the stage. I finish fast, hoping for some better stories once I join the crowd.

Thousands of people are on their feet, joining the band onstage in song:

Jesus, we love you, Oh how we love you.

You are the one our hearts adore.

This church is not the Potter's House; it is not a black church. There are some blacks here, but very few. This is a white church, and the level of energy and passion here does not reach what I witnessed in Denver. But what they are lacking in energy they compensate for in production value: lots of lights, dozens of lighting effects, amplifiers that are very loud yet very comfortable to the ear, TV screens, comfortable seating, a modern stage – and stagecraft second to none. Simply put, the service here is a production that could easily compete with every Broadway show in history.

The singing continues:

I believe in the resurrection,

That we will rise again.

For I believe in the name of Jesus.

Lights flicker and shine, lines light the stage, and the party goes on. The thousands of people raise their hands up to the ceiling, singing: "We will rise again."

When the songs end, the sermon starts. The pastor says that Christianity is a unique religion because it does not relate to a specific geographical area. Islam is rooted in the Middle East, Judaism in Israel, and Buddhism in the Far East, but Christianity has no one unique location and is equally connected to any place.

He's not totally right, but theologically speaking he has a point. As I look at the praying and singing people around me, it hits me – and for the first time: "American" is very "Christian."

Americans like to say that what unites them is not a race or ethnic identity, not even a land, but an "idea." But isn't their idea actually rooted in Christianity? "There is neither Jew nor Gentile, neither slave nor free, nor is there male and female, for you are all one in Christ Jesus" (Galatians 3:28). Why didn't I think of it before?

And here's the corollary: the modern-day ideology of "human rights," as well as the idea that tribalism is essentially bad, is not "liberal" thinking but an old Christian doctrine.

It goes without saying that both liberals and conservatives would commit you to a mental institution if you dared say this to them.

Especially human rights activists, many of whom do not follow Jesus. Yet, whether they like it or not, none of them was born in a vacuum. They are the children or grandchildren of believers, and while they don't follow Jesus it does not mean that they don't follow his teachings. They do. They follow an "idea."

• • •

I enter the belly of Captiva, a Car on the Move, and drive south. On the roads I see big signs: "Worry less, pray more." "In God We Trust."

After an hour or two of driving I park my Captiva – what a gorgeous name! – between Jesus road signs and an Indian casino, the most important Indian cultural institution of our day.

A few feet ahead of me is an RV outside of which stand an older couple and a young lady, the older woman's daughter from a previous marriage. The man is a Native American ("Assiniboine Sioux"), the wife is a white American and the daughter, Robin, is a former US soldier who, for a time (2003–2004), was deployed to Iraq as a supply sergeant with a quartermaster company supplying a base with water.

How was it in Iraq? What did you find out while serving there?

"I found out that the media, as far as America goes, was pretty much wrong on the way they portrayed the events happening in Iraq."

Tell me!

"Things were not always as bad as the media made it out to be."

For example?

"There were a lot of good Iraqi people there that were being mistreated."

By whom?

"Unfortunately, by US military. Also by their own people."

Give me an example of US military treatment of Iraqis.

"Whenever they would be captured as prisoners they were very mistreated. They were starved – "

Starved for how long?

"Weeks!"

What do you mean? Were they given just water…?

"Barely even water."

She gives me more examples, what she calls "hearsay," meaning things she did not personally see: "Iraqi people were beaten with frozen fish."

What did you, personally, see?

She saw the starvation and "a lot of horrible things."

Give me an example of that.

"Little kids, on the side of the road, were begging for food, and American soldiers threw cans and bottles of water at them."

Just for fun?

"Just for fun."

Robin informed her superiors of these abuses, but no abuser was arrested and the abuses continued unabated.

Do you think that the Iraqi invasion was justified?

"No."

Robin's stepfather, who served in Vietnam, puts an Indian head-dress on my head and we pose for pictures.

For the record: Robin supports Obamacare, does not believe in climate change and supports Israel.

Before I leave, Robin thanks me for talking with her. "It is very humbling," she says, "that you are interested in American culture and that you are asking me about America, because so many people don't like Americans."

She pauses for a second, looks at me, and says: "We are not all bad."

Robin is one of those people who touch me very deeply. She is among the finest that I have met. She loves her country and is pained by its misdeeds. She loves America, yet she is not lost in blind admiration. She is part of this huge and powerful country, yet "humbled" by a stranger's curiosity about her country. She combines pride and humility in admirable portions, making America look so much better than most will ever succeed in doing.

I think that Captiva, a proud American, is a bit ashamed listening to Robin's account, and she wants to leave. As we drive off I take a look at the casino's reflection in my mirror and think of the people inside who feed the slot machines with a never-ending supply of greens. Take me, Captiva, to the next casino you see!

• • •

Sulphur, a little city of five thousand residents, has a casino. I park Captiva near the casino's entrance and just before I get out another car pulls in next to me, driven by a man who calls himself "Sooner."

He loves this casino. "Last time I was here," he tells me, "I made $1,900."

How did you do it?

"You have to understand the machines."

Do you make your money on slot machines?

"That's part of it. I also have my own business."

Do you really make money playing the slot machines?

"Oh, yes."

How often do you play?

"Two, three times a week."

How long have you been doing this?

"A number of years – four or five."

In total, how much have you lost or made?

"About $150,000."

In winnings or losses?

"Winnings!"

Is there a system to it?

"Yes. Ignore all the lights and the flashes and look for the numbers."

What numbers?

"At the bottom of the machines there are numbers of last winnings. If the number is high, I know this is a machine that gives money and I play it."

Interesting.

"There are other things you have to know."

Such as?

"You have to tip the girls well." If you do, he says, they'll tell you which machines give the best returns.

I ask him which machines. "The Cats."

I have no idea what he's talking about.

Would you mind if I go with you and watch you play? I ask him.

He would love me to, he says. Sooner and I enter the casino. I see the expected: old white ladies. There are free drinks around and I take a cup of cola.

Sooner walks around the machines, checking them out. He does his magic and picks a machine. He puts a hundred dollars in. His golden fingers press the buttons, and in less than three minutes he loses $99.70.

Got to try the Cats! He goes for the Cats. Don't ask me what the Cats are. Perhaps it is a way to lure pet lovers into playing the machines.

Sooner puts in another hundred dollars, plus the thirty cents he had in credit. He plays. The girls are smiling. It takes about four minutes and he loses it all: $100.30.

"You must be in it to win it," he tells me, and moves on to yet another machine. He puts in a one-hundred-dollar bill and in a few minutes the number jumps to $186. He is smiling. Lady Luck is on his side. He plays with renewed energy. He is smiling more, he's happy and he presses play again and again.

Until it goes below one hundred dollars.

"Time to stop," he says. I bid him farewell. As I walk away I look back for a second or two. Sooner goes to another machine, trying his luck again. I leave. Let the cats play.

What games would Americans play if their forefathers had not butchered the Indians?

• • •

The casino, Artesian, is owned by the Chickasaw Nation. Here in Oklahoma, I am told, there are no Indian reservations; here there are "nations." Why? It goes back to the forced relocation of Native Americans from their homes almost two centuries ago, along what is known as the Trail of Tears, into an area of what is Oklahoma today, and it is here that the Indians established their "nations." What are these nations known for? If I'm getting it right: Cool Cats.

Not far from the Indian casino is the Echo Canyon Spa Resort, where I am going to rest for the night. A beautiful place!

A couple, Joe and Carol, are the owners of the resort and they have a crew of dedicated and beautiful girls – for a moment I think I'm in Salt Lake City – who take care of the place. The food is very un-American, which means that it's excellent. I have a filet mignon, the best filet mignon offered on this side of the Atlantic, and I'm so glad that I chose these accommodations.

I am curious about Joe and Carol. Their own home is on the property and I go to pay them a visit. As I enter I see they are watching a TV program called *The Voice*, a singing competition in which young singers go on the stage to showcase their "voice." The show, in its ninth season, is reportedly watched by over twelve million people. Unlike American TV shows of the past, which took artists to create – scriptwriters, actors, various designers – and consisted of storylines, ideas and messages, the "reality shows" are cheap to produce and have a tendency to kill every cell in the viewer's brain.

I watch the competitors sing and I think of Oscar, the soul man of Chicago, aka SoulO. Oscar touched me deeply with his music, with his voice, with his soul. No one here on this screen reaches Oscar's toenails. Oh, Oscar! "Go south, my man. Go south. Go to Georgia, go to Mississippi, go to Texas. The good people live there. Go south. South is the place," Oscar said to me then, and his echo rings in my ears now.

Yes, Oscar: I hear your echo loud and clear. When the sun shines I will head to Texas, to the Lone Star state. Wait for me there!

Here's an item from the *New York Times:*

> The Justice Department will release about 6,000 inmates from federal lockups in less than a month, many of whom were nonviolent drug dealers. It's part of a bipartisan effort to reduce prison overcrowding in the US, which has a quarter of the world's prison population.

A quarter of the world's prison population is safely housed behind bars in the Land of the Free.

Gate Twenty

If you misbehave, the Jews will come and eat you
– Fifty million Germans are gone, all melted

THE FIRST THING I SEE UPON ENTERING TEXAS FROM OKLAHOMA IS A WORLD
War II memorial. On the memorial I read: "The German 19th Army
surrendered to the [103rd Infantry] Division 5 May 1945 at Inns-
bruck, Austria." Why should people think of Nazi Germany as they
enter Texas? I don't know, but this is what it is. I keep on driving,
and soon enough I get to Dallas.

Have you ever driven in Dallas? First off, whoever designed
the roads in Dallas is probably either a Talmudic scholar or a Greek
philosopher, but he should have been fired on day one. One road
melds into another road, and then another road, which then becomes
another road that comes out from yet another road – and all these
roads are multilane roads.

But forget the roads; consider the Dallas drivers. They will cut
you off from every direction without a second's hesitation. "Dallas
drivers are children of cowboys and they think that cars are horses.
That's why they drive the way they do," a young man explains to me.

Lady Luck is with me, and I survive the road. As I reach my hotel,
the Highland Hotel, I relax in the smoking area. There I meet a guy
who tells me that he's a Republican. A few feet from me I spot another
smoker, a lady, and I invite her to join us. I tell her that the other guy
is a flaming Republican and ask her if she's also a flaming Republican.

That's too much for her, to be labeled a Flaming Republican. She promptly tells me that she's a Democrat.

I ask the two of them to explain to me, a fat tourist, the difference between themselves.

They oblige.

The Republican says: "Being American means thinking of yourself first, which is the essence of capitalism."

The Democrat says: "Healthy societies care about their weaker parts. I don't mind paying taxes as long as my money goes toward helping the poor."

Personally, I agree with the lady. The guy is too cold and too selfish for my taste. But there's something in the way that the lady phrases her response that frightens me. She's willing to pay more taxes, and she says it. She's righteous. And righteous people scare me.

Historically speaking, righteous people, knowing and proclaiming their righteousness, don't have and don't see any stop signs. When they believe in something, they will force their way through. Righteous people have done this from day one, when man first appeared on the planet – and, oh boy, how many people ended up dying because of the righteous! If you don't believe me, open the annals of history and you'll read it on almost every page.

I light up a cigarette and watch these two argue with each other. Neither convinces the other, and each passionately hates the other, which makes it fun to watch.

After a while, and to add a little fuel to the fire consuming these two, I throw in my "climate change, Israel-Palestine" question and ask both to respond. The Republican believes there is no "new" climate change, arguing that the climate has been changing for thousands of years, and he supports Israel. The Democrat asserts that he is utterly wrong on both counts.

Yeah.

• • •

Before I make my acquaintance with more of the good people of Texas, I go for a little history lesson. Presidential history, in this case.

In November 1963, President John F. Kennedy was shot to death from the sixth floor of the Texas School Book Depository in Dallas by Lee Harvey Oswald. Two days later Oswald was shot to death by a nightclub owner, a tough Jew by the name of Jack Ruby.

This is more or less what the US government has been saying ever since, but no matter how often the government argues this case, there are more conspiracy theories out there than the total number of abortions and gay marriages all across the USA.

The Book Depository of old is no more. In its stead is the Sixth Floor Museum, which I now enter. Here, on the sixth floor, in an area enclosed by glass barriers, visitors can see the exact location from which President Kennedy was shot, or not, but they can't stand on the very spot. Why? I don't know.

Barriers or not, Americans flock to this place. Old and young, male and female – mostly white – they are here. Why are they here? I approach an older lady who is walking around the various exhibits at this museum, and I ask her: Fifty-two years have passed but you Americans are still thinking of JFK's assassination. Why?

"We don't preserve buildings, like the Europeans. We preserve events. You are European, aren't you?"

I can't believe she's said this, so I try a retort: I'm German, and I think that you're Jewish. Aren't you?

"I was born Jewish, if that's what you meant."

What does it mean, "born Jewish"? Are you no longer Jewish?

She points to her husband, standing next to her: "He is an Italian."

It takes her a while, but in the end she says: "Yes, I'm Jewish." Her name is Ruth.

I'm sure that any hypothetical mutual acquaintance watching Ruth and me right now would be exploding in laughter at the sight of two Jews hiding behind Germany and Italy.

Just as I'm thinking of this I hear JFK uttering the eternal words "Ich bin ein Berliner" from one of the TV screens on the floor.

The Sixth Floor does a great job in presenting not just the assassination but also JFK the man. In pictures and moving images we see JFK using the emerging new medium of his time, TV, to his advantage: "And so, my fellow Americans: ask not what your country can do for you – ask what you can do for your country."

Classic JFK!

I leave the past behind, exit the building and am ready to make my acquaintance with the Texans living here and now. I walk just a few feet on the streets of Dallas when right before my eyes I see a Holocaust museum. What's a Holocaust museum doing in Dallas?

• • •

The Dallas Holocaust Museum occupies the first floor of an office building. It is a small museum, really small, but it's visually striking. At the entrance there is a graphic installation that depicts Europe in World War II. European countries are displayed in different colors, representing, for example, those who participated in Jew killing and those who resisted.

When you see in such a stark visual how almost every European country joined the Kill Your Jew party, it hits you: this is the face of European culture.

It is time I leave both JFK and the Holocaust aside and live in the real world, the one of today. I exit the building.

I ask a white man walking by for the best spot in Dallas where I could witness the soul of the city. "Definitely you should go to Deep Ellum."

What's that?

"In Deep Ellum you will see the real Dallas, not the Dallas of the stories. Dallas is much more liberal and diverse than what the media will make you believe. In Deep Ellum you'll see the diversity of our city: African Americans, gays, great bars and cafés; you will hear live music – jazz, blues, soul – and you'll love it. Just go there. Listen to me."

Oscar of Chicago: I'm going to listen to music in the heart of Dallas!

A few feet further down the sidewalk I meet a black man, whom I ask to tell me about Deep Ellum.

"Deep Ellum? That's the crime capital of Dallas!"

These two people, the white and the black, live on different planets. I go to Deep Ellum. What do I see?

"This is a gentrified area," a white lady tells me. "If you go south from here you'll hit a very bad neighborhood. Don't go there."

Who lives there?

"Blacks and Spanish."

The gangs are over there?

"Yes."

Gentrified. Gentrification. To the lady here, a white lady, "gentrified" is good. To the cabbie in Washington, DC, a black man, gentrification is bad.

Gentrification, to put it mildly, means getting poor residents out and putting in rich residents in their stead. In other words: getting the blacks and Spanish out, putting whites in. Real estate people like to do this. They buy out (usually for a low price) or evict poor people living in low-rent neighborhoods, then renovate the properties and rent them out or sell them for high sums. That's how they make their millions.

The new residents, whites, are often self-described liberals or progressive liberals who tell everybody listening that they dedicate their lives to helping the poor blacks and Spanish of America. In reality, they are the very ones who drive the blacks and the Spanish into homelessness. To blind you, and themselves, to this reality, they frequent a local bar where a black guy plays the blues, and they feel really, really good and very, very liberal.

It is good that Captiva is not listening to any of this. Had she done so, I'm afraid, she would have rammed herself into one of the newly expensive homes and totally destroyed it.

• • •

Captiva and I move to Fort Worth, another city in the huge state of Texas. Fort Worth bills itself as a city of cowboys and culture, two things I've been missing for a long time. Will I find them here?

In downtown Fort Worth my feet take me to the Sid Richardson Foundation, which houses an exhibition of cowboy paintings by Remington and Russell, kind of a cowboy and culture combo.

Darlene, an attractive lady with tons of energy, welcomes me. "What can I do for you?" she asks.

I would like to know, I tell her, which of the paintings I should try to steal in order to get rich fast? Without blinking an eye she shows me her favorite painting in the exhibition.

I like this lady. She is the sort of woman Oscar had in mind, the thought occurs to me.

Who are you, Darlene, and what do you stand for?

"I'm a Zionist."

Excuse me? What?

"A Zionist."

Why are you a Zionist?

"I grew up in Turkey, because my father worked in Turkey, and I traveled a lot in the Middle East. If a child misbehaved, the parents would say to him: 'The Jews will come and eat you.' Everything they blamed on Jews. That's why I'm a Zionist."

Are you Jewish?

"No. I'm agnostic."

Are your parents?

"I grew up in a Catholic family."

I wanted cowboys; I get Turks.

• • •

Will I, at least, get a little culture in this Fort Worth? Across the street from Darlene's, my eyes spot a small local theater, the Jubilee. Theater is culture, isn't it? I cross the street.

The Jubilee Theatre is a small black theater (147 seats) and this season it celebrates its thirty-fifth year of existence with the play *Lady Day at Emerson's Bar and Grill,* which appeared on Broadway last year. The play is a solo performance about the great black American singer Eleanora Fagan, known as Lady Day and, most famously, as Billie Holiday.

When I enter the house I notice that most of the people in the audience, about 80 percent of them, are white.

As a play *Lady Day* lacks structure, and, drama-wise, it's poorly written. But, still, it offers some great lines. For instance: "In this country, getting arrested is a colored tradition." Likewise, when Billie talks of her days in Philadelphia: "Philly's been rat's ass for me. Shit. I used to tell everybody when I die I don't care if I go to Heaven or Hell long's it ain't in Philly."

These lines are what you would call razor-sharp. But as performed here, even taking into account that this performance is a preview, the lines get lost long before they leave the stage. And despite the fact that the script deals with the awful treatment of blacks at the hands of whites, not one iota of pain registers here.

Who directed this piece? I wonder. A white lady did. And it shows. None of the blacks' pain registers on the stage, because it could not. You'd need a black director, one who can understand this unique pain, to extract it from the actor.

When the show is over, a black guy affiliated with the production points to the audience and says to me: "These white people will tell their friends tomorrow that they saw a black show in a black theater last night. That's why they come here. It makes them feel 'progressive.' It's all fake."

I give up on culture and go to see a rodeo. Rodeo, at least here in Fort Worth, is very much like baseball – a fun place where people sing, drink and eat. Moments after I enter, hundreds of people stand as one and sing:

> And I'm proud to be an American
> Where at least I know I'm free....
> I love this land
> God bless the USA.

The "Star Spangled Banner" follows, with its immortal words: "O say does that star-spangled banner yet wave / O'er the land of the free and the home of the brave."

The rodeo itself, at least as performed here, is pretty boring. God bless the USA.

• • •

Next morning, Captiva says, Let's go! We go. Direction: the good people.

On the road, like on many other roads in this big country, there are pawn shops all over. One after the other. To have all these pawn shops you need many poor people.

Sad. Is this the powerful America? Yeah.

Even Captiva doesn't feel good seeing these, and she picks up speed until we reach Fredericksburg. Fredericksburg? Sounds German. We stop to take a look. Gotta find the fifty million!

Fredericksburg is one of those cities founded by Germans and to this day it celebrates German, whatever that is. There are stores here that have distinct German names, but when I try to speak German with some people, they think that I'm speaking Japanese. They don't even know what German sounds like.

Not far from me is a guy standing next to his Harley-Davidson, a Harley man. He could be one of the Harleys who participated at Greg's father's funeral procession; you never know. I ask Mr. Harley for the best restaurant in town. I want to have some good German food! "Ashander," he says. Ashander? Yeah. Actually, he's not so sure how to pronounce the name. "It's in German," he explains to me.

I try to find the address of Ashander but it doesn't exist. Mr. Harley says he just ate there. We check together, Google and Shmoogle, and discover that the name of the restaurant is actually Ausländer ("foreigner" in German).

To Ausländer I go. Upon entering, I see three men dressed in Wehrmacht (German military) uniforms from the Nazi era, drinking beer with much pleasure. Am I seeing what I'm seeing? Pinch me, *bitte*. Nobody does, and so I go to meet the soldiers in person.

Lance, whose Wehrmacht uniform fits him extraordinarily well, speaks perfect German, and he is quite surprised that I know what his uniform represents, since everybody else in town thinks that it is of the US military. While we are talking about the subject he tells me that neither he nor his friends are Nazi soldiers. They are, he explains to me, actors whose job it is to "reenact" some of the Wehrmacht's activities during the war.

Yes, he knows German, but only because he studied the language. As for his ancestors, they were English.

Lance loves politics. He believes, he tells me, that climate change is a process that's thousands of years in the making; he's pro-life and pro-Israel. "Palestinians," he tells me, are a work of fiction. Listening to him talk you'd think that he was a right-wing Jew, not a twenty-five-year-old man with a perfectly tailored Nazi uniform.

I order some food. What can I tell you? The food here is nothing to brag about. I eat little. This ain't really "German" food, even though it looks like it.

And that's Fredericksburg, a cemetery of the German culture – a culture dead and buried.

Perhaps it's time I get in touch with a culture that's not melted, just to see the difference.

I consult with Captiva and she agrees to drive me to Laredo, a border city to Mexico. When we arrive I leave Captiva at my new hotel, La Posada Hotel in Laredo, and start toward Mexico on foot.

• • •

"After you cross the border you can walk only in the first five blocks but no further," Mexican Americans tell me. "It's dangerous there. Shootings, robberies. Drugs. Murders. Drug cartels." I listen and I keep moving toward Mexico, approaching the bridge that separates the two countries.

Crossing into Mexico requires some investment on my part, as might be expected. The Mexican government – or the US government, I'm not sure which – charges me seventy-five cents to cross the border. I pay the whole sum in cash and cross into the Latin world, or whatever this new world is.

The first sight that catches my attention in this border city, Nuevo Laredo, is the Mexican soldiers – or are they the police? – who either stand around or patrol this entry point with an impressive array of machine guns. I snap a picture of these beauties, and one of them, with a big gun, immediately crosses the street toward me, demanding that no pictures be taken in this obviously top-secret location.

Abruptly, I get a call from my belly. "Gimme food," it says.

Okay, I'll try.

Back in the States I do everything humanly possible to avoid Mexican food. My personal experiences with Mexican food, long and painful ones, always ended badly. But I am in Mexico now. Maybe, just maybe, in Mexico they have different Mexican food than the Mexican food in the USA.

I walk in search of food. The first five blocks, where it's "safe," are guarded by armed Mexican security personnel. But after the fifth block I don't see them anymore. I keep walking, another twenty blocks or so, just to see how many times I'll be killed, drugged, robbed and taken hostage by the famed Mexican drug cartels.

Before any of them has the chance to shoot me, I try some local food from a street vendor. It costs less than one US dollar, but is divinely delicious. I don't know what it is, was, but this is the best return I've ever made on one buck.

I keep walking, block after block, in search of that elusive perfect restaurant. These streets remind me of eastern European and Middle Eastern countries. Everybody walking around here, all Mexicans, behave as if they were members of one family, one big family. I look at them and I can tell that each of them shares something with the other, something that's bigger than themselves.

And it hits me: a tribe.

These Mexicans share a culture. When they communicate with each other, their communication is not made only of words but of other elements, such as gestures and body language. They understand each other in ways I never will. There are layers to their communication that are under the surface, known only to them.

They are a tribe, not a "diverse" society. Mexico resembles a barrel of old wine, its people savoring the taste of time. America, as I see it now that I am outside of it, is a melting pot of sour grapes mixed with pizza and asphalt.

American society is a man-made society, like the ponds and lakes of Qatar. Somewhere deep inside, Americans must know this. Maybe, a thought comes to me, the real reason why so many Americans refuse to discuss politics and religion is because they are afraid that the artificial glue that binds them together will dissolve the moment they start talking and reveal what they really think.

Who are they? Not one society, but many – many competing societies, each one afraid of the other.

I keep walking. Walking, walking and walking. So far, nobody has even thought of robbing me. What's wrong with these Mexicans?

I finally settle on a restaurant, whatever its name, and order food that I can't pronounce.

When my plates arrive I carefully try the food. Look: here is a bowl of melted heavy cheeses, something I've never been served before.

What can I tell you? Melted cheese taste a whole lot better than a melting pot. What else can I tell you? Mexican food is awesomely delicious. Blessed be Mexico! I fall in love.

I ask two ladies, busy eating over at the next table, if this city is dangerous. "It's dangerous in America, where they shoot students in school," is the answer I get.

Oops.

I try a bowl of soup, made of heavenly ingredients, and get myself a glass of whiskey to feed my soul as well, and then a cheese-cake – the best cheesecake on planet Earth.

Sorry, Jewish Federation of Chicago: the food here is much better, and they have cake too!

• • •

It's getting late and I slowly make my way back to the United States, leaving the Mexican Nuevo Laredo in the direction of the American Laredo.

Separating the two countries is a river, Rio Bravo (Mexican name) or Rio Grande (American name); one bank belongs to one country, and the other half to the other. Above the river there are bridges, one of which I will have to cross in order to enter the "New World." I walk back over the same bridge through which I entered Mexico, only in the opposite direction.

The border crossing within the USA, where the people and their documents are checked, is not an appealing place, to say the least. It's an iron structure surrounded by wire fences. To put it pictorially: it's a stable.

The inside of the building, where US Customs and Border Protection officers are processing the incoming people, reminds me of an abandoned property in a 'hood. I look around me. To my right I see a group of people sitting on the floor, surrounded by an interior fence. It looks like a prison within a prison. Who are they? I ask an officer.

"They are Cubans."

What are they doing there?

"Waiting to be processed."

How many hours will they stay there?

"More than that."

God and Castro know what this means.

A visibly bored blond officer stands a few feet from me, and I approach her. How long will it take till I can get out of here? I ask her.

"I can't tell. Last night, at this time, it took about two and a half hours."

This border crossing is worlds apart from passport checks in the average American airport. Laredo crossing is not an airport, and the people coming in are not English or Japanese but Mexican.

The line barely moves. I ask an officer with a mustache why this takes so much time.

"If you don't like it, go back to Mexico," he replies. The word *service* does not apply here.

I wait, wait and wait. Lord knows how much time has passed.

There are many people here, all waiting their turn to legally enter the country, but the officers are a bunch of lazy creatures. Most of the windows, where these officers interview the people, stand empty. At times, all of them are empty. When I check around to see where they are, I find them schmoozing with one another, as if this were a class reunion.

Even the cashier window, where all kinds of fees for visas and permits are collected, is often empty. When a clerk does show up, he or she seems to expect thanks for taking the people's money.

If I'm not wrong, it's faster to cross into this country illegally than to stand in endless lines like these. The only time that the officers show any desire to do anything is when they "catch" me writing notes on my smartphone. An officer speedily approaches me, demanding that I immediately turn it off. An iPhone, don't you know, is an illegal device in this part of America.

Freedom. Liberty. Diversity. Three words that mean not a thing at this entry point to the USA.

When my turn arrives, I present my passport – an America passport – to the immigration officer. "Why are you coming to this country?" he asks me.

Excuse me, but can you explain to me the nature of your question? I gave you an American passport; I can go in and out any time I want. What's your problem?

He won't let me through unless I answer him. This man is accustomed to abusing Mexicans and it's hard for him to break the habit.

I'm a journalist, I tell him. Media. Press.

"Have I offended you?" he now asks, giving me a smile that's an exact replica of a Yellowstone grizzly bear's. He lets me through.

I walk back to the La Posada Hotel – and I can smoke in my room! My room is cool, cozy and beautiful. The hotel staff (all Mexicans) did a great job. So clean and so nice!

There are millions of Mexicans living illegally in the United States, and if not for them rich Americans would have to clean their toilets themselves.

And I'm proud to be an American
Where at least I know I'm free....
I love this land
God bless the USA.

• • •

The next day I walk along Rio Grande, on the American side. It's hot, it's humid – about a hundred degrees – but I want to see the river under the bridge. Ahead of me I spot a Border Patrol van and I walk over to see who's inside. Just like that.

As I approach, a Border Patrol officer lowers his window and looks at me. I assume that he's here to catch illegals.

You are sitting in your van midway between two pretty close bridges, both of which I assume are well guarded. Do you think that anybody in his right mind would try to swim into America here?

"You never know."

In the distance I can hear a Border Patrol boat coming in our direction. The Border Patrol boats, at least here, make louder noises than helicopters. Why are they so loud? I ask the man.

"They are old," he answers.

We talk some more, about this and that, when suddenly we notice a clear plastic bag and a hand swimming toward us. The Border Patrol man gets out of his van and we follow the plastic, which is soon accompanied by a head, and later by a torso. It's a man, alive and well, and he is trying to enter the United States in the fastest, coolest way possible. The Border Patrol officer tells the man to come inland, but the man won't. The officer radios his base to send the boats to catch the swimmer, but it takes a while for the boats to arrive.

I look at the man. He stands in the water and he lifts his hands, showing two clear plastic bags, the kind you would pick up at the vegetable department in an average supermarket, but I can't tell what's inside them. Besides his little bags he has nothing, and I am amazed by the scene unfolding in front of my eyes: A lonely man leaving everything behind, who, if not caught, would have entered this land with nothing. All he has are his wet clothes – one set – and two tiny bags. He is a one-man operation who fights water and the strongest army in the world, because he wants to be here, closer to the dollar.

The Mexican guy, a "wetback" in American slang, swims closer to land to take a closer look at us. The officer again tells him to get out of the water and come up to land. The Mexican won't. He knows that nothing good will come to him if he lands.

In the distance the sound of the "helicopter" is audible and the "wetback" immediately turns and starts swimming in the other direction. Now it's a race between him and America's tough guys:

Who will reach his target first? If the man gets to the Mexican side first, across the river's midpoint, the officers on the boat won't be able to arrest him; if they get to him first, he will be in their custody and at their mercy.

The man with the plastic bags wins. Just as the boat is about to snatch him, he reaches the Mexican side of the waters.

• • •

After two televised debates of the Republican contenders to the White House, Americans are finally given the opportunity to see a Democratic debate, this one broadcast on CNN. Contenders criticize America's ills, each claiming he or she will solve America's problems.

Hillary Rodham Clinton says that "we lose ninety people a day from gun violence," and that's why America must have tougher gun-control laws; Bernie Sanders says that "we have more people in jail than China," and that's why America must stop arresting people so quickly, so often.

Taken together, this is the picture: if you have fewer people in prison, fewer people will die from gun violence.

Bernie, a self-declared socialist, looks like a nice grandpa on the TV screen, and he seems to be an ideologue – perhaps the only one among the various contenders of either party.

But Hillary wins the debate hands down. Not because she's so good but because the other contenders are not as polished as she is. With time, you never know, the others might improve.

Months before, as we all know, nobody thought that the Donald would make it this far.

He did.

The world of politics is never predictable, as it never follows a straight, logical line. Bottom line: at any given point nobody, but nobody, can tell who will be the next president of a nation whose people are afraid to tell strangers which president they have voted for in the past.

Of course, this intrigues me further, and I want to take a peek at American politicians of the past. To this end, I go to Houston to meet a man who should know.

The name of this man is Chase Untermeyer. Don't get confused by his last name; he's an American. And he has a title: ambassador.

As I get off the elevator on his floor, I see this sign: "All visitors must register with the Secret Service in Suite 950." Fortunately, the Secret Service agents are out. They are in only when Chase's next-door neighbor, former president George W. Bush, is around – which is not the case today.

Ambassador Chase Untermeyer is a former ambassador. His Honor served as the American ambassador to Qatar for about three years, from 2004 to 2007. I ask His Honor to explain to me why many Americans won't tell me which president they have voted for or what candidate they will vote for?

"A vote for president of the United States," he responds, "is the most personal vote that any American citizen can cast. The guiding force of their vote is very personal, having to do with the personality of the candidate."

Voting for a senator and voting for a president, he teaches me, are two different things. A vote for a senator is about issues, but a vote for a president is a deeply personal matter having to do more with a sense of sympathy for the candidate, a feeling for personality, than with issues. This, of course, might explain why at this point in time America has a president who is a Democrat while both the House and the Senate are in Republican hands.

Good. This Untermeyer is no idiot. Let me ask him more questions.

Moving from national to international affairs, I ask Ambassador Chase Untermeyer to explain to me why the United States is more pro-Israel while Europe is more pro-Palestine, as seems to be the case based on the various countries' voting records in international forums. Are the people of America and Europe different, or are the leaders of Europe and America different?

"I say to many of my Arab friends who suspect that the reason America is so pro-Israel is because of the influence of Jews in America: if Israel's future and support by America depended only on Jews, it would never have the same support it does."

Why, then, is America supporting Israel?

"Because so many Christians are admirers of the Israeli spirit, which they see as a kindred spirit to the American spirit."

What do you mean?

"Going to another country, being a pioneer, facing dangers."

Ambassador Chase also shares with me his belief that peace between Israel and Palestine is possible and that he personally knows many Arabs who view the Jews as the "people of the book."

I tell him to stop dreaming, since the reality on the ground proves his knowledge worthless. The other day, I relate to him, I was traveling to Doha on an assignment from *Die Zeit*, and when I landed the Qataris gave me a visa in which they changed my place of birth to "New York," despite the fact that my American passport states very clearly that I was born in Tel Aviv. They wouldn't write "Tel Aviv."

"This is news to me," he says.

Some years ago, I also share with him, I was about to fly to Riyadh and faced difficulties getting a visa because the Saudis required travelers to state in which religion they were brought up, but "Judaism" did not exist on their list. Why? To them, obviously, Judaism does not exist.

He didn't know about this, he says to me.

I ended up getting the visa, but only after the White House intervened on my behalf. He is surprised. Actually, despite being in the Arab world for quite some time – he's flying to Qatar tomorrow, for example – he knows next to nothing about the Arab world.

And he admits it.

Are there no people in the State Department who would tell you what's going on, I ask him, or is America consciously deluding itself?

"The nature of politicians and policy makers is to try to make reality conform to theory, or reality conform to policy, rather than the opposite. In the American government there is always a tendency to make facts conform to philosophy and facts conform to policy, in order to either justify that policy or to justify changing it."

But you know this doesn't work; you can't change facts –

"It does not work, but this does not prevent political people from doing it."

Why?

"Because it serves their interest."

In other words, America's foreign policy is based on Cinderella tales concocted at the highest levels of government.

This is bizarre, very bizarre, but Ambassador Untermeyer is probably right. Almost everywhere America gets too involved, its efforts backfire in the end. America invaded Iraq, bombed it to pieces and killed thousands upon thousands, but ended up achieving not one of its stated goals. On the contrary: ISIS would not exist if not for that invasion, and Iran wouldn't be the powerhouse that it is today.

America bombed Libya day and night, inflicting colossal death and destruction, only to see Libya worse than it has ever been. Egypt would today be much more peaceful had America not intervened diplomatically. Not to mention Afghanistan, where the Taliban rules supreme, or Korea and Vietnam, and a host of other international problems.

Why is America failing in almost every move it takes overseas? Because facts don't matter.

Genius.

When I leave Chase's office I think that America's bombing of foreign countries must have a more sensible reason than what he had argued; perhaps it has to do with leaders' pleasure of watching big bombs explode somewhere at their command. Regular citizens, like Andrea and her husband, love to fire guns in Wisconsin, but high-ranking officials, Republican and Democrat, like to use bigger bombs.

• • •

Of all the wars America is engaged in, either at the moment or in the recent past, none has the feel of a crusade like the war on smoking. This one is a total war. Hotel after hotel, sidewalk café after sidewalk café, in almost every state I visit, is 100 percent smoke free. The modern-day lepers and pariahs, the smokers living in our day and time, must seek out places to satisfy their addiction, usually twenty-five to fifty feet away from either a café or a hotel's entrance.

It is in one of these "lepers' squares" that I now join other smokers, all Europeans. And they talk. The Americans, they tell me, are certifiably dumb. What makes Americans so dumb? "They don't know where Netherland is on the map," a Dutch man tells me. A French lady sitting next to him agrees. Americans, she says, don't know where Paris is on the map. Americans, in short, have no culture.

What's the name of the first state west of New York? I ask the educated Dutchman.

"North Dakota."

The other Europeans agree.

Where is Israel?

"In Africa."

Sure?

"Yes!"

Europeans, at least these, are very educated.

• • •

One of the issues that is unique to America is the black-white issue. It refuses to die. But there are blacks, a minority of blacks, who are doing well, drive expensive cars, live in nice villas and have enough money. How do they feel?

Ask Darryl. I meet Darryl, a lawyer and lobbyist who also happens to be black, in one of Houston's better restaurants, at a table packed with rich Texans. A black lady who works for a local TV station had just told us, a mostly white crowd, that there's no racism in America, that blacks are responsible for whatever problems they have, and that if there's racism it's by blacks against whites. As Darryl listens to this, his blood pressure shoots up. He asks if he could talk to me in private, and so we go out to the street to talk.

He wants to set the record straight. He lives better than most people in the world, he starts telling me, just by virtue of being an American. In America, he says, "there is no ceiling and no floor," and anyone who aims high has a chance to reach as high as their dreams. But he is discriminated against because of his skin color, and on a daily basis.

"My brother, who is older than me, is in prison for over thirty-two years, accused of raping two white women. Blood evidence and hair evidence don't match. Pubic hair pulled from both women do not match his, but he was convicted. Twice. And in Texas, if you are convicted of raping a white woman you are gonna spend the rest of your life in jail. And, essentially, that's what happened."

You say you're being discriminated against on a daily basis. How? Are you pulled over by police?

"That too! I've been pulled over 129 times since I was fourteen years old. I'm now fifty."

When was the last time that you were pulled over?

"Last Friday."

What happened?

"I was coming down the street, going home. There's some guy tailing me, right on my tail. I sped up, trying to pull into the garage to get away from him. As I sped up to my driveway the guy gets out, runs to his trunk, and pulls out an AR-15."

A gun?

"An automatic rifle that can take out everybody at this restaurant with one clip. When I saw the gun I pulled off. A cop comes. He drives by the man with the gun, ignores him, and comes after me: 'What the hell are you speeding for?' I say: 'The guy pulled an AR-15.' He says: 'What guy?' I say: 'The guy in the middle of the street.' He looks back. There is a group of people, neighbors who happened to be white, and they tell him: 'Officer, you drove by a guy standing with a gun in the middle of the street.'"

The guy with the gun was white. Darryl is black. The officer only saw the black speeding but not the white guy with the rifle right in front of his nose. Darryl is upset, and he wants me to know.

Another black man, from the same party, comes outside and tells me a similar story. Their message is clear: the black-white division in America is not a poor-rich division, but racial.

It's all about race.

Which raises the question: What race am I?

I'm in Houston, and in Houston you have all kinds of businesses, not only oil companies. One of those other businesses is called Family Tree DNA.

Many Americans are busy taking DNA tests these days because they, the "diverse" people, want to know who they really are. There are blacks, I'm told, who take this test to find out if they have white genes, which would mean that they are actually white. Makes total sense.

Who am I? Am I a Jew, or perhaps I am really a Saudi. Personally, I'd like to be a Saudi sheikh.

I go to take the race test. The DNA test is fast and almost painless. I get a kit, which identifies me with a number, and I am given something that looks like a set of two toothbrushes. All I have to do is take these brushes and rub them on the inside of my cheeks. Rub, rub, rub, rub, rub, rub, rub. Then I put the brushes in little containers on which my number is assigned. In a few weeks, I'm told, I'll be given a detailed report of who I am and where I come from.

I can't wait.

• • •

Oscar, Oscar! Where are the good people of Texas? Did you, by any chance, mean the people of Vidor? Vidor, I hear, is a racist, skinhead city, where the Ku Klux Klan used to have a number of parades.

I have never seen any KKK characters up close, and I would love to see them now, parading or otherwise. I drive to Vidor, in southeast Texas. My Captiva can drive anywhere and everywhere.

Captiva is not white; she's gray, kind of silver, and I really hope that silver is an okay color in KKK land. She's not black, and I hope that's good enough.

When I reach Vidor I stop at the first parking place I find, a consignment shop parking lot, get out of Captiva, tell her to honk if she gets into trouble and walk inside. What can I see in Vidor? I ask in the shop.

Neither the shoppers nor the owner are used to having a stranger pop into their lives with such a question. I assure them that I'm not a cop, an NSA agent or even an FBI agent. I'm just a fat tourist from Europe. They smile and talk to me.

As far as they know, they say, there's nothing special to see in Vidor. Is there anything specific you're looking for? they inquire.

Honesty is the best policy, goes the American saying, and I tell them that I'm looking for a couple of KKK sweethearts.

No one can help me. "I don't think they are alive anymore," a young man tells me. "My old grandfather was a Klan member," but that belongs in the past. The KKK, others tell me, left town ten, twenty or thirty years ago.

Are there any skinheads around?

Oh, those types abound, about one thousand of them.

Great! Where exactly could I find them?

"They are on crystal meth," a man volunteers, and I had better avoid them.

No chance. I want to see them.

You'd better not go there, he tells me, unless you have a gun on you. I don't, and I don't plan to buy one today.

It's a dangerous place out there, he warns me, and he who goes there should expect to be shot, robbed or both. "You don't want to meet them," he says. "They are the type who'll rob you and steal everything. They're no good."

The skinheads, a young lady tells me, are members of the notorious Aryan Brotherhood gang, and they live in mobile homes, trailers. They are white trash, and they are dirty as well. "Nobody goes there," she says sternly. The other people in the shop concur.

Logically, I should heed their advice. But the possibility of facing one thousand anti-black, anti-Jew individuals in one setting arouses my curiosity, and I turn deaf to their warnings. Not only that. I would love, *love*, to see an Àsatrú service. I missed the service in the North Dakotan prison; I shouldn't miss one again, oh, no!

Where exactly, ask I, should I drive to reach the meth-consuming, trailer-living white supremacists? They give me directions: drive south, cross the rail tracks, pass the church, make a left and a right and you'll see them there.

I drive. Two minutes later, when I look to my right, I see a number of police cars surrounding two young white people. This is an arrest, I guess.

I drive there.

The cops handcuff a young blond girl and push her into a police car. Once done, they do the same to the blond guy. Their vehicle, an old pickup truck, is being impounded. Crime? Narcotics. The skinheads in the area, one of the cops tells me, are very upset today because the police have arrested a number of them.

I think of Andrea, who told me that cops shoot more white people than black people, and wonder: Is this true? I don't know.

I do a little research and this is what I find: during 2015, as of today, almost 250 blacks and close to five hundred whites were killed by US law enforcement personnel.

Where are the skinheads located exactly? I ask the cop.

Don't go there, he tells me, adding: "I wouldn't go there!"

Captiva and I drive on.

I make a right, a left, a reverse, a right, straight, left, straight, over and over and over; I drive all around. No shot is heard. No one bothers me. When I stop to ask for directions, I get friendly responses and helpful instructions.

Where are the skinheads? Where are the guns? Where are the crystal meth folks? Where are my Aryans? Where are the Àsatrú worshippers?

There are trailers here, some with big American flags; but that's it. I spend a considerable amount of time in search of racists and anti-Semites, but I find none. This part of the world is as dangerous as Dearborn.

Yes, it is possible that some real nuts live here. It is also possible that some real nuts study in UC Berkeley.

While driving out, I notice a restaurant by the name of Schnitzel. Must be Germans, part of the fifty million. Let me go there.

When I stop at Schnitzel the owner is having a smoke break outside, and I join her. Her name is Monika, and she is originally from Germany but has been living in the United States for many years. She tells me that whatever I heard about Vidor has no basis in reality.

Maybe it was like that a generation or two ago, but the neo-Nazis that lived here have either left on their own volition, were forced to leave by one or another government agency or simply passed away.

As we chat more, over two more cigarettes, she tells me about many of her thoughts, including that she supports Israel. Yeah. If you want to meet a German who supports Israel, come to Vidor, Texas.

Cigarettes done, we walk in. It's late in the evening, about one hour before closing time, and there are only two people at the restaurant now. Both are children of German parents, one is an older man and the other middle-aged, and both are monks from a nearby city. Last night, one of them tells me in perfect German, ninety-seven people stayed at their monastery. Both are very happy that they have the power to influence people.

Not all people, as you know, think proper. For example: Monika. Supporting Israel is wrong, damn wrong, they say.

Why?

"The Palestinians have been living there for seven hundred, eight hundred years," and that parcel of land belongs to them.

Didn't the Jews live there as well? At least, this is what the Bible says, isn't it?

Hearing this, they get upset with me. Why, in heaven's name, am I bringing the Bible into this discussion?

Well, I tell them, you are monks, aren't you?

This gets them even more upset. I am intruding on their privacy, they suddenly say. They just had great food, the food mama used to feed them, good German food, and I had to come here and mention the Bible? What a chutzpah! "The Bible is not a history book. What the Bible says are just allegories," says the younger monk, who is now very, very upset.

Perfectly okay with me, I say. But since the Bible's stories are just allegories, could we also conclude that Jesus himself is just an allegory?

The discussion is over, declares the younger monk. Now I have really crossed all boundaries. The older one adds that the media is controlled by the "rich people."

Do you mean the Jews?

Obviously he does, and so immediately the younger monk motions the older monk to stop talking; he gets up, and they both leave.

I tried to chat with Vidor racist skinheads and I end up with two old outsider monks who feed their bellies with schnitzels and their souls with hatred.

When I entered Texas, a monument for the dead who fought hatred stared at my face. When I leave Texas, I stare back and what I see are living haters eating schnitzels.

Adios, Texas; hello, Louisiana.

Gate Twenty-One

A man with no teeth has a heavenly smile

AS I REACH LOUISIANA I STOP BY A LITTLE RESTAURANT. I HOPE THAT Louisiana will finally save America's reputation for me and that I'll find some good food here. Louisiana, many people have told me before, is a state where people love to eat and they know how to make food, good food.

The waitress comes to my table and starts talking. Oh, Lord of lords, I have no idea what she's saying. There are many accents across the USA, and I thought I understood them all. But oh, was I wrong!

I try to strike up a conversation, just to get my ears used to this new accent. What's the best thing in Louisiana? I ask the lady.

"Bores," she says.

Bores?

"Many bores."

That's all you have, boring people?

Now she has no clue what I am saying. It takes me some time, of sheer confusion and delight, until I successfully decipher the accent. Bars, she said, not bores. It takes another ten minutes, and by then we understand each other perfectly well.

Bars.

Out the window is a big sign about Jesus. I have seen more Jesus signs during this journey than I care to count, but this one is special. Here goes:

Jesus

There is power When you just Say His name.

Thank you Jesus.

The food arrives. Fried and delicious. Thank you, Jesus. Somebody in this country knows how to make food. Hallelujah!

On the top news of today's American media, written in a clear accent, I read these:

Washington Post: "Palestinian protesters set fire to a Jewish holy shrine in the West Bank." *Fox News*: "'How to Stab a Jew': Palestinian leaders condemned for violence."

Can't American media get busy with other things, let's say Red Zone, and with other people, let's say Mad Dog?

• • •

The temperature in Louisiana is about thirty degrees lower than in Texas. I love Louisiana! I drive on.

Somewhere along the roads, I think it's called Pierre Part, I see people in boathouses and I stop. I pay a visit to one such boathouse. The owner, Pam, is sitting on the porch with a few ladies, her guests. "My husband killed a deer this mornin'; he went deer huntin'. We freeze it and then we cut it," she says. "He's gonna go back huntin' this afternoon to kill another one. We'll put it in our freezer and then we got our meat for the year. Would y'all like some coffee?"

We all do. In the north they say *you guys*. In the south they say *y'all*.

Are you a proud American? I ask Pam while sipping her American coffee.

"Very proud! For Labor Day we had some wounded warriors come down. Some with no legs. You know, that far foul country."

Iraq?

"Africa, Afghanistan, and all that; you know. And they came down here, and my husband took 'em on airboat tours. They were just – and before they left they gave my husband a purple heart. Yeah! I mean, it – it was – it was sad, but I was so happy I got to meet these people."

What did they tell you about Afghanistan?

"Oh! He got hurt, he had a leg blown off, but he was so worried about his friend that he saw was bleedin' that he crawled to him, just tryin' to save his life. I mean, they told us – "

Did he explain to you why America is fighting in Afghanistan?

"No."

Do you know why America is fighting in Afghanistan?

"No. Because it look like it's not helpin' any. They just keep on fightin' and fightin' and fightin'."

Did he tell you what's going on in Afghanistan, what's the reason America went to Afghanistan?

"There are certain things they want to talk about, and there are things they don't want to talk about."

They never told you why?

"No."

Do you know why?

"No. I don't have no idea why they fightin'."

But you stand by them?

"I stand by my troops. Yeah."

She thinks for a second, how to best explain her feelings to a stranger, and then says: "My uncle, he went to Korea."

She did not vote for Obama, she tells me, even though she's a Democrat, because she despises him. You don't like blacks? I ask.

"Oh, I don't mind blacks. Not at all."

Pam's two female friends drink coffee and tell me why America went to war in Iraq. The reason? The Iraqis came in and blew up the Twin Towers in New York. I tell them that they were not Iraqis but Saudis, but they don't see the point. What's the difference, after all? Saudis, Iraqis. It's all the same. One of the ladies has fifteen to twenty guns in her home, the other one has thirty. Why not? If you can afford more than one gun, why not have thirty?

What I see here is not a common sight: Americans socializing with one another. Most often, as far as I have seen, this is not the case. Blacks and Spanish tend to socialize more, even in the 'hoods between shootings, but whites are usually into their own, befriending their TV sets and socializing with their cars. It is nice to witness this exception.

When I leave them I think of Robin. Robin doesn't stand by her troops, she stands by justice. Not everybody is Robin.

• • •

In an hour, maybe two, I reach New Orleans. We're just driving, Captiva and I. We can't stand still.

The first man I meet is Mike, a tall, fat black man walking around with a cup of beer. Could you, my friend, tell me what's New Orleans about?

"In New Orleans you can drink like a rock star, eat like a pig and party like an animal. Any way you slice it, it's a good time."

He has a good time. He even counts for me, in case I want to know, the total number of fingers he has on both his hands: "Six on one hand, half a dozen on the other."

New Orleans, others tell me, is about football. To be more exact: the New Orleans Saints, which is the local professional team. New Orleans, with its long history of brothels and drunks, slaves and jazz couldn't come up with a better name for its professional sports team.

Saints. Yep.

For tourists, New Orleans is about the French Quarter, where they drink big glasses of beer and dance to music performed by mediocre musicians and singers of jazz and the blues. I'm on Bourbon Street, one of the French Quarter's most recognized streets, and I get bored pretty quickly. It's such a tourist trap!

I walk away from the quarter into the rest of the city of New Orleans, looking to meet real people, and soon enough I meet Frank. Frank is riding his bike in a black New Orleans neighborhood, and when he sees me he stops. He seems to be over seventy years of age and is missing almost all of his teeth, but there is a smile on his face that refuses to die.

Who is this man?

In 1971, Frank tells me, he went to Germany, where he stayed for four years as part of his military service. He was, as they call it here, a "GI" (Galvanized Iron/Government Issue, US military personnel).

You speak German?

"*Kinder Deutsch* [children's German]," he answers in German, laughing heartily.

What did you do when you came back?

"Truck driver."

What can you tell me about America?

"It's a great country to live in, one of the best in the world."

It takes a few minutes for Frank to feel comfortable with me, and when he does he tells me a different story, the real story.

Years back, about ten years ago, Frank now tells me, he worked in construction and he was told that he "may not use the bathroom" in the house.

Why, because you're black?

"That's right."

So what did you do?

Well, if there was a restroom in the garage, he could use it, but not the one inside the house. "You work for some people, and if you ask the people if they would let you use the bathroom or not, they might fire you because you actually asked the people to use the bathroom."

Does this still happen today? According to Frank, yes.

Frank doesn't like President Obama. "For me," he tells me, "he hasn't done anything." Under Obama, he says, his food stamps were taken away and his only income nowadays is what he gets from Social Security, which totals $762 a month.

I'm trying to calculate how he lives off such a small amount.

How much is your rent?

"I'm homeless."

Where do you live?

"In the street."

Where do you take a shower?

"At the Mission."

A church?

"Yeah."

And where do you go to the bathroom?

"Burger King."

But he has healthcare.

Frank has four daughters and fourteen grandchildren, but he doesn't ask his children for help. He wouldn't "take food out of their mouths," he explains. He doesn't want his daughters to know that he's homeless. And to make sure that they don't find out, he doesn't keep in touch with them. But from time to time he rides around their houses just to take a look at his grandchildren.

It is not easy listening to Frank, a man of no teeth and a big smile. Yes, Oscar: I have found good people, right here in the south. I'm gonna stick around for a while in the south. I want to meet more good people.

Gate Twenty-Two

If you are planning on having sex, wait for your partner's
verbal permission before each successive step

MISSISSIPPI. I'M DRIVING IN MISSISSIPPI. "WHEN LIFE GETS TOO HARD TO
stand, kneel," reads the big sign at the First Baptist Church in Gautier,
Mississippi. A bigger sign, on the right, states: "We Support Israel.
Genesis 12:3, Psalms 122:6."

Here's the Genesis verse (NIV): "I will bless those who bless
you, and whoever curses you I will curse; and all peoples on earth
will be blessed through you." The Psalms verse (NIV): "Pray for the
peace of Jerusalem: May those who love you be secure."

For two thousand years, most Christians did not view these
verses as applying to a Jewish state, or to Jews in general. This Mississippi church, like the people of CUFI, are certain that these verses
apply to today's State of Israel. How did this change come about?

I get out of beloved Captiva and go to the church, where I meet
Pastor David, the boss of the place. I ask David if the support for Israel
is just because of the Bible, or if there is also some kind of inherent
support for the Jews. He won't answer. Why?

The church is a tax-exempt organization, he says, and it might
lose its tax status if he, the pastor, answered this question. Period.
But if I want to know what he thinks, he goes on, he'll willingly share
his opinion provided I stop recording him.

I turn my iPhone off and we have an interesting conversation which, sadly, I cannot share. This is called freedom of speech, American style.

Not that people are not allowed to talk in this country. Sometimes, surprise, they are requested to talk nonstop.

Case in point: Governor Jerry Brown of California has just approved legislation that would require schools offering health classes to teach a "yes means yes" doctrine in sexual relationships. This means that people who are engaged in sexual activity must ask for a "yes" from their partner for every step in their sexual contact.

It would go something like this: May I tell you what I feel for you? – Yes, you may.

I am attracted to you. – Thank you.

May I touch your hands?

Yes, you may.

May I caress them?

Yes, you may.

May I kiss you?

Yes, you may.

May I touch your knees?

Yes, you may.

May I touch your nose?

Yes, you may.

May I take off my shoes in front of you?

Yes, you may.

And so on, and on and on, and on and on and on, until a baby comes along – if at all.

This is part of liberty, California style. I don't think that anybody in Mississippi will ever abide by such rules.

A gallon of gas here in Mississippi costs $1.74. In Castro, San Francisco, it cost $3.89.

What else is new these days? Canada's Prime Minister Stephen Harper lost in the general elections, and he will be replaced by Justin Trudeau. The *Huffington Post*, in a byline by the Associated Press, describes Harper thusly: "He gradually lowered sales and corporate taxes, avoided climate change legislation, supported the oil industry against environmentalists and backed Israel's right-wing government." Climate change, Israel. What a nice salad.

I stay the night at the fabulous Beau Rivage Resort and Casino in Biloxi, Mississippi, where I bet one dollar at a slot machine, lose eighty cents immediately and allow the young girls with the sexy smiles to supply me with never-ending free drinks, and in the morning Captiva says: Let's go to Montgomery, Alabama! No problem, Captiva. If you're into it, I am too. Let's go!

Gate Twenty-Three

*For $10 million, 23 percent would become a
prostitute for a week or more and 16 percent
would give up their American citizenship*

WOULD YOU LIKE TO KNOW AT WHICH HOTEL I STAY IN MONTGOMERY? I'LL tell you. The Hilton. And they give me a smoking room. God bless Montgomery!

I sit down, smoke in the room, feeling free in the Land of the Free, and only then get up to walk the streets of Montgomery, the Home of the Brave.

Montgomery was the first capital of the Confederate States of America. It is out of Montgomery that the order for the first shot to be fired in the American Civil War was issued. It is here that Martin Luther King Jr. had his church, the Dexter Avenue Baptist Church. And it is here, in this city, that Rosa Parks refused to give up her bus seat to whites, which prompted the Montgomery bus boycott and set into motion the civil rights movement in this country.

How do I know all this? Some locals tell me. What locals? I'll tell you soon.

At the beginning of my journey through America I thought that Philadelphia represented the most "historic" city of this country, and then I thought maybe it was Gettysburg, but now that I'm here I think that the title "America's Most Historic City" should in fact belong to Montgomery.

Yeah.

I go to visit the Dexter church, which is practically a museum and charges a $7.50 entrance fee. Have you been here? Martin Luther King Jr.'s office, right here, is an interesting sight to see. The desk, Martin's original desk, is the most prominent item in the room, and there's also a bookcase with a few books. I check out the books. Most of them are scattered volumes of an old Jewish encyclopedia. How did they get here?

It is here that I learn that Martin Luther, both Sr. and Jr., did not start life with this name. They used to be called Michael, but following King Sr.'s 1934 travels to Berlin and Jerusalem the names were changed to a loftier one: Martin Luther.

I stick around for a while, and then I exit. Outside I spot two black people on a small vehicle that looks like a mowing tractor, and I ask them to tell me when blacks were first allowed to vote in this country: Was it after President Lincoln's Emancipation Proclamation in 1862, or only after the 1965 Voting Rights Act?

They don't know. They gotta mow, not vote.

An attractive young black lady with pink lipstick also says, "I don't know." What she does know is this: "My first crush was Martin Luther King Jr."

Who was your second?

"Obama, but not anymore."

Why not?

"I'm disappointed with him."

Why?

"Don't get me started."

Who knows everything about black history?

Now I'll tell you. The locals who know everything about voting rights, King, Parks, and the rest of this country's black-white history, the locals who tell me all about it, are the local Jews and their leaders. These Jews support the blacks and have dedicated their time to helping them.

How many blacks are on the side of Jews in their struggles against anti-Semitism? I ask them.

They can't name one.

Soon, "they" will be no more.

The Jewish community in Montgomery is gradually disappearing. These days the Jewish talk in Montgomery is of combining the two remaining synagogues into one, due to the dwindling number of Jews in the area. They want to delay the inevitable demise of the Jewish presence here, but they know that the end is near. It is the story of American Judaism that I have already seen: people who dedicate their resources to help others and to fight themselves are doomed to succeed on both fronts.

I get to talk to a number of them, off the record, and I share these thoughts with them. They don't take it lightly.

"You are forcing us to look at the mirror," a Southern Jew tells me, "and it's hard, very hard. It's not a comedy. There will be no happy ending."

I get to feel it personally. A week or two ago I sent my monthly column to the *Forward*, this time about blacks and Jews: about the Jews in St. Paul who are busy talking about helping blacks and ever busier criticizing other Jews. I have been writing for the *Forward*, a liberal Jewish publication, for some years by now and never had any problem with them.

This time, writing on this sensitive issue, is different. The story is being censored. Liberal Jews, I guess, can't stomach a mirror. What shall I do? I quit on the spot. I don't like censorship; I'm not built for it.

Liberals were my first crush, but they have been disappointing me ever since.

• • •

I keep on driving and reach Mountain Brook, a city that's practically all white. "Here," a resident tells me, "you will be pulled over by police if you are caught driving DWB." I know DWI, which stands for Driving While Intoxicated (and in some states: DUI, Driving Under the Influence). What's DWB?

"Driving While Black." Funny people.

• • •

On Sunday morning I go to pray for the peace of Alabama. The best prayers, I already know, take place in megachurches. Alabama, as you might expect, has got the best of them: the Church of the Highlands in Birmingham, the state's largest city, has more than thirty thousand members.

Just yesterday I had no idea that such a church existed; today I'm driving to attend its services. It is a sight to behold. As I advance close to the church at about nine o'clock in the morning, I see a huge line of cars leaving the area on one side and another huge line queuing up to go into it.

Am I in Penn Station, New York? No. This is God's Station, Alabama. The cars leaving and coming are of people attending different services. The church has five services on Sunday.

I have heard much about the Evangelical and Charismatic Southern Christians. Jews of the South have been telling me that these people are in love with Jews and will support the Jews until their last breaths. I want to meet such idiots, creatures who are ready to help those who won't help themselves.

Before I join the nine-thirty worshippers I stop to chat with some of the eight o'clock flock, who are on their way out. Right next to me I see two well-dressed young couples on their way to their cars and I ask them the easiest question I can think of: Who are God's Chosen People?

"God's Chosen People are the people who follow Christ," one of the young women says, and the rest agree.

That's you, right?

"Yes."

Aren't the biblical Chosen People from somewhere far from here?

"The first Chosen People were the Israelites, yes."

Remembering my discussion with William Atkins in Utah, I ask: Are the Jews in America the same people as the "Israelites"?

"No."

So, they are not chosen?

"No."

Only the Israelites?

"In the past they were the Chosen but not anymore."

Where was Jesus born, in what country?

"Bethlehem."

Where is that?

"In Jerusalem." All agree.

Jerusalem is a city, and Bethlehem is a city. What country is Jesus from?

No one knows more than they have already shared.

What country will Jesus return to?

"He will return and all will see His glory."

What country?

"What's the difference?"

The Bible gives a location, doesn't it?

No one knows.

There's only one issue that not all of them agree on. Three of them say that they support Israel "because of the history of the Israelites," and the fourth person has not made up his mind yet. These are the young Christians. Maybe their parents were in love with Jews; they are not.

I go to join the service. The church is packed with thousands of people. As I enter, they sing: "I was bought by Jesus' blood." How lovely.

There are five singers on the stage: a black male and female, two white females and one white male. All that's missing here is a Chinese LGBT and they will be completely "diverse."

The founder and senior pastor, Chris Hodges, appears on stage. He is white. He delivers a sermon. About money. The church, he says, has existed for fifteen years and is growing, without ever undertaking donation campaigns to raise the money.

This is church talk, by the way. Which in this case means that soon, very soon, ushers will move in with buckets to collect donations.

As in every other church that doesn't raise funds, there is an envelope in front of every seat in which worshipers are called upon to give a tithe to the church. A tithe is 10 percent of gross income.

Chris keeps talking. He also presents some survey results to the believers. The question is: What would you be willing to do for $10 million?

The responses:

Twenty-five percent would abandon their entire family.

Twenty-three percent would become a prostitute for a week or more. Sixteen percent would give up their American citizenship. Ten percent would withhold testimony letting a murderer go free.

Seven percent would kill a stranger.

Three percent would put their children up for adoption.

Surveys, like other statistics, must add up to 100 percent, yet this one adds up to eighty-four only. But who cares? The people are impressed and go on to pay the tithe.

Once the prayer service ends, one of the pastors of this church, who goes by the name of Kory, approaches me. He has been told by security that I interviewed people outside, and he would like to know what my story is.

I have a question, I say to him, and I'm looking for an answer; that's my story. The question is: Will the Jews go to Heaven or to Hell?

"To Hell."

Do you support Israel, by the way?

"Yes!"

But they will go to Hell?

"If they don't want to go to Hell they must start believing in Christ."

Bingo.

I thank him profusely and leave.

• • •

As I'm getting ready to leave Alabama, fate dictates that I meet a charming Orthodox Jew, a Jew whose business it is to lend money at extraordinarily high interest rates. Anti-Semites have been accusing Jews of doing exactly this kind of business for the past six million years, and now I get to meet a professional.

Bob Nelson is his name. At least that's the name he goes by when making his deals.

Bob didn't start out his life being a loan shark. His previous job, interestingly enough, was in the rabbinate. The problem was that this former rabbi's flock was not bought by Jesus' blood and they would never even entertain the thought of giving him 10 percent of their gross income. Which left him very poor, his wife very upset and his children ever more demanding. A stressful life. To get out of his bad situation, he became a loan shark.

No. He doesn't call himself a loan shark.

What do you do? I ask him.

"I make a living."

How does Bob make a living?

"Through commercial finance."

What does that mean?

"Commercial finance means supplying businesses and corporations with working capital. If a company needs money they can be supported through our business."

How does it work?

"Let's say you need $10,000."

How long does it take to get such a loan, by the way?

"Twenty-four to forty-eight hours."

How much interest do you charge?

"Between 15 and 40 percent."

Not 49 percent?

"In certain circumstances."

He looks at me, feeling a bit uncomfortable, and he tries to explain himself a bit better. "This is America," he tries his hand at explaining, "a land of opportunities. It is in America where a person can one day be a rabbi and the next day a 'commercial finance specialist.'"

So be it.

He doesn't stop here. He does not give the actual loans, he says. Simply put, he doesn't have this kind of money. What he does is more like "matchmaking," as he calls it. He matches the people who have lots of money, Orthodox Jews like him, with the people who need big sums of money very fast. He is, in other words, a broker. As a broker, he gets his cut the moment a loan is made, and he doesn't lose his share if the borrower defaults.

Are Jews, compared to other ethnicities, more into finance than other groups?

"Yes."

How come?

"It requires a *Yiddishe kop* [Jewish mind]."

Explain to me this *Yiddishe kop*.

"In general, in lending, there's always a risk attached, because you need your money back – and it takes a *Yiddishe kop* to mitigate your risk."

Give me an example.

He does. And it's genius.

Once a borrower has paid, let's say, half the initial loan plus the interest, Bob calls him and offers him an additional loan in an amount that is double the unpaid balance, for a lower rate. When this second loan is approved, the borrower must immediately pay the rest of the first loan, which is automatically deducted from the second loan by the lender. The borrower now pays a lower overall interest rate, calculated on the total amount of the second loan, but in reality he's paying a far higher total amount of interest because he's left with only half of the second loan.

In short: everybody feels happy, and the Jews get richer. Jews, you see, have to work much harder than pastors to make a living.

My Captiva is outside, on the road, and she doesn't hear any of this. Good. But she misses me, my Captiva, and I go to see her.

We have a little meeting and both of us decide that it's time to move ahead. Where to? Tennessee.

Where in Tennessee? Lynchburg. Why? No particular reason.

Gate Twenty-Four

*When the atomic bomb fell on Hiroshima, people went out
to the streets, yelling and dancing and having a good time*

ONCE WE ARRIVE, MY CAPTIVA WANTS TO REST A LITTLE, AND SO I WALK
on foot. In Lynchburg's historical district I see this poster on a
window: "Homeland Security. Fighting terrorism since 1942."

Cute.

Here they also sell cute t-shirts, like this one: "I'm the God fear-
ing, gun toting, flag waving conservative liberals warned you about!"

Speaking of flag waving, by the way, here's a news item from AP:
"The University of Mississippi quietly removed the state flag from
its place of honor on Monday, heeding the calls of those who say the
banner's Confederate battle emblem is hurting the school's future."

The Confederate flag refuses to disappear. Nobody remembers
the Iran nuclear deal anymore, and nobody cares. But the Confederate flag is serious business. The repercussions from the shooting at
the black church in South Carolina refuse to ebb.

I keep moving on and I meet Dianne, a retired lady who has just
finished lunch with her husband, and she asks me where I'm from.
I tell her I'm an Israeli.

Oh, she loves Israel, she says. Christians, she informs me, love
Jews. Have I been to Alabama? she asks.

What's in Alabama? I ask.

"Jews."

Nice.

"I checked my DNA in Ancestry.com," she joyfully tells me, "and I discovered that I am one percent Jewish."

Wow!

I wonder what she had for lunch, beer or brandy. Captiva doesn't wonder about anything now. She just wants to move. We drive to Nashville, "Music City."

• • •

I've always been intrigued by Nashville for the simple reason that I like country music. Yes, I do. Years back it was my dream to be a country singer. I fell in love with the image of it: female lovers with sexy accents, stallion horses, expensive whiskey and ranches that make New York look like a small village. Sadly, fate stood in the way and I never actualized my country dreams. But now I am in Nashville, and maybe my old dream will become a reality soon.

You never know! This is America, where anything can happen.

The State of Tennessee Department of Tourist Development is nice to me. They get me a hotel about ten miles from here, and I am told that the visitors center can provide me with suggestions about places to see and people to meet.

I go to Nashville's visitors center, officially known as Nashville Convention & Visitors Corporation, but the ladies at the front desk, to my surprise, won't respond to most of my questions. Even a simple question, such as "Who's your favorite country singer?" is met by a reply of "I'm sorry, but I'm not gonna answer this question."

Why not?

"Because we can't really do that."

It's against company policy. I try to be friendly and ask them to name some of the famous singers in the city, but they fiercely object to the question.

Why?

It is against company policy to name famous singers. That's it.

When I'm done with them, Martha, an official with the corporation, comes to talk to me about "our" city, but once she opens her mouth her Los Angeles accent reveals that she is a transplant. Going for the small talk, I ask her how it feels to move from a liberal state such as California to a conservative state such as Tennessee.

I don't get a clear answer to this question.

The corporation, by the way, is an all-inclusive enterprise. On its shelves I find a nice brochure, "sponsored in part by the Nashville Convention & Visitors Corporation," called "The African-American Guide to Nashville." I ask the ladies if they also happen to have a Native American Guide to Nashville. They have no answer.

These are not the female lovers with the sexy accents that I've been dreaming of.

Outside their office is a place called "Honky Tonk." What's honky-tonk? I ask Martha.

"A live music bar."

What does it mean literally, "honky-tonk"?

"I don't know what it means. It's just a name."

Who came up with it? Why not Ponky Shmonk?

"It's a great question; I'm not sure."

I proceed to downtown Nashville.

Nice, cute and awfully small. For about five blocks on Broadway, live music can be heard from eateries or bars, which is nice, but most of these places are almost empty. I go to a joint called Honky Tonk Central. What's country music? I ask Paul, one of the two singers now performing.

"Country music is about storytelling."

Could you sing one of these stories to me? He gladly does. He sings George Jones's "He Stopped Loving Her Today," a song that will make a romantic soul cry for at least a month because it tells the tale of a man who has died and hence will no longer love.

What happened to the beloved girl afterwards? I ask Paul.

He's not sure, but then an idea pops into his head: "Fell in love with the mailman?"

Great answer!

In a honky-tonk joint down the road a young singer is singing: "I want to be like you, walk like you, talk like you." What's the story here? No story. This is "modern" country, I'm told, and in modern country it's not about a story but about a message. I'm not sure if I get the "message" here, but what do I know?

The question I have is this: Since the bars are almost empty, where are all the country lovers? I know they are around, because the hotels in Nashville are packed.

It takes me some time, but I catch up with the crowds later on in places such as the Johnny Cash Museum and the Country Music Hall of Fame and Museum, where they longingly look at Elvis Presley's "solid gold" Cadillac and watch short video clips. There are more people in each of these locations, which offer trashy celebrity memorabilia, than on all of Broadway.

Once upon a time, perhaps, Nashville was a great cultural city; it no longer is. Today's Nashville is kept alive by a highly effective PR machine and big businesses that milk huge amounts of cash from naïve tourists who stupidly enough still flock to Nashville. Hotels in downtown Nashville charge hundreds of dollars a night, and people think that if it's so expensive it must be worth it.

Ponky shmucks.

Here, by the way, is how the Urban Dictionary defines a honky-tonk: "A loud, rowdy bar that plays 'honky-tonk' country music. Typically full of drunken hillbillies having a good ole' time. To go out 'honky-tonkin' is to go out on the town to honky-tonk bars and get drunk."

Full of drunken hillbillies? I wish!

Later on I meet an older woman and ask her to tell me what honky-tonk is.

"Honkies," she says, "is what blacks call whites and is a derogatory name."

And what's "tonk"? This she doesn't know.

Tomorrow I'm scheduled to meet some interviewees, thanks to the efforts made by Tennessee's tourism office, and perhaps they will have a better explanation of honky-tonk.

● ● ●

As I wake up the next day I get an email from a representative of the State of Tennessee's tourism office, telling me that I better leave the hotel this very day: "In case you have not already checked out, my friendly advice to you is to make sure to check out in time." In addition, all scheduled interviews made by the tourism people are cancelled.

In other words: the PR machinery wants me out of Nashville, and the sooner the better. Effective immediately I am persona non grata in Nashville. What happened? It takes me a few hours to find out, and when I do I explode in laughter. The State of Tennessee regards me as a dangerous person because I asked Martha a "political" question. Yeah. Asking an American citizen how it feels to move from liberal California to conservative Tennessee is an offense.

And they get mean.

To make sure that I promptly pack my belonging and disappear, their representative calls the hotel and tells them that I'm leaving my room today.

I don't.

I spend the next two days having the time of my life with the hotel employees and a number of guests, drinking and singing together. Then I slowly advance with Captiva to a new distillery in Tennessee that goes by the name of Short Mountain Distillery, which sells all kinds of "moonshines" with funny names such as Apple Pie and Prohibition Tea.

• • •

The man behind this distillery is a California transplant by the name of Billy Kaufman. Billy, who is the great-grandson of the Samsonite company founder, is happy to be gay and delighted to be a farmer. He walks around in a black T-shirt and boots while his dog is busy making rough love to another dog. Billy is fully ready to sit down with me and chat about his life among the trees and about his distillery venture that he hopes will soon become a household name. If Jack Daniel could do it in this state, why not Billy Kaufman?

Before I try out his drinks, while I am still sober, I ask Billy the most important question a journalist could ask a new distiller: What does it mean to be an American Jew? What is the meaning of Judaism? Billy is Jewish, an American Jew, and I'd love him to explain to me everything there is to know about this group of people and their belief system.

"Jews are international people; we integrate ourselves in so many cultures but we retain intellectualism and an understanding of where we come from so that we never become fully integrated."

I'll probably understand the full meaning of this answer once I drink some moonshine. In the meantime, I ask him: What's Jewish in you?

"Oh, I look Jewish!"

Billy has a moustache that looks similar to the prophet Muhammad's, and perhaps that's why he thinks he looks Jewish. I tell him that he doesn't. Hearing this, Billy now tries to explain to me in exact terms his "Jewish" part.

"You are Jewish by blood, so your brain is Jewish."

I love this "Jewish by blood," which is in complete harmony with the Indian blood quantum. What's a Jewish brain? I ask Billy.

In reply, Billy stretches both hands forward, brings them close to one another as if he was holding a soccer ball or a skull, and then moves his hands in circular motions a number of times.

Yeah, that's the "Jewish brain." Bob Nelson would love it. I taste some of Billy's Tennessee moonshine products and I actually like them; I even buy a small bottle for the journey ahead, in case I get thirsty.

• • •

By now, as you've probably noticed, Captiva and I are very tight. We get along extremely well, thank you. She's never been thirsty since our first day together; I take good care of her. And the best thing is this: we both like to go places we've never been before and meet people we don't know. Yeah, it gives both of us immense pleasure.

Today is no different.

Today in Oak Ridge, Tennessee, I meet Bill Wallace, a former pastor whose father worked in Oak Ridge during the forties. What's Oak Ridge? I just found out, and let me share this with you. Oak Ridge served as a major site for the Manhattan Project, a secretive experimental operation dedicated to the production of atomic weapons that would later be dropped on two Japanese cities toward the end of World War II.

At the time, when Bill was a baby, Oak Ridge was something like a military city, a secret city, where no one could enter without a pass.

Everybody in the city, excluding the children, was involved in the making of weapons powerful enough to instantaneously kill untold numbers of people and decimate cities long into the future. Baby Bill didn't know what Papa's job was, and neither did Bill's mama. In fact, nobody in town knew what the neighbors were doing, and if anybody asked he or she would be handled by security officers at once.

Baby Bill, a smart cookie, had an inkling that where he lived was not a normal place. And to this day he remembers that when the atomic bomb, made possible by Papa and friends, was dropped over Hiroshima, "that's when we knew what we were working on. Exactly." He was three. It is interesting to me to hear him use the word *we*, like Nancy from Tulsa, as if he were one of the people who developed the atomic bomb.

I want him to explain to me, if he still remembers, what he saw on that day as a little child. He obliges. Everybody in Oak Ridge, he tells me, "was excited. It was just like a Fourth of July celebration. People were on the streets, they were yelling and dancing and having a good time."

I ask Bill if America has a right to get involved militarily in other countries.

"I think a lot of this goes back to the foundation of America. The fact is that America was founded because of oppressions of different kinds in other nations and that's what brought people to America."

Are you saying that because of the way America was founded, the USA today has the obligation to get involved in foreign countries? Did I get you right?

"That's a fair observation."

It's time for me to drink a Moonshine or two. Hey, Oscar! Are you still singing there in Chicago?

• • •

I take Captiva and drive to my new lodging, a cabin near the Smoky Mountains. My cabin is nice, and in it I have everything a guest needs: three American flags, two Bibles, and three crosses of different sizes. The Internet doesn't work here, but who needs Internet when you have flags and crosses?

I open Billy's Moonshine and take a long sip, the first of many...

When I wake up the next morning, Captiva decides to get in touch with nature, and we drive into the Smoky Mountains. What a beautiful ride it is! In this place, at this time of year, the trees offer a marvelous sight. The leaves come in multiple colors, clouds hang between trees, and the valley as seen from the top of the mountains offers the loveliest of images Captiva has ever seen.

It's rainy, and at times we drive into clouds, but Captiva doesn't mind. And no matter how far or close the visibility is, the gorgeous scenery encircles us and engulfs us through a majestic dance of nature and man. Slowly, I reach Cherokee, North Carolina.

Gate Twenty-Five

Liberals live much longer than conservatives

CHEROKEE. WHAT A NAME. MUST BE AN INDIAN PLACE. IS THIS A reservation? No, a local lady who goes by the name of Dawn tells me. This town, she says, belongs to the Cherokee tribe, and no one but the Cherokee people can buy property here. Who is a Cherokee? "If you are one-sixteenth Cherokee by blood."

At this point in my experiences with Indians, after hearing this logic in Michigan and Montana, I try to see what happens if I challenge them on the basic tenet of their thinking. I ask Dawn how she'd feel if she were told by white people that she couldn't buy property in their neighborhoods. Wouldn't that be considered racist?

"Yes."

Here, in an Indian city, whites cannot buy property. Is that racist too?

"Oh, no!"

Why not?

"Whites can buy anything they want; they just can't own the property."

Why not?

"We bought the property!"

When?

"In the 1860s."

Why can't you sell it?

"We can, to each other."

Why not to whites?

"Because it's our property!"

She must be a graduate of Chief Dull Knife College in Lame Deer. There's no point in arguing this any further. But I do get from her a quick course about the benefit of being a Cherokee and living here. Twice a year you get a $6,000 check from the tribe, just because you're a Cherokee.

Poor Cherokees! In Michigan the Indians get $64,000 a year.

Cherokee is different in other ways as well, I learn. History, you see, plays a big part in this place. If your ancestors lived here but were forced by the American government of the time to depart to what is today Oklahoma (along the "Trail of Tears," 1838–39), you will get one big zero from the tribe.

I talk a bit more with Dawn. How many Indian tribes are there in the country? I ask her.

"There are 565 tribes," Dawn says, and she tells me that each of the tribes has a different language. Almost no one here speaks the Cherokee language, except for about two hundred people.

Bo Taylor, who is the executive director of the Museum of the Cherokee Indians in Cherokee, which here means a great deal, is one of the two hundred. How do I know? He tells me.

He also tells me that "I speak at least sixty languages, at least a little bit."

Bo is more than just an Indian. "I'm not really an Indian," he tells me. "I am a Giduwa. That's what we traditionally call ourselves."

What does that mean?

"It means to be set up, above. Like to be raised up on a platform."

Like the "Chosen People"?

"Yes, someone like that. We believe that we are chosen."

I would love to arrange a sporting event for a match between members of the Church of the Highlands and Bo, where they can fight it out for the title Chosen People.

By the way: Chosen People would be an excellent name for a sports team. We have the Pirates, the Warriors, the Saints, and all other manner of similar diseases. Chosen People we don't have. Isn't it time to have a baseball or football team named "the Chosen People"? They would win every game!

What does it mean to be a Cherokee? I ask Bo.

"It's my identity, it's my history, it's my way of seeing the world, it's – "

What's your way of seeing the world?

"Let me finish! I'm trying to get there. It's, what's important is, you know, we see the value not in money but the fact of – of family, the clans, the world we live in."

I apologize in advance, but it's strange to hear you say that your values are not about money when you have all those casinos. That's pure money –

Bo is visibly upset when I say this. He mumbles some half sentences and half words, trying to find the right accusatory terms in the English language, and once he does he spits them out: "You are brutish," he says to me. He also accuses me of coming to an Indian town for the sole purpose of speaking badly of its people.

My impression is that this Bo is used to white people who get mushy-eyed when they see him, and he's shocked to see a white man, this fat Jew, who does not bow down to lick his toenails. In addition, Bo cannot grasp the idea of anybody out there questioning the existence of the skyscrapers that he and the rest of the Indians have been building in mid-air for centuries now.

He composes himself and tries a new trick. "The place we live in, the Smoky Mountains, is the most diverse place in all of North America for plants and animals," he preaches to me.

This Bo must be anticipating that I will now burst out in tears of happiness and total acceptance at the very mention of the word *diverse*.

Even Captiva is laughing. She should be crying.

Later in the evening I go to a local Indian restaurant and order authentic Indian food: fried trout and coleslaw. I can't believe that they call this "Indian" food.

When I give the waitress my credit card she tells me that she is not allowed to take it from me. Why? Waitresses in this area have been robbed on their way from the table to the cashier, and the restaurant's owner has had enough of it.

Welcome to Indian culture, pure Native Americanism.

At night, in pitch darkness, I hear loud sounds coming from a security system across the road from my hotel room: "Burglary! Burglary! Burglary!" But nobody is paying attention; they are probably used to it. It must be part and parcel of the Chosen People's way of life.

• • •

How can it be that in our day and time, blood quantum and other forms of Indian racism are accepted by Americans, people who view themselves as anti-racist?

Perhaps because the real culprits are not the Indians. Who made it possible to have dirty Indian ghettos, populated by the ignorant and the drunk, with glitzy casinos in their midst? The nice non-Indian American elite.

Not being able to face the cruel murder of countless Indians committed by them, or their ancestors, they allowed those still alive to settle here and there, as if compassion had suddenly filled their hearts. It doesn't bother the privileged whites that the reservations, and all other forms of sovereign appearances, are nothing but hot-beds of ignorance and crime as long as they, the non-Indians, look good and cool.

But perhaps there is something deeper here than first meets the eye.

The truth is that America is not the only country or culture on the planet that was founded on the fresh blood of those who came before. Every country, every nation, every culture was founded by butchers. Sorry, that's life. Western people who today fly high the flag of human rights are the very children and grandchildren of yesterday's rapists and murderers. I know. Most of my family was murdered by them in cold blood long before I was born.

In truth, murderers don't change their nature, and the shameless butcheries of yesterday did not stop yesterday. At any moment when the Western human-rightists feel threatened by another culture, they will annihilate the "offending" culture with the most sophisticated of weaponry without blinking an eye.

This is the world, whether we like it or not.

This does not mean that you or I will soon turn into murderers or victims, but our respective societies will. And every society is the same: north, south, east and west.

Yet only America, an extremely powerful country, feels bad about its history of conquering this land. Why?

As far as I can tell, there is only one logical answer to it: Americanism is a culture of the fearful. American culture, a social experiment in creating a culture based on an idea, instills fear in its citizenry. To keep America as one entity, even though its people are glued to each other by artificial means, America's leaders force the citizenry to be "nice" to each other and be "sorry" if they were not nice in the past. Nancy and Bruce, like a zillion other Americans, feel bad for what "we" have done to the great, lovely, highly spiritual, brilliantly charming Indians of yesterday and today.

Captiva, born and raised in the USA, is totally hurt when she hears this, and she wants to drive out of here fast. Somewhere along the path of our white flight I see an auto body shop, and in honor of Captiva's curiosity we stop in.

• • •

The city we are in at the moment is Shelby, North Carolina. In the middle of the shop is an antique-looking red Chevrolet pickup truck. The engine is from 2012, the body is from 1965 and the parts assembled to rebuild it are for the most part new. Price tag: $60,000.

There are three people working on the pickup at the moment, and all seem pretty happy. What's special about Shelby? I ask them.

Jason, the owner of the shop, answers. Shelby, he says, has the "best barbeque in America."

What's special about North Carolina?

"You can be on the beach, and then you can be in the mountains in about five hours."

And what's special about the people here?

"Nice people. The South is a good place to be."

Do you have rednecks in this state?

"Oh, yes, sir!"

What's a redneck?

"Beer drinkin', deer huntin', nice car lovin'," replies one of the workers. "That's about it, really."

Jason is a redneck, he says, but he doesn't drink because of "my morals. I'm a Christian," he says.

What do you think of the State of Israel?

"We need to support Israel."

I ask Wayne, one of the workers, if he agrees.

"They got to cure their problems themselves," he says. "We can't be no police for them, first of all. That's what I feel about the United States. But, on the other hand, a Jew is a Jew and a Christian is a Christian. We can't get those two things mixed up, in my opinion. But I do believe it's God's Holy Land."

We talk some more and they explain to me what they think of the big picture: all three believe that the United States should support Israel, and all three believe that the Jews murdered Jesus Christ.

There's one Jew, though, that the three of them like. He is a German Jew, half German, half Jewish, and he's good. Why is he good? Because he believes in Christ. Jews who believe in Christ are the exception, and these people get along with them just fine.

To Captiva, this body shop feels like a hospital, and she has had enough. She wishes a speedy recovery to the red pickup and we drive on to Charlotte, North Carolina's largest city.

Before we reach Charlotte, I get a call from Enterprise. What's the problem? They want me to drop Captiva off at the nearest Enterprise branch. "This car was sold. We need it off the road."

They are jealous bastards. They don't like it that Captiva and I are so close. Captiva is crying, I can tell, but we have no choice.

• • •

We reach Charlotte and we separate. So quickly! I feel like an Indian, thrown out of my abode, divorced from my dearest American mate.

To compensate me, the Enterprise people say that I can take a pickup truck for the same price. Captiva is watching, I can see, and so I say no. I'll take a van, a minivan, in memory of my beloved mini SUV.

We say goodbye and hope we'll soon reconnect again.

• • •

A survey published today by the Pew Research Center asserts that 89 percent of Americans believe in God, a drop from the Pew's last survey of seven years ago. The survey, based on responses by thirty-five thousand Americans, also claims that there are significantly more nonreligious people among the Democrats than among Republicans and that the younger generation tends to be less religious than the older generation. The survey is not totally conclusive, as in some areas it points to stronger faith in large segments of American society.

All in all, religiously speaking, America seems to be closer to Iran than to Sweden.

That said, based on what I've seen while traveling the country, surveys are limited in scope.

As already mentioned in these pages, the people of this land are afraid to speak up when first approached, and this applies even to homeless people, such as in the case of Mad Dog in Hawaii. As strange as it may sound, Americans would sooner drop missiles on a foreign country than tell you who they voted for in the last election.

I do hope that my DNA test will confirm that I'm a liberal. Why? Liberals live longer. How do I know? I read it.

The *New York Times*, in a piece written by Paul Krugman: "Life expectancy is high and rising in the Northeast and California, where social benefits are highest and traditional values weakest. Meanwhile, low and stagnant or declining life expectancy is concentrated in the Bible Belt."

In simpler words: liberals will live forever, and conservatives will be dead in an hour.

My new car, a Dodge Grand Caravan, is my biggest car yet. It reminds me of the Dodge in Maryland. Naturally, we are strangers to one another, and in order to make our acquaintance I drive without stopping. Just drive. Direction: more south. Happy, SoulO?

I drive, drive, drive and drive. And when I get hungry, I stop next to a Waffle House in Rock Hill, South Carolina. Yes, I've just entered another state.

Gate Twenty-Six

People who talk to the Lord eat muffins.

I'M IN WAFFLE HOUSE AND I MEET SOME LOVELY WAITRESSES WHO SPEAK in a wonderful accent, real Southern. I ask them how much they make per hour. I know that the federal minimum wage is $7.25, and that in some states it's higher, up to fifteen dollars an hour.

How much is it here?

Three dollars an hour, they tell me. How come?

Their bosses are aware of the $7.25 minimum, but they claim that with tips the wait staff will make $7.25.

Unbelievable.

Is that legal? I ask around, and am told that it is. Actually, it's legal to give waiters a base salary of $2.13 an hour because somebody figured that with tips they will get the minimum.

Not one waitress at the Waffle House, by the way, is complaining. They work six and sometimes seven days a week to make ends meet. But they love their job because they like to work with people. "Two-bedroom apartment here costs $450; this is not New York," one of them says to me.

I give them a big tip and drive on, moving further south, and I reach Charleston. I came here for a reason.

• • •

Charleston is the city where, last summer, nine blacks were shot to death in the church by Dylann Roof, the guy whose photo with a Confederate flag has caused a chain reaction that's being felt to this day. I started my journey with this story, but only now I feel that I can "handle" it.

The name of the church is Emanuel AME Church. What's AME? African Methodist Episcopal. What's that? I have no clue. I park the Caravan and go to the church.

It has been months since the murder took place here, but when you pass by the church it seems as if it had happened only yesterday. There are flowers on the metal gate in front of the church, quite a big church, plus photo displays of black people with quotes inscribed on their bodies. "Across cultures, darker people suffer most. Why?" reads one of the inscriptions. Another reads: "To be a Negro in this country and to be relatively conscious is to be in a rage almost all the time. –James Baldwin."

Services in this church are held on Sunday and there is a Bible study on Wednesday, but today, Tuesday, nothing's going on. The office is open and I talk to one of the people working here, Maxine. The church has "about 550 members," she says.

Did membership increase after the murders?

Not really. "Just in small numbers," she says. But "people come to the service on Sunday; they want to be in the building, they want to be in the church. Since the incident we have anywhere between seven to eight hundred people attending the service."

Is this a black-only church?

"We don't have white members at this time."

I've heard it before, the fact that whites are not eligible for membership in this church – yet it still rings strange in my ears. "But on Sundays," she adds, "we do have white people who come."

How many whites come on Sundays?

"Two hundred or more. But before the murder we had no whites."

A similar thing, she tells me, happens in the Bible study, where presently about one hundred people attend. Almost all of them are white. At the time of the shooting, in June, only twelve people had showed up for Bible study.

Do you get more donations now?

"We have gotten a number of donations from all over the world."

Probably double or triple what you used to get…

"It's quite handsome."

Ten times more…?

"I'm not at liberty to say."

What she is at liberty to say is this: "The sympathy that came as a result of the murders did lead to the [Confederate] flag coming down in many places."

• • •

Outside the church I meet a tall black man who wears a yellow shirt and a big cross. His name is Johnny and he tells me that the murders "brought whites and blacks together and made Charleston known all over the world."

Do you have white friends?

"A lot of them!"

Johnny is not part of any denomination, he says, but "my teacher is Minister Louis Farrakhan," the leader of the Nation of Islam. Denomination or not, Johnny is a Muslim.

Why are you wearing a cross?

"This is not a cross, this is an ankh, an old Egyptian symbol that represents life!"

But, he says, he also attends services in a church down the road, and I ask why.

"Because we draw no distinction. They are our family!"

That's an interesting concept. I wonder how far this "no distinction" stretches, especially since Minister Louis Farrakhan is a known anti-Semite, a man who has repeatedly spoken out against Jews and Judaism. And so I ask Johnny how he feels about Jews.

"As a group?"

Yes.

"Not all of them are bad."

What do you think about how the Jews treat Palestinians?

"This is stuff that's going on for centuries!"

Israel was founded in 1948, but I don't mention it.

He knows Jews and thinks they are good people. Some are rich, he says, "like in our government. You got Jews in the United States government. Lot of them!"

They run the government?

"Yeah!"

Do they run President Obama?

"Oh yeah! He can't make decisions without them. He is like a puppet."

If President Barack Obama heard you saying that –

"He know! That's why he's all gray-headed now!"

Because of the Jews?

"Yeah. They run this country. For their own gratification. That's life."

So good to be a Jew!

Jews or no, Charleston is one of America's nicest cities. Here you have big white buildings with grandiose columns, lovely houses, small streets, tons of fine stores and, according to the US Department of the Interior, Charleston is also home to Kahal Kadosh Beth Elohim synagogue, "the country's second oldest synagogue and the oldest in continuous use. The American Reform Judaism movement originated at this site in 1824."

Interesting.

I go to see this temple. The thing I like the most about it is the sign outside: "Thou Shalt Not Park Here." So biblical. I love it!

I don't know why, but every time I pass by an old Jewish building I start getting hungry. Where can I find good food in Charleston? Charleston, I hear, is damn proud of its four-block City Market, a tourist destination and a "must-see" for every visitor.

I go to the market, hoping that it will offer the best food available in the world. Well, here I can buy handmade baskets, shirts, necklaces, jewelry and more handmade baskets. I don't want baskets, I want food, and the food choices here are quite limited.

Can you tell me, I ask a black guy who sells three million types of home-prepared oils, where a fat man like me should eat?

"The best food in Charleston," he says, "is at Hyman's. When I feel like treating myself, I go there."

I keep on walking, hoping to find Hyman's once I'm out of the market, and when I reach the end of it I meet a lovely black lady, who tells me that she believes in Jesus. She also tells me that Jerusalem is next to Israel, that the Jews are the richest people in America, and that I should try the food at Hyman's, which is owned by a rich Jew.

Hyman's again. I go there.

Eli is the owner of this restaurant, and I get to meet him before I eat his food. He was born in this city, lived in Israel for a few years, even served in the Israeli army, and in truth he would like to still be living there. He doesn't because his wife, a Jewish lady from Sweden, wouldn't move with him. "She wears the pants in our house," he tells me.

I don't want pants, I want food. Eli serves me.

This restaurant, just so you know, is a Southern restaurant. Fried this and fried that, delicious this and delicious that. Eli feeds me various fish dishes, each of them better than the one before. This guy is a magician, let me tell you. I don't know how he does it, but he does. Here I eat the best Southern food in the United States. Thank God that he has a bossy wife who wouldn't let him move out of here.

Food finished, I have the urge to find some non-Jews in this city.

• • •

I step into the house of the Trinity Worldwide Outreach Ministries. Don't ask me what it is; I like the name, and that's enough for me. I meet Minister John.

Minister John loves everybody, he tells me, and so does the Lord. Good to know. Minister John also tells me that "the Jews own everything in New York."

How about Charleston?

"Also in Charleston!"

• • •

It is Wednesday and I go to the Emanuel church's Bible study, where I will have the pleasure of meeting one hundred mostly white people who, since the murder, have been attending the Wednesday Bible study.

In reality, there are about twenty people here, half white and half black, plus a policeman and a BBC reporter on assignment to witness the whites who out of sympathy come to study the Bible here. Like many things in America, this church's PR is one thing but its reality is another.

In a row behind me there's a Jew from Massachusetts. He didn't come to study the Bible, he came to "sympathize." The BBC reporter, who finds his very being here newsworthy, immediately runs to him and asks for an interview.

Today's study, in case you're interested, is about prayer and fasting. Next to the speaker, a female pastor, is a big cross with the nine names of those murdered here nailed on it. Jesus was nailed on a cross, and so are they. Next to the cross is an American flag with this line above it: "One flag, state, nation."

The speaker asks the audience to share their thoughts on fasting. "I was just talking to the Lord," one of the participants starts to answer. Yes. There are people out there who claim to have real, actual conversations with God; they talk to Him, He talks to them and they exchange views.

Don't ask me.

At the end of the study we are treated to a gift from a local bakery: breads, Danish, cookies, muffins. It's good to talk about fasting as long as it ends with a muffin.

It's also good to speak of racial equality in a church that allows whites to attend services and accepts donations from whites, but will not accept whites as members.

The African Methodist Episcopal Church, if I understand correctly, was actually founded in the early nineteenth century in Philadelphia, Pennsylvania. That's enough time, one would assume, to start practicing racial equality and open the Church's doors to all colors. But, I guess, not everything we assume turns out to be reality.

Gate Twenty-Seven

In the turtle hospital, every turtle has health insurance

I KEEP DRIVING SOUTH, AS IF THERE'S GOLD THE FURTHER SOUTH I GO. YES, I'm still in the South, Oscar! I enter Georgia, driving in the direction of Savannah, where the gold should be.

Hotels in Savannah, in the downtown area, charge hundreds of dollars per night. But I want to beat the system. I go online and find myself a hotel room a few miles from downtown Savannah for thirty-nine dollars a night. I like the hotel's description: "Simple chain hotel offering extended-stay deals, an outdoor pool and a computer for guests."

I park the Caravan next to the hotel, Masters Inn in Garden City, and go to pick up my room key. There's a big sign on a high pole with the hotel's name, but I can't find the actual hotel. It takes me a while to find it, and then I see a small structure with the hotel's name on it.

This cannot be the hotel, unless this hotel has only one room. I walk in there anyway. It's the hotel's reception area. Where's the hotel? I have no idea. But before I have the chance to open my mouth, the lady at the desk looks at me, takes notice of my white skin and asks if I really want to be here.

What's the problem?

"Would you like me to give you the key and you see for yourself?"

Do you have smoking rooms?

"Yes, but you wouldn't want to be there."

Why not?

"Trust me!"

Where's the hotel?

The lady points to some big, dark structures and says that the hotel is there. "I give you the best room I have, but you'll have to tell me if you want to stay here."

What's going on, lady?

"Go and see."

I go.

Poor families, all black, congregate in different spots of this Masters' hotel, and young men sit down on the floor and on the stairs in various places, each of them extremely busy doing nothing. As I pass by them they look at me, wondering what the hell I'm doing here.

What is this place? I enter one of the buildings, looking for my room. In the stairway I see notices on the walls warning people that if they misbehave they will be thrown out of here at once.

What the heck is going on here? Better that I not know. I go back to the car and move on. Hotel after hotel, each looking worse than the other, decorate the roads I drive on. Some are rumored to be the abode of whores; others are beyond rumors.

What's going on with this Georgia?

Just before I'm ready to give up on hotels I find the Deluxe Inn, a hotel with an almost empty parking lot. I have never been to a hotel where I'm its only guest; it's time I try.

On the small refrigerator in the room I read this: "Alarm + Police = Jail." What is this? Better that I not know. The good thing is that all rooms are smoking rooms. Perfect for me. I unpack, light up and try to take my mind off of where I am.

I start with *Fox News*. They are often entertaining, and I need that now. Fox reports that "Eight ISIS terrorists wielding AK-47s and wearing suicide belts carried out coordinated attacks at six sites around Paris Friday night, killing at least 127 people and wounding at least 180 others." Oops. This is not exactly entertaining.

Eighty-nine of those people died in a concert hall where the American rock band Eagles of Death Metal performed. What a prophetic name for a band.

The good news is this: As far as I know, ISIS is not planning anything spectacular in Georgia. This hotel is empty.

• • •

When the sun shines on the next day, it's Saturday. Time to get out of this hole and explore Savannah with Mr. Caravan. Right off Martin Luther King Jr. Boulevard is St. Luke Baptist Church, also known as St. Luke Missionary Baptist Church, and there I see people going in. Are they having their service on Saturday instead of Sunday? It sure looks like it, and I stop by to watch this wonder.

An attendant stops me and asks if I have locked my car. Some folks around here are praying, and others are stealing. I walk in.

Oh, God! I almost get a heart attack in this wonder church. Right in front, by the podium, lies a dead man. This is not a "Sabbath" service; this is a wake!

A dead black man in a white coffin, half his dead body on display.

My first reaction: Run out of here! I've never seen a dead person and I don't want to do it now. But as soon as I run out, I walk back in. It's called curiosity.

I sit down in the back, as far away as possible from the dead. About twenty people are in attendance. Nothing is happening. No dead is moving, and neither are the living.

Time passes. More people come in.

All are black. I think of the black theater in Fort Worth and what the guy told me about the whites who attend black events. This ain't

Sunday, I say to myself, when the whites might show up so that a day later they could brag about their "diversity." Not a single white.

The clock is moving. Over the next half hour or so, more and more people come in. And slowly a crowd forms, numbering well over one hundred. Not one of them is white. Didn't this dead man have one white friend, or acquaintance, who would come to pay last respects, to say one final goodbye?

Above the coffin, on the front wall, is a painting of Jesus and John the Baptist, both in a pool of water, and both are dark-skinned.

The service starts.

The cover of the coffin is lowered and we don't see the dead anymore. A female singer and a choir are on the stage. "Praise the Lord, Hallelujah," they sing. Everyone on stage is clapping, as if this were a wedding, and the audience joins in. Speeches and stories follow.

The audience members in the church are old and young, male and female, and all are black. The deceased, Henry C. Edwards Jr., was born in 1945 and died of heart disease one week ago.

I stick around for over two hours in the hope of seeing one white person, but, alas, the only white here is me. In American English this is called diversity; in other languages they call it segregation.

"This is a celebration of life," says a speaker, and the audience applauds. A lady opens in song, with resounding words that repeat over and over: "I say, thank you." This lady knows how to schlep out a tune. Her *I* goes longer than the train to Alaska. Oscar would be a good match for her. This is a black church, and when the lady sings well, the audience roars in approval. Whites usually don't do that – their loss.

A preacher goes to the stage and speaks. He knows when he hits the right chord because the audience will respond with "yeah," "right" or "amen." What's cooking here is a dialogue, not a monologue.

"Whatever you need your God to be, the Lord will be for you!" he says, and they say, "Yeah!" Henry, who won't be part of this again, will surely miss it.

In due course the service is over and the procession starts out: a sea of blacks and one white. Just like it was on the Red Line train in Chicago. Outside, ready to enter his car, I meet Albert, Henry's cousin, who came down here from Brooklyn, New York.

There is not one white person here, I say to him, and I ask him why. "That's a good question," he says. "I never paid attention to that. Henry had white friends; they didn't come in."

They are not real friends –

"This is America!"

Is *diversity* just a word, a PR word?

"Yeah. Exactly. And New York is the same way. Brooklyn is pretty much the same way. Whites do their own things, and blacks do what they do."

I tell him that the event in the church touched me.

"We all gotta go through this one day. Gotta make that journey!"

A group of people stands not far away, most of them women, and I ask them the same thing: How come not one white person showed up to say goodbye? They nod with their heads, but have no words. Reality hurts.

Diversity.

A minute's drive from here is downtown, where the expensive hotels are and where people, enlightened whites, come to feel they are in the midst of diverse America. I drive back and forth in downtown, looking at them. The color here is almost all white.

Cafés, shops, more cafés and more shops. The whites have a good time. They have come from every corner of America to feel Southern culture firsthand. They are wined and dined by black waiters and they feel "diversified."

But Henry is gone and no white "friend" has come to say good-bye. It hurts to witness all this.

Downtown Savannah is similar to downtown Charleston, but now both ring very hollow to me, as both tell a tale of illusion and delusion.

• • •

I drive on, learning more about the Caravan as we go. As the day is about to pass I get on the highway and drive in the direction of Florida. Somewhere on the highway I see a road sign leading to a visitors center. Am I in Florida already? I get off the highway and stop off at the center.

There I see a brochure called the Golden Isles official visitor's guide. Is this Florida's nickname? No, I'm still in Georgia. "You should visit Jekyll Island," a lady tells me.

What's Jekyll Island?

"That's where the richest people of America once lived, and no one but the richest people could enter the island. One day they were sitting and drinking, and after some drinks one of them threw out this idea of creating the Fed [the Federal Reserve]. That's how the Fed started."

In the brochure I read:

> The island has long been appreciated for its historic landmark district coined the "Millionaires Village."... The Jekyll Island Club Hotel and the surrounding cottages were once home to the most exclusive club in the world, consisting of America's most influential, the Morgans, Pulitzers, Vanderbilts and Cranes, among others. It was used as a hunting and golf resort and has been the setting of many historic moments, including the making of the first transcontinental telephone call and the first meeting of the Federal Reserve.

America: from the first swivel chair to the first transcontinental telephone call. Jekyll Island. That's a place for me. It'll be good medicine after a wake.

I drive there. What an amazing place! Jekyll Island is a Garden of Eden on earth. Here's where real Chosen People, the ones with the healthy pockets, come to refresh. I walk on the beach, which is clean and beautiful, and feel like the luckiest man on the planet.

The streets here are narrow, with the greenest of grass and trees all around, and the overall effect here is a "life as a dream" reality.

I see a young couple playing with their children on the grass. Who did you vote for in the last presidential election? I ask them. They look at me and then at each other, each waiting to hear what the other will say.

Why? Neither of them knows whom the other voted for, they tell me. It's such a "controversial" issue that they don't discuss it even between themselves.

Oy!

The Jekyll Island Club Hotel, which has a number of properties on the island, looks like a nice hotel. I think I should stay here a bit.

• • •

The *Savannah Morning News* reports today that "Georgia Gov. Nathan Deal has issued an executive order declaring that no state agency can accept refugees from Syria in the wake of the Paris terrorist attacks, due in part to concerns that terrorists might use the refugees as cover to sneak across borders."

The *News* also reports that "Gov. Nathan Deal is scheduled to arrive today in Jekyll Island for what's been billed as a 'rededication' ceremony touting all that's new at the state-owned island park." This island was privately owned in the past, but now it's owned by the state.

This event is just a few feet from my hotel room, and so I go to check it out. When I get there I see a big tent with hundreds of people.

Most of them sit, some stand, and I take a look at the attendees. In the front rows, almost all of them are white. In the back portion, there are about fifty blacks and they are wearing tricolored robes: maroon, gold and white.

I walk to where the blacks sit, and I sit with them. Before I can figure out who they really are, a speaker goes to the podium and tells us that this event is in celebration of the $195 million investment for the revitalization of Jekyll Island. I don't know what he's talking about but, personally, I'd be much happier if part of that money went to buy me a robe.

His Excellency Governor Deal approaches the stage, from where he thanks all those who, over the years, have passed through this island and collectively made it what it is. Among the thanked: the Native Americans and the "Millionaires Club."

He doesn't thank me. Toward the end of his speech the blacks get up and start marching. Where to? I don't know, but I join them anyway: a lone white in a little sea of fifty blacks. It's my new habit: where there are blacks, there am I.

Where are we all going to? Oops, to the stage.

Okay with me, as long as it's not another wake. They sing:

Oh, happy day

When Jesus washed

When He washed

My sins away.

I join them in song and dance on the stage.

A PR lady for the event, watching this in horror, quickly approaches me and asks that I dismount the stage at once. S--t. The blacks get to wash their sins away, but I don't. They sing a little more, and when their sins are all washed away the ceremony is over.

What was this all about? Why was this choir brought in to sing Jesus songs in an event that has nothing to do with Christianity? Ask the PR lady. I have more burning questions. For example: Why is it that when whites get to make tons of money, blacks break out in song and dance?

I should find me someone who understands these things better than me – Governor Nathan Deal, naturally.

To make our acquaintance, I ask His Highness to explain Georgia to me. "We are, for those who are interested in business, we have been for the third year in a row designated as the best state in the United States in which to do business."

Who designated them? I have no idea. But it doesn't matter; it sounds good, and that's enough.

From what I have seen in Georgia, I share with His Excellency, there is a huge divide between blacks and whites, especially in terms of the distribution of wealth. Is my impression wrong?

Wrong, of course.

His Excellency asserts that "We have extended great opportunities to our minority community," and that "Georgia doesn't get the designation of 'best state in the country with which to do business' unless we are distributing that wealth appropriately. I think we are."

I can't say if this true or not, but what I can say is this: turtles are well taken care of on this island and they get their fair share of the wealth here, no matter what anybody says.

Yes, Turtles. Forget blacks, think turtles. Yeah, there is a "Sea Turtle Hospital" on Jekyll Island. I go to see it.

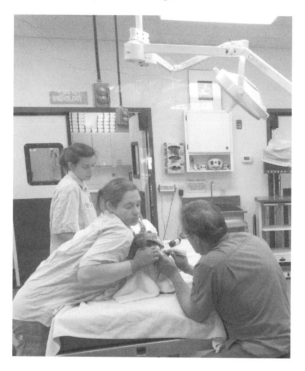

A "surgical removal of fungal mass" is taking place at the hospital when I enter the facility. A nurse holds a turtle tightly while a doctor performs the procedure with surgical scissors. The turtle pushes out its dark front flippers. It's amazing to watch. Who's paying for this? I don't know. Maybe the turtles have Obamacare.

> Oh, happy day
> When Jesus washed
> When He washed
> My sins away.

Rich folks love turtles. Don't ask me to explain.

• • •

A short boat cruise, or a longer road drive, will take you to Sea Island, a private island where the super-Chosen live, the Millionaires Club of today. You can't get in unless you live there or have a reservation at the local hotel – for which you will have to pay an extraordinary number of Dead Presidents. Another class of people who can enter this exclusive place are those who have some official capacity that requires them to be there.

The fourth and the fastest way to get in: hook up with one of the three above. Which is exactly what I do. I find me such a person, and he's driving me around. We pass by the hotel property and I take a look at the guests, not one of whom is black. Blacks go to the Masters Inn. We drive on.

Sea Island, where the leaders of the G8 Summit (Group of Eight) convened in 2004, is where the richest of Americans, often called the "one percent," live their special lives. If you are into more precise terms, you may refer to the residents of this island as the "0.001 percent."

Houses here run in the millions of dollars – three million, ten million, nobody really counts. But you will be hard-pressed to find grandiose mansions here, such as those in many of America's other exclusive neighborhoods. The residents of Sea Island, my new friend tells me, are not stodgy, pretentious people. Their homes are understated because no one on this Sea Island is trying to impress anybody else. There's no need. If you were not of the 0.001 percent, you wouldn't be living here.

Still, I can't but be impressed by these "simple" homes. Even though they are not that big, each and every one of them looks like a rare gem – made of masterfully drawn colors, shapes and designs.

The most unique feature of this place is that you can see zero percent of its residents. Nobody's out, except for the occasional worker. Where are the people? The rich are hiding inside their fortresses, sitting by mirrors and talking to themselves.

The cloud of loneliness is Sea Island's best friend. I close my eyes and I hear Randy Newman singing his "It's Lonely at the Top."

> You'd think I'd be happy, But I'm not...
>
> Oh, it's lonely at the top.

Gate Twenty-Eight

*The most beautiful women in the world live in
Puerto Rico – The Jews are busy counting cash*

I GET BACK TO MY CARAVAN, MR. GRAND CARAVAN, AND DRIVE NONSTOP
until I reach Florida, the Sunshine State, and the last state in the
Union I will visit before I return to New York.

There are born-again Christians and there are born-again drivers; I belong to the second group. From having almost no driving
experience just a few months ago, I have turned into a driving addict.
I love it. Man belongs with machines, let me tell you.

Another of my discoveries is this: the car is man's best friend.

Where shall I go in Florida? I ask Caravan and Caravan says,
Let's just drive. We drive, here and there, there and here, stop there
and stop here, until we reach St. Augustine.

Over half a century ago, amidst mounting civil unrest, the
Reverend Martin Luther King Jr. was taken to jail here, from where
he wrote a letter to a Jewish rabbi, asking him to come down to St.
Augustine with as many rabbis as he could bring along to join the
protests. They came. Does anybody here still remember this?

I go for a walk on the streets of St. Augustine, which I think
is the oldest continuously occupied city in the United States, and
within the first five minutes of my walk I'm stopped by a lady who
asks me if I'm a Floridian.

388 | The Lies They Tell

Of course I am. Always was, always will be. I'm German, I'm Jewish, I'm Jordanian, I'm lesbian, I'm a Saudi. Anything anybody would like me to be.

The lady is happy to hear that I'm a full-blooded Floridian. She shows me some papers, constitutional amendment petition forms, and says that it would be great if I signed the petitions. If she and her comrades collect enough signatures, she tells me, the amendments will be voted on in next year's election. Since the number of signatures must be in the high thousands, she and her friends have already started to collect signatures.

What are the petitions about? One is about solar energy and the other is about legalizing medical marijuana. In short: climate change and weed. She is, I assume, a caring individual who's committed to higher social and ethical values and driven to ensuring a more positive society.

I ask her if she lives here, in St. Augustine. This is a touchy subject. She is from Florida just like I am. She is, let's cut to the chase here, from Michigan.

Why does she care so much about Florida? Well, she doesn't. This petition drive, she confesses to me, has nothing to do with values and everything to do with profits. Business entities, whose core values are higher profits, hired her and others to come here and pretend that they are caring Floridians. I am a naïve lesbian Floridian. I never entertained the thought that climate change, at least in part, is a huge financial issue.

I keep on walking in the historic district. There are lots of crosses around: here's a statue with a cross, there a monument with a cross, and here a cathedral.

I try to engage in a conversation with some people next to a statue that looks like Jesus, to see if they remember the rabbis and Martin Luther King, but they only remember women. They are from Puerto Rico, which has "the most beautiful women in the world," as they promise me.

I keep on walking, discovering other things. For example: an old fort by the name of Castillo de San Marco. According to the National Park Service, a US government agency (a bureau of the US Department of the Interior), "America Begins Here."

Great. But wait, there's more: "Castillo de San Marco symbolizes the clash between cultures which ultimately resulted in our uniquely unified nation." I am, I guess, at the biblical sixth day of creation – of America. Entrance fee: ten dollars.

Bobby from New Jersey, enjoying the sight of the fort, is upset that he has to pay money to see such an important national treasure. "I think that Jews are running this place and that's why it costs money to enter," he tells me. At closing time, he muses, the Jews must sit around counting all the tens and the fifties, because that's what Jews do. "I've been dodging Jews all my life," he says, "because all the Jews want is to take money from people they are in contact with."

Bobby is a religious man, a good Christian, and a flaming Democrat to boot. He adores President Barack Obama and he even has a nickname for him: Barry.

Forget the protesting Jews, and let's concentrate on the "rich Jews." About three hundred miles from here is a place called Boca Raton, where some rich Jews live. Let me meet them. Let me see, with my own eyes, the Jews in this country who "give money to politicians," as the US government official told me in Alaska, the same Jews who control Obama and make his hair gray, as Johnny of Charleston said.

• • •

Mr. Caravan must have more testosterone than my dear departed Captiva, because we reach Boca Raton faster than a "wetback" swimmer reaching Mexico. Boca Raton. What kind of a name is this? Peter, a Jew living here, tells me that Boca Raton means Rat's Mouth. And he also tells me that "Boca Raton is the 'Promised Land' of the Jewish people. The Promised Land is not Israel; it's Boca Raton."

Boca Raton is not just one unit. Here you have gated communities, protected around the clock by security personnel. Each community is different. Some have golf courses and tennis courts, others have gorgeous waterfalls on their streets, plus assorted clubs with funny names where "members" go to be spoiled a little more than usual.

Boca Raton, by the way, is not Sea Island. The rich of Boca Raton make sure that you know how rich they are, and they will do everything possible to ensure their home looks better than yours.

I get myself into one such gated community, where I go to visit Alvin. Alvin is Jewish, and he has tons of money. He has a beautiful home, one that looks more like a splendid museum than a house, and there he lives with his wife and a Peruvian lady – whom I believe is their maid. I can't tell because Alvin and his wife are progressive liberals and they will never say "maid." A Peruvian who cleans your house, please remember, is never a maid but a Friend of the House, Our Dear Friend or even Just Like a Member of the Family. Like the Hilton's engineers.

What I want to find out about this rich Jew is how he views his Jewishness and what being Jewish means for him. Here's what he says: "I care about being Jewish. I'm not happy with the way the Israelis treat the Palestinians."

Tell me, Alvin: What else makes you a Jew besides your criticism of Israel?

"I'm Jewish in my heart."

Alvin, who is not a religious person by any means, expands on this statement by saying: "I don't think the Jews have the message of Jesus Christ. Jews don't have that message. The Jews are not as focused on helping others as the non-Jews."

Caravan, my Dodge Grand Caravan, listens to this outside and I can hear him sing:

Dodge the father

Ram the daughter.

You stay home and stroke it

I'll go to her house and ram it.

I walk out to calm Caravan down, and we drive on. Until I reach Coral Springs, where I meet Miriam Hoffman, a Jewish intellectual, who for twenty-five years had taught Yiddish and various courses on Jewish topics at Columbia University in New York. Miriam, born in 1936, is one of the smartest people I know. I first met her about twenty years ago, but have not seen her in ages. Today we meet again.

"My impression of the Jews that I'm surrounded by in this area is that they are ignorant and primitive," she tells me. "I come from New York. I never knew such primitivity and ignorance among the Jews. In New York I never came across ignorant Jews. I came across ignorant professors, Jewish professors…"

Miriam knows American Jews; she's one of them. "Many Jews in America are liberal," she tells me. "They are not sure what 'liberal' means, actually. Loving 'Negroes' is liberal. Hating Jews is also liberal. Something is wrong with us."

• • •

Here's a tidbit from today's *Haaretz*:

The American Anthropological Association overwhelmingly passed a resolution Friday to boycott Israeli academic institutions. The association's 12,000 members worldwide will now be asked to approve or reject the decision, which delegates at the association's annual conference in Denver, Colorado passed by a vote of 1,040 to 136.

It doesn't matter what the "members worldwide" will decide. What matters here is this: 1,040 to 136 of America's elite have nothing better to do than mess with the Jews. Americans won't learn from the Europeans how to cook, but they learn from them how to hate Jews.

• • •

Before I leave Florida, I finally find diversity. Location: Ocean Drive, Miami's South Beach.

From about Fifth Street to Fourteenth Street there are endless eateries and drink joints all at the ready to serve the world's tourists, of whatever race or ethnicity, and to lighten their wallets. Cruising lovingly on the street is a stretch limousine tempting the eaters and drinkers with "all nude adult entertainment," if they so wish, once their bellies are full and while there's still something left in their wallets.

Ocean Drive of South Beach is where diversity is most triumphant. Near me is an old white man shouting at a young Russian girl: "You know you want to!" Ahead of me is a black guy who tries to sell me cocaine (and if I don't want cocaine, he assures me that he can get me weed just as easily). To my left is a Latin girl in a bikini that shows off her breasts and her ass, inviting all who marvel at the size of her treasures to come in and eat while staring at them. A few feet ahead is a stage where a tall white girl in a bikini stands with a mirror to her back so that no Cuban patron loses sight of the full size of her behind.

Yet, I soon discover, the diversity here is not totally complete. The police, for example, are not represented here at all.

Why? I don't know. Joe doesn't know either, and he's trying to do something about it. Joe, sitting in a park across the street a couple of blocks down, is a Cuban American, and he is a success story.

Almost.

Born in Cuba, Joe studied in college, was a businessman, and for years raised a wonderful family. He even bought his daughter a business in north Miami Beach. Then, Joe got on drugs – marijuana, cocaine, heroin (in that order) – and lost everything. He served years in prisons and now he is homeless, spending his days where I meet him: in a park right off the beach.

He became homeless in 1985, and since then he hasn't seen his children and doesn't know what his grandchildren look like. His daughter hasn't come even once to say hello. Classified by the local authorities as a "habitual violent offender," he was arrested numerous times in this park as well. What had he done? "Beat up crack dealers" in the park. In the old days he served time for drug offenses; now he occasionally serves time for beating up pushers.

It was rainy the last few days, and Joe lays out his clothes on the grass to dry out. People in the area know him and give him food every day. That's his life. He reminds me of the immortal words of Blanche DuBois in Tennessee Williams's *A Streetcar Named Desire:* "I have always depended on the kindness of strangers."

Joe tells me that he doesn't want to live in a house. A house for him is a prison, where he feels confined. The park is good. He points to the beach behind him, which he calls "my backyard," and he says that he likes it here. He sits on a box and watches the ladies go by. Could life be any better? This is not New York; here you can look at the ladies.

There is a public toilet a few feet behind him, and that's where he goes when nature calls. If it rains, he has a place with a roof over it, a place he keeps to himself so nobody steals it from him. He has invited Pinky, a blond homeless lady, to sleep there as well to protect her from the rain. Pinky is newly homeless, doesn't know the ropes yet, but Joe is sure she will learn soon.

Life on the street is good, life on the street is free.

Every morning at six thirty Joe goes to a nearby grocery, where he takes the trash out to the dumpster, and for this service he gets a free breakfast. What else can a man ask for? This is total freedom, and Joe is happy.

So he says. Joe is a religious man, a Catholic, and he believes in life after death.

How many more years will you be here? I ask him.

"I hope," he says, "I can go to Heaven today."

You want to die?

"Yeah. One of these days."

Henry, maybe, will be waiting for him there. When Mr. Caravan hears this, he cries. I wish I could do something to help you, I say to Joe.

"Don't worry about it. If I can't take care of myself, nobody else can," he says.

Can I give you something? I think he mumbles a "yes," but I'm not sure. He looks at me and he is quiet, like a fish. I give him a twenty-dollar bill, just so that he has something on this earth. His eyes shine; he didn't expect it, and he's thoroughly thankful.

"I can eat for three days with this! Thank you very much. God bless you, man."

What a kind man this Joe is.

I get into Caravan and we drive. Direction: Miami International Airport. Once we arrive I leave Caravan at the rental place, to take care of Miami's Cubans. But as I walk away, Caravan looks at me one more time and says: Dude, who are you for real? German, Jew, Saudi?

Thanks for reminding me, Caravan! Let me check if the DNA results are in. Oh, yes, they have arrived. On my iPhone!

Here's what the report says, Caravan. Listen: 94 percent Jewish Diaspora, 6 percent Eastern European. Not even 1 percent Saudi! Can you believe it?

I thought so, says Caravan. You didn't strike me as a Saudi. Caravan knows. He has driven around a lot of people during his lifetime.

Caravan will miss me, I know. We are buddies. I fly back to New York. No Captiva, no Caravan, no Versa, no Fiesta, no Malibu, no Cruze. Back to the subway, with the rest of the 5,597,550 riders.

Gate Twenty-Nine

One thousand people come to say "I hate you"

TOWARD THE END OF MY JOURNEY, MANY THINGS ARE HAPPENING IN the States and worldwide. Take, for example, the climate change summit in Paris. As reported in the *Washington Post*: "Negotiators from 196 countries approved a landmark climate accord on Saturday that seeks to dramatically reduce emissions of the greenhouse gases blamed for a dangerous warming of the planet." Carter Stewart of Montana probably wants to kill them.

According to *Newsweek*, "More than half, or 58 percent, of Republicans surveyed said they approved of US efforts to work with other nations to limit global warming." If I phrased my questions like this, I'd most likely get the same percentage. You can try this out: ask Americans if they would approve US efforts to work with other nations to limit global sand dunes, and you'll get 59.7 percent of Americans approving this measure.

Time magazine chooses Angela Merkel, chancellor of Germany, as its Person of the Year. *Time's* people love Merkel for opening Germany's gates to about one million refugees. Isn't this impressive? I ask an American investment banker.

"*Time* magazine loves the Germans; they also picked Hitler as their Man of the Year," he replies.

In other news: A Muslim couple, followers of the teachings of the Islamic State (ISIS), storm a holiday party in San Bernardino,

California, and randomly shoot its participants. Fourteen die, twenty-two are injured.

The Donald, what a surprise, suggests that the United States bar all Muslims from entering its soil. At the same time, the Donald suggests that half of Jerusalem be given to the Palestinians and hints that all Jews are businesspeople.

As for me, now that I'm in New York, I am invited to countless parties and events, but say no to all – except one. US ambassador to the United Nations Samantha Power is to speak at the Roosevelt Hotel as part of a conference organized by the Israeli newspaper *Haaretz* and an American Jewish organization, New Israel Fund (NIF), both avowed progressive liberal institutions.

I enjoyed listening to Samantha months ago in New York, at Abe Foxman's tribute at the Waldorf-Astoria, and I'd like to hear her again. I go to the conference. I'm not alone. About one thousand people, almost all of them liberal American Jews, are in attendance.

I'm a little early for Samantha's speech and so I stand outside and smoke. Near me is a top NIF official and we talk a bit. She tells me that about 70 percent of American Jews hold the same views as NIF, and she also tells me that there are fifty speakers at this conference, forty-nine of whom are liberals and one of whom is conservative.

What happened to the liberals? They are progressing, it seems, to the Stone Age. Be that as it may, it does arouse my attention and I go up to hear some of the forty-niners.

What a show! Here I hear a lady, by the name of Suhad Babaa, who talks of "Palestinian boys killed in broad daylight by Israeli soldiers" as an example of the brutal and lawless Jews. The audience, liberal American Jews, applaud. Don't ask me to explain.

Amira Hass, a *Haaretz* columnist, tells these American Jews: "Anybody who intends to emigrate to Israel is about to commit a crime." The Jewish state, if you didn't know, is a criminal state.

The Jews applaud.

Bridget Todd, a black lady who is associated with Black Lives Matter, shares the stage with Amira. What is she doing here? I can't tell, but it's definitely an effective visual tool to illustrate to Americans what the Jews are doing worldwide: murdering non-whites.

What else do I see here? Roger Waters is sitting in the front row of the main hall, being glorified by a *Haaretz* fellow who tells him how pleased he is to see such an important man at this conference. Roger, cofounder of the old favorite English rock band Pink Floyd, is still in the music business. But besides music, he has some other things on his mind, such as comparing Israel to Nazi Germany and engaging in endless activism against Israel.

The Jews here love him for that. And they applaud at the mere mention of his name.

This conference is called *Haaretz*Q, where the "Q" stands for question, but nobody is questioning anything. Everybody here has the answers, all the answers. And they talk. The forty-niners say, for example, that Jewish Voice for Peace, whose activists I met while in DC and by whom I was told that I'm a fat, filthy Jew, is an exemplary organization.

All in all, it is bizarre to watch. Every time someone says that the Jews are horrible, are criminals and thieves, one thousand American Jews applaud.

When I met Abe Foxman, over six months ago, he talked to me about the Jews who wouldn't produce shows or films about Israel and other Jewish issues. But this belongs in the past. Today's American Jewish liberals speak loud and clear about Israel and the Jews: they would love both to disappear. What's "liberal" in this? I have no idea. I think it's the opposite of anything liberal.

An Austrian Jew, now living in New York and active in liberal causes, tells me that he's enjoying every moment of being here. What's here to enjoy? Every speaker says that the Jews are horrible, and you are enjoying it? I ask him. "I'm a masochist," he replies.

If I am to believe what the people here say, then the Jewish state is made of ruthless killers and sadistic butchers. Yes, as simple as that: Jews are sadistic butchers. Period.

I'm not going to pass judgment but if this is true, Adolf Hitler was right and it's too bad that he didn't finish the job.

Samantha: What exactly are you doing here?

When an administration joins in the self-destruction of its citizens – be it the self-killing of the black, the self-hatred of the Jew or the self-rape of the Native American – it automatically becomes an accomplice to their annihilation.

Hello, Samantha, do you hear me?

• • •

The America I find is not the America I wished to find. It is racist, it is hateful and its citizens are bound to destroy themselves. Be they blacks and some Spanish who have nothing better to do with their time than shoot each other in the head; be they Jews who are possessed by a terrifyingly psychotic illness of self-hate; be they Indians who have given up any semblance of spirituality in exchange for acres and casinos; or be they all the others: whites, the rest of the Spanish, Muslims, Mormons and others who live in fear of one another.

What about diversity?

Yes, American society is diverse, but this does not mean that Americans are not segregated; they are. The "melting pot" of America has been quite successful in forcing individuals to forsake their ancestors' cultures, but it has given them nothing worthwhile in return. Through the process of forcibly dumping its citizens into a giant boiling pot of diversity and shaming them if they are not proud of it, America's democracy succeeded in instilling fear in the minds of its citizens and effectively created a stench of segregation that reaches the highest heavens.

One side effect of this process, which only outstanding psychologists will be able to explain, is the high degree of patriotism found within this country's borders. These American patriots, by a strange psychological coincidence, convince themselves that they are the only true guardians of culture and morality and therefore it is their duty to invade and bombard foreign countries that do not abide by their sense of morality and ethics. Knowingly or not, they rush to commit and undertake every failed deed ever committed by the Europeans.

A telling effect of the forced melting pot is the majority of Americans who are afraid to share their political and religious views with strangers. In the Land of the Free, the Brave are quiet.

There is a component of the melting pot that often bewilders me: people who passionately argue that America is not a "melting pot" but a "mosaic" of cultures or, as others prefer to call it, a "multicultural" society. Those people have, however, been so thoroughly melted that for the life of them they can't identify a single part of their mosaic or one unique culture of the "multi" – no matter how many times you ask them.

I'm no authority on climate change, as I have said, but from a social perspective America is definitely getting warmer, melting in the blazing fires of its own making.

Sometimes, I must admit, as I drove around meeting people I had this feeling that America is one huge Ponky Shmonk, a kindergarten otherwise known as the USA. Like misbehaving little kids, Americans are ever worried that somebody out there will "out" them one day and tell everybody what they really think. But the problem is that Americans are not children; they have huge bombs and sometimes they like to drop them. America is also one of the strongest economies in the world, and at times the strongest of them all, but can humanity rely on this country?

I wouldn't.

My observations, needless to say but I will say anyway, are based on my experiences and apply to the majority of Americans, but not to all of them. Not "all" Americans, just like any other grouping of people, are the same.

• • •

As I write this, the Greek parliament has just voted to recognize Palestine. Forget the economic austerity, the financial hardships and the suffering of its own people. Who cares? What's important is Palestine.

Yeah.

President Joachim Gauck of Germany delivers his Christmas address. Speaking of the refugees whom Germany welcomed into its borders this year, he brags that "we have shown what's in us."

Yeah!

Here in the USA, the *Wall Street Journal* reports that the National Security Agency (NSA) has been eavesdropping on the Israeli prime minister, on American Jewish leaders and then on some American lawmakers. Why? Well, firstly because the NSA had nothing better to do this year, and secondly because President Obama wanted to know everything that's cooking around the world with his Iran deal adversaries.

When I want to know something like this I use my driver's license. President Obama uses the NSA.

That's democracy, in case you didn't know what to call it. A deeper understanding is this: now that Homeland Security has pulled the plug on rentboy.com and America is getting ever safer, it's time for the NSA to sniff around American lawmakers and make sure that they aren't engaging in dirty talk.

And thusly, on this dubious high note, we are about to end the year.

I fly to Britain, America's old mama.

Epilogue

AMERICAN AND EUROPEAN MAINSTREAM MEDIA OFTEN REPORT ABOUT Jews, and related topics such as Israel, far more often than their numerical representation ought to justify. I didn't think that I would follow the same pattern but, surprisingly to me, almost every American I met had strong feelings about Jews and the Arab-Israeli conflict. I put down what I heard and saw, parts of which are found in the preceding pages, and as the year drew to a close I presented my findings to an international gathering of Jews in Birmingham, England. I shared with them my other findings (about blacks, Indians, etc.) as well.

After I finished speaking I invited the attendees to share their thoughts with me.

Once allowed to speak, some American and English participants went ballistic: How dare you criticize the great America? How dare you say that there's so much racism in the wonderful United States? How dare you say that many American Jews are self-hating? How dare you put down the Native Americans?

To them, America and Americans are beyond criticism, and words such as mine should not be uttered in a country as great as Great Britain. They were loud, they were hostile, and they went personal.

Emotions were high, very high. Facts, data, numbers did not matter. I slaughtered their sacred cows and this was not to be forgiven.

And to make sure I got the message, I was "disinvited." As far as they were concerned, the rotten fruit is Israel – which by this point in the conference they had lambasted back and forth for days. The United States and the United Kingdom, by contrast, are great.

Let them believe it.

I left the conference and went to my hotel, the Genting Hotel in Birmingham. Late at night I went to smoke a cigarette outside. Nobody was around. But just as I was about to walk back to my room, an elegantly dressed young white couple came my way. They asked me what I was doing in Birmingham, and I told them that I had come to take part in a Jewish conference. The girl, a tall blond, took out her smartphone and asked for a selfie with me. I was her first Jew, and she wanted to have one Jew on her phone. Okay with me.

The young man didn't want a selfie; he wanted information. "You hate Arabs, don't you?" he asked.

No, I said; I don't.

"You have money, don't you?"

Not really.

"Jew!" he raised his voice, as if yelling at a dog. And then he proceeded to tickle me. Jews should be tickled, I guess.

I pulled his ears in response. This surprised him. "Jew!" he raised his voice again.

I'm no Jew, I'm a journalist, I said to him.

"What paper?"

It's a German paper, you wouldn't know it, but it's something like the *Guardian*.

"So, you are like us!"

Yeah! I'm liberal like you!

"So you are not a Jew?"

No.

"You have blond hair. Are you Aryan?"

You bet!

I went back to my room, leaving the well-mannered English couple perplexed. Kicked by the Jews, tickled by a Brit, I returned to the USA the next day.

Across the Atlantic, in the Europe I've just left, some New Year's celebrations went awry. In central Cologne, Germany, for example, hundreds of young males sexually abused hundreds of young German women and robbed them as well. Who were the males? Very hard to know, especially if you are in the habit of reading or watching German media. Some German media outlets, such as the mighty and highly respected *ZDF*, waited days before reporting any of these crimes.

Why? Well. According to international reports the abusers, at least a big number of them, happened to be refugees. But you can't say this, because it's really not nice, and democracies are all about being nice. Aren't they?

Yeah, yeah. Didn't you know that?

I am in New York at the moment, and I read the *New York Times*. Here's a quote:

> The pension board of the United Methodist Church – one of the largest Protestant denominations in the United States, with more than seven million members – has placed five Israeli banks on a list of companies that it will not invest in for human rights reasons, the board said in a statement on Tuesday.

Suddenly, after decades of Arab-Jewish infighting, the American Methodists awake from a deep sleep to realize that, oh my God, there are Jews in the world.

Pastor Kory, who declared to me that the Jews will go "to Hell," is probably happy as hell.

Americans are trying to be European. Educated, smart, just. Like all the Europeans.